THE COMMON SECURITY INTERESTS OF JAPAN, THE UNITED STATES, AND NATO

THE COMMON SECURITY INTERESTS OF JAPAN, THE UNITED STATES, AND NATO

JOINT WORKING GROUP OF THE ATLANTIC COUNCIL OF THE UNITED STATES & THE RESEARCH INSTITUTE FOR PEACE AND SECURITY, TOKYO

U. ALEXIS JOHNSON, Chairman

GEORGE R. PACKARD, Rapporteur

Foreword by
KENNETH RUSH and MASAMICHI INOKI

BALLINGER PUBLISHING COMPANY
Cambridge, Massachusetts
A Subsidiary of Harper & Row, Publishers, Inc.

Copyright © 1981 by The Atlantic Council of the United States, Washington, D.C., and The Research Institute for Peace and Security, Tokyo, Japan. All rights reserved. No part of this publication may be reproduced, stored in a retrieval system, or transmitted in any form or by any means, electronic, mechanical, photocopy, recording or otherwise, without the prior written consent of the publisher.

International Standard Book Number: 0-88410-698-5

Library of Congress Catalog Card Number: 81-1527

Printed in the United States of America

Library of Congress Cataloging in Publication Data

Main entry under title:

The Common security interests of Japan, the United States, and NATO.

   Includes index.
   1. Japan–National security. 2. United States–National security. 3. North Atlantic Treaty Organization.
I. Johnson, U. Alexis (Ural Alexis, 1908–
II. Packard, George R.
UA845.C66   355'.033052   81-1527
ISBN 0-88410-698-5   AACR2

CONTENTS

List of Figures and Tables ix

List of the Joint Working Group Members xi

Foreword—*Kenneth Rush and Masamichi Inoki* xv

Preface—*U. Alexis Johnson* xix

Editors' Note xxiii

Chapter 1
The Policy Paper 1

Chapter 2
The Balance of Power in East Asia and the Western
Pacific During the 1980s: An American Perspective
—*Ralph N. Clough* 27

Chapter 3
The Balance of Power in East Asia and the Western
Pacific in the 1980s: A Japanese Perspective
—*Makoto Momoi* 43

Chapter 4
Japan's Foreign Policy and Areas of Common Interest, Possible Cooperation, and Potential Friction Among Japan, the United States, and Other Western Countries
—Seizaburo Sato   51

Chapter 5
U.S. Interests and Policies in Asia and the Western Pacific in the 1980s—Richard L. Sneider   63

Chapter 6
The U.S.-Japan Alliance: Overview and Outlook
—John K. Emmerson and Daniel I. Okimoto   87

Chapter 7
U.S.-Japan Relations in Retrospect and Future Challenges—Fuji Kamiya   131

Chapter 8
Japan's Self-defense Requirements and Capabilities—Seiichiro Onishi   143

Chapter 9
Soviet Policy in East Asia
—Gaston J. Sigur   165

Chapter 10
An Outlook on China in the 1980s: A Political Turnabout at Home and Improvement of Relations with the USSR—Mineo Nakajima   185

Chapter 11
Comprehensive Mutual Security Interests of the Major Industrialized Democracies
—James W. Morley   197

Appendix
Data Tables   219

Glossary	223
Index	225

LIST OF FIGURES AND TABLES

Figures

9-1	Soviet Military Deployment in the Far East	173
9-2	The Baykal-Amur Main Railroad	174
9-3	Outline of Soviet Ships and Military Aircraft Movements around Japan	181

Tables

6-1	Japanese Import Quota Restrictions, 1962-1973	98
6-2	U.S. Japan Bilateral Trade, Trade, and Current Account Balances 1953-1974 and 1975 First Two Quarters ($U.S. million)	100
6-3	Japan and U.S. Dependency on Imports and Share of Total World Imports of Major Basic Commodities	102

JOINT WORKING GROUP ON THE COMMON SECURITY INTERESTS OF JAPAN, THE UNITED STATES, AND NATO

CHAIRMAN
U. Alexis Johnson, director, Atlantic Council; former under secretary of state and ambassador to Japan

RAPPORTEUR
George R. Packard, dean, SAIS, Johns Hopkins University; former deputy director, Woodrow Wilson Center for Scholars, Smithsonian Institution

PROJECT DIRECTOR
Joseph W. Harned, deputy director general, Atlantic Council

MEMBERS
Robert W. Barnett, resident associate, Carnegie Endowment for International Peace; senior fellow, Asia Society; former deputy assistant secretary of state for East Asia

Ralph Clough, fellow, Woodrow Wilson Center for Scholars; former member, Policy Planning Council, Department of State

John Emmerson, senior research fellow, Hoover Institute on War, Revolution and Peace, Stanford University

William H.G. Fitzgerald, vice-chairman, Financial General Bank Shares

Henry H. Fowler, partner, Goldman Sachs & Co.; former secretary of the treasury

Andrew J. Goodpaster, superintendent, U.S. Military Academy; former supreme allied commander, Europe

JOINT WORKING GROUP MEMBERS

Lincoln Gordon, senior fellow, Resources for the Future; former assistant secretary of state

John E. Gray, president, International Energy Associates Limited

Marshall Green, former assistant secretary of state for East Asian and Pacific affairs

Eric W. Hayden, vice-president and senior economist, Bank of America

Martin J. Hillenbrand, director general, Atlantic Institute for International Affairs, Paris; former ambassador to Germany

James Hodgson, chairman of the board, Uranium Mining Corporation; former ambassador to Japan

Masamichi Inoki, president, Research Institute for Peace and Security, Tokyo; professor emeritus, Kyoto University

Fuji Kamiya, professor, Keio University

Lyman L. Lemnitzer, former supreme allied commander, Europe

Winston Lord, president, Council on Foreign Relations; former assistant secretary of state

David W. MacEachron, executive director, The Japan Society

Harald B. Malmgren, consultant; former deputy special representative for trade negotiations

Edwin M. Martin, former assistant secretary of state and chairman, OECD Development Assistance Committee

Makoto Momoi, professor, National Defense College, Tokyo

James W. Morley, professor of government, Columbia University

Mineo Nakajima, professor of international relations and modern China studies, Tokyo University of Foreign Studies

George S. Newman, manager, International Programs Department, BDM Corporation; former deputy chief of mission, U.S. Embassy, Korea

Paul H. Nitze, former secretary of the navy and deputy secretary of defense

Kazuo Nukazawa, senior assistant director, International Economic Affairs Department, Keidanren

Daniel Okimoto, assistant professor of political science, Stanford University

Seiichiro Onishi, secretary general, Research Institute for Peace and Security, Tokyo; former head, Japan Defense College

Robert E. Osgood, Christian A. Herter Professor of American Foreign Policy, SAIS, Johns Hopkins University

David Packard, chairman, Hewlett-Packard Company; former deputy secretary of defense

Henry S. Rowen, professor of public management, Graduate School of Business, Stanford University

Seizaburo Sato, professor, Tokyo University

Robert A. Scalapino, professor of political science, University of California at Berkeley

Thomas C. Schelling, professor of political economy, JFK School of Government, Harvard University

Cortlandt V.R. Schuyler, former chief of staff, Supreme Allied Command, Europe
Brent Scowcroft, former assistant to the president for national security affairs
Gaston J. Sigur, director, Institute for Sino-Soviet Studies, George Washington University
Richard Sneider, consultant; former ambassador to Korea
Richard Stilwell, former commander, Eighth Army, Korea
Leonard Sullivan, Jr., consultant, System Planning Corporation; former assistant secretary of defense
Tadae Takubo, foreign news editor, Jiji Press, Tokyo
Nathaniel Thayer, director of asian studies, SAIS, Johns Hopkins University
Philip H. Trezise, senior fellow, Brookings Institution; former assistant secretary of state and ambassador to OECD
William C. Turner, former ambassador to OECD
Franklin B. Weinstein, director, Project on U.S./Japan Relations, and professor of political science, Stanford University
Martin Weinstein, professor of political science, University of Illinois
Seymour Weiss, former director, Bureau of Politico-Military Affairs, Department of State
Thomas W. Wolfe, senior researcher, The Rand Corporation

INVITED GUESTS

Michael Armacost, deputy assistant secretary of state
David E. McGiffert, assistant secretary of defense
Hisahiko Okazaki, director general for foreign relations and intelligence, Japan Defense Agency
Nicholas Platt, deputy assistant secretary of defense
Naotoshi Sakonjo, former secretary general, Joint Chiefs of Staff, Japanese Self-defense Forces
Marshall D. Shulman, special adviser to the secretary of state
John Stremlau, assistant director, international relations, Rockefeller Foundation
Katsuichi Tsukamoto, former commanding general, Western Army, Japanese Self-defense Forces
Roy A. Werner, principal deputy assistant secretary of the army

EX OFFICIO

Theodore C. Achilles, vice-chairman, Atlantic Council
Kenneth Rush, chairman, Atlantic Council
Francis O. Wilcox, director general, Atlantic Council
Joseph J. Wolf, director, Atlantic Council

PROJECT ASSISTANT

Eliane Lomax, staff member, Atlantic Council

STUDENT INTERNS

John B. McGrath, graduate student, Columbia University
Ian O. Lesser, M.S. London School of Economics; candidate for Master of Law and Diplomacy, Fletcher School of Law and Diplomacy
Neile L. Miller, candidate for M.S.F.S., Georgetown School of Foreign Service

FOREWORD

The United States and Japan, and their friends and allies, together face truly awesome challenges in the 1980s. The confluence of recent international events and changing domestic perceptions has enhanced our political will, strengthened our sense of purpose, and today enables us to take new initiatives on the problems and opportunities that we share. History will judge us by how we respond to these challenges.

Soviet militarization of strategic islands off the coast of Japan; the Soviet invasion of formerly neutral, independent Afghanistan; Soviet use of surrogates to fix a grip on countries of Africa and the Indian Ocean—all are new elements of the long-term Soviet expansionism we have seen before in Berlin and Hungary and Czechechoslovakia. While negotiating limits on strategic weapons, the USSR and its satellites have piled up arms, seeking superiority over the United States and its allies. In the process, the Soviets clearly threaten to take advantage of our dependence on the Middle East for energy, thereby compounding our interlocking problems of inflation, employment, productivity, and trade.

The basic structure for cooperation to meet these challenges exists. The U.S.-Japan alliance, ANZUS, NATO, and the OECD in the fields of defense and economic cooperation attest to our mutual recognition that none of these problems can be resolved by any nation acting alone.

The hope that negotiation can dissuade the Soviet Union from pursuing its manifest effort to gain strategic superiority and political advantage must not diminish our resolve to match deployed Soviet power with deployed power of our own. The Soviets have not been known for trading clear advantage for unilateral concession.

The allies of the United States can rightfully expect America to stand by its commitment to their common defense. The United States can rightfully expect its allies to bear a fair share of that common defense effort. These expectations can be met only by close and increasing consultation, based on mutual confidence and reinforced by shared planning and capability. The basic structure of cooperation between Japan, the United States, and Western Europe needs to reflect this.

These three great power centers would seem to be as interdependent for their ultimate security as they are for their economic prosperity. What is needed is a mutual understanding among them that the maintenance of adequate deterrent force in the Atlantic, the Pacific, and the Middle East theaters is vital to the security of each of us. This issue has taken on a special urgency because of the steady increase of Soviet military power and the greater willingness of the Soviet Union to use its own or proxy forces to attempt to shift regional power balances in the Third World.

If deterrent balances are not kept, the Soviets may feel encouraged to undertake hostile action or to shift forces to the theater of allied weakness. Consider the situation that may develop if deterrence is weakened in one theater; an attack does come, either in that theater or in another; and the response is to "swing" forces away from the unthreatened theaters to the threatened one. The war could immediately escalate in the theater of first action, while a new danger is incurred that it may well spread to the other theaters to deter the "swing." Finally, consider the situation in which a "deterrent balance" is kept in each theater. The likelihood of war is seriously reduced; and even if it should come, there is a greater chance of discouraging its escalation and spread, since an aggressor would be hindered from concentrating its forces lest they be counterattacked in other theaters. The essential point is that it is very much to the advantage of Japan and Western Europe as well as the United States to keep the Soviet theater forces divided, facing three fronts—the European, the Middle Eastern and the Pacific—and pinned down on each by forces sufficiently strong to deter any Soviet moves to concentrate forces and cross borders.

But the common security interests of Japan, NATO, and the United States are considerably broader than this concept of "balanced deterrence." They include the areas of supply security—the assurance of adequate foodstuffs and raw materials as well as energy supplies. They include our responsibilities toward the developing countries of Asia, Africa, and Latin America. They include our relations with the People's Republic of China (PRC), North Korea, Vietnam, and Afghanistan as well as with Eastern Europe and the Soviet Union. They include economic and monetary cooperation as well as security and defense. In short, we are dealing with problems that are not amenable to unilateral action; but we are also dealing with problems that elicit national decisions and national initiatives daily. The need for effective and rigorous consultation has never been greater.

It was with this understanding that the Atlantic Council of the United States in Washington and the Research Institute for Peace and Security in Tokyo have collaborated for the past two years on a joint project to identify more clearly our common security interests and to recommend policies for cooperative action. U. Alexis Johnson, who has chaired this joint project, describes in the following Preface the scope and methodology of this work program. We would like to congratulate Ambassador Johnson on the results and to extend our deep appreciation to the members of the working group in the United States and Japan who have contributed their considerable expertise and their continuing commitment to the success of this project. We are also indebted to those who provided substantive and financial support—The United States Department of Defense, the Rockefeller Foundation, the Henry Luce Foundation, the Bank of America Foundation, the Earhart Foundation, and the Matsushita Electric Industrial Company Limited. Finally, very special thanks go to Hisahiko Okazaki for bringing our two institutions together at the start.

Kenneth Rush
Chairman
Atlantic Council of
   the United States

Masamichi Inoki
President
Research Institute for Peace
   and Security

PREFACE

As Dr. Inoki and Ambassador Rush have pointed out in their Foreword, it is now two years since the Atlantic Council of the United States and the Japanese Research Institute for Peace and Security (RIPS) decided to undertake a joint policy project on The Common Security Interests of Japan, the United States, and NATO.

After obtaining George Packard's agreement to be the rapporteur of the project, I readily accepted the invitation to act as chairman of the joint working group. The objective of the group fit well with my own views, developed during more than forty years' service in Asia, Europe, and Washington—experience from which I derived my conviction that just as there is now only one world in economic affairs, so is there only one world in security affairs. Thus, as far as the United States is concerned, loose talk of "swinging" forces from one theater at the expense of another in case of a major conflict with our principal opponent is just that—talk devoid of realism, talk that confuses and disconcerts our allies. Further, there is the general failure of our Asian allies to recognize that what is done or not done in Europe can have a direct effect on their own security and the concomitant failure of our European allies to recognize that what is done or not done in Asia can directly affect their security.

All this was given increased urgency and importance when, during the course of the study, orderly government broke down in Iran, and the Soviet invasion of Afghanistan brought Soviet forces within 350 miles of the Persian Gulf. It took no sophisticated geopolitical analysis to see that with the overwhelming dependence of both Japan and the European members of NATO on oil originating in or passing through the Persian Gulf, and with the United States having the only significant sea and air power available for deployment to the area, the term "common security interests" was given an immediate and sharper meaning.

As this was the first joint study of any kind undertaken by either the Atlantic Council or RIPS, and as their offices were 7000 miles apart, it was necessary for both organizations to develop new ways of doing things. In this, Fuji Kamiya very ably represented RIPS on the organizational as well as the substantive sides. In Tokyo, Seiichiro Onishi helped to guide and facilitate the project throughout its course. I am profoundly grateful to both for their cooperation and assistance. The substantive results of the project strongly reflect the consistent wisdom and good counsel of Dr. Inoki and Ambassador Rush, the heads of the two sponsoring institutions.

In selecting the American members of the Joint Working Group, we deliberately went beyond members of the Atlantic Council to enlist additional expertise. Although not as numerous, the Japanese members were drawn from an equally broad spectrum. It was originally anticipated that the Joint Working Group would consist of about fifteen members, but interest in the project was so great that eventually fifty-three persons, both Japanese and Americans, became members. The list on pages xi–xiv indicates the exceptional qualifications and experience that they collectively brought to the project. In addition, we drew on the wisdom of seven invited guests, as well as the four ex officio members. Three student interns contributed much useful research. Without the untiring and cheerful assistance of Eliane Lomax, the mass of paperwork and the organization of our meetings could never have been accomplished. Finally, but not least, the experience and energy of our project director, Joseph Harned, was invaluable.

At the first meeting of the Joint Working Group, in January 1979, agreement was reached that the project should be broken down into eight subjects. The writers assigned to each subject from among the members of the Joint Working Group were as follows:

1. The Balance of Power in East Asia and the Western Pacific During the 1980s—Dr. Ralph Clough and Professor Makoto Momoi.

2. Japan's Foreign Policy: Current and Projected into the 1980s—Professor Seizaburo Sato.
3. U.S. Interests and Policies in Asia and the Western Pacific during the 1980s—Ambassador Richard Sneider.
4. The U.S.—Japan Relationship—Dr. John K. Emmerson with Dr. Daniel Okimoto, and Professor Fuji Kamiya.
5. Japan's Self-Defense Requirements and Capabilities—Mr. Seiichiro Onishi.
6. Soviet Policy in Asia and the Pacific during the 1980s—Professor Gaston Sigur.
7. The People's Republic of China: Foreign Policy in the 1980s—Professor Mineo Nakajima.
8. Areas of Common Interest, Possible Cooperation, and Potential Friction among the United States, Japan, and other Western Countries—Professor James W. Morley and Professor Seizaburo Sato.

The individual studies were subjected to vigorous criticism in a series of meetings of the Joint Working Group in Washington and in Tokyo, as well as correspondence from members of the group not able to attend some meetings. The authors then reviewed and revised their papers in the light of those discussions, but retain responsibility for their individual papers. The results are all of the exceptionally high quality and interest befitting their distinguished authors and are published in full in this volume.

From the working group discussions and the evolution of these studies, George Packard, as the rapporteur, drew the substance of a summary Policy Paper. The drafts of the Policy Paper itself were, of course, also discussed in meetings of the Joint Working Group, and the penultimate draft was transmitted to each member of the group for concurrence or comment. Dean Packard, Joseph Harned, and I carefully reviewed all of those comments and incorporated the many excellent suggestions that were submitted. Others that we were not able to incorporate, but that were, nevertheless, substantively important, have been included as footnotes. In no case was there an effort to compromise the text down to the "lowest common denominator" of meaningless rhetoric; rather, the effort has been to identify problem areas and to make realistic policy recommendations on issues of importance.

It is hoped that this end product, which forms Chapter 1 of this volume, will stimulate debate and action. It is noteworthy that on a subject of such high political and emotional sensitivity in both countries, the discussions in the Joint Working Group and the written comments did not divide along American and Japanese "sides": Differing points of view were well represented on both sides.

It is also the hope of many who worked on the project that it may be a prelude to subsequent efforts that could include representation from Europe and Canada. In this connection, the members of the Joint Working Group were pleased to note that during the course of their work, a representative group of parliamentarians from the North Atlantic Assembly visited Japan at the invitation of members of the Japanese Diet. In turn, members of the newly formed Security Committee of the Diet have begun to participate in the debates of the assembly.

While no individual members of the Joint Working Group can be charged with responsibility for every word in the Policy Paper (Chapter 1), it does represent a "best effort" at recording the consensus that emerged from many hours of discussion and correspondence among informed and thoughtful Japanese and Americans. It is in that spirit that we commend it, together with the substantiating analyses that follow, to the peoples and governments of Japan and the United States and to the European and Canadian members of NATO.

U. Alexis Johnson
Chairman
Joint Working Group

EDITORS' NOTE

At the first meeting of the Joint Working Group in January 1979, agreement was reached that the project should be broken down into eight subject areas. Nine working papers—in addition to a collective policy paper—were commissioned from among the members of the Joint Working Group and are listed in the table of contents.

The nine individual papers were subjected to vigorous critique in a series of meetings of the Joint Working Group in Washington and in Tokyo, as well as through correspondence from members of the group not able to attend some meetings. The authors then reviewed and revised their papers in the light of those discussions but retain responsibility for their individual chapters. Each chapter, therefore, continues to reflect the author's style, translation, and spelling of foreign names. For the reader's convenience a glossary of acronyms and other specialized terms is provided at the end of this book.

From the working group discussions and the evolution of these papers the rapporteur drew the substance of the policy paper, which appears here as Chapter 1. The drafts of the policy paper itself were, of course, also discussed in meetings of the Joint Working Group, and the penultimate draft was transmitted to each member of the Joint Working Group for concurrence or comment. We carefully reviewed all of those comments and incorporated the many excellent suggestions that were submitted. Others that we were unable to incorporate but were substantively important, have been included as footnotes. In no case was there an effort to compromise the text down to the "lowest common denominator" of meaningless rhetoric; rather the effort has been to identify problem areas and to make realistic policy recommendations on issues of importance.

1 THE POLICY PAPER

INTRODUCTION

The United States and its allies—Japan and the NATO nations—all advanced industrialized democracies, have many interests in common and hold similar views about the kind of world that will enable them to pursue those interests. They share a belief in the preeminent value of self-government through representative institutions and respect for basic civil liberties and the rights of individuals. They share an interest in maintaining stable, healthy, and growing economies capable of raising the quality of life for all their citizens. Living in a world in which nations are interdependent, they share an interest in the continuing and orderly growth of trade; access to markets, raw materials, and investment possibilities; and sound international monetary arrangements that facilitate that trade and investment. They share concern for development of the poorer nations, since the advanced industrial nations cannot in the long run live peacefully in a world in which the gap between rich and poor grows greater by the day. Most of all, they share an interest in preserving world peace in a climate favorable to the flourishing of democratic forms of government and individual dignity.

History has taught that the maintenance of peace requires that no single nation or bloc of nations with expansionist tendencies be tempted to launch aggressive actions against others. The right of and need for collective defense is a cardinal principle of the Charter of the United Nations and forms the basis of the North Atlantic Treaty and of the U.S.-Japan Security Treaty.

Yet in the face of recent aggressions, the allied democracies have done surprisingly little in concert to maintain the balance of strength that will preserve the kind of liberal world order in which they can survive and prosper. The Joint Working Group of the Atlantic Council of the United States and the Research Institute on Peace and Security of Japan has examined this state of affairs and in this Policy Paper makes a series of recommendations for action aimed at harmonizing the policies of Japan, the United States, and the other NATO nations. In so doing, the Joint Working Group wishes to emphasize the importance it also attaches to the United States and Japan maintaining and improving relations with friendly countries of East and Southeast Asia, several of which have important security arrangements with the United States, and with Australia and New Zealand.

Since the early 1970s, many students of U.S. foreign policy and national security have argued that the common interests of Japan and NATO should encompass not only economic and cultural matters but security affairs as well. Despite the adverse events of the 1970s, however, these democracies did little to articulate or act upon their common security interests. The war of 1973 in the Middle East, the dramatic rise in oil prices dictated by OPEC, growing social and political unrest in South Asia and the Middle East, the clear increase in the military power of the Soviet Union and its evident ability and willingness to project this power into troubled areas far from its own borders (Vietnam, Angola, South Yemen, Ethiopia, Cuba), all failed to bring these democracies into a more cohesive grouping. Not even the more recent danger of a cutoff of oil from the Persian Gulf area following the fall of the Shah of Iran, nor the advent of a militantly anti-Western regime in Teheran, nor the Soviet invasion of Afghanistan (which brought Soviet fighter planes within striking distance of the Persian Gulf) have caused the allies to act effectively in concert.

SHIFTING U.S.-SOVIET BALANCE

The reasons for this situation are complex. The United States, long having recognized its role as a power with global interests, has nevertheless permitted its military power to decline during the past decade in relation to the strength of the Soviet Union. Also, during the 1970s, the atmosphere of détente raised unrealistic expectations about the willingness of the Soviet Union to moderate its expansionist activities. The Soviet Union, by continuing to build up its military forces, has been challenging the clear-cut American superiority in nuclear forces that prevailed from the end of World War II and has taken the lead in some categories of weapons. Some observers believe that the Soviet Union already possesses overall superiority in strategic forces, and others believe that if it is not superior today, it soon will be. There is no question that it possesses superior ground forces relative to those of the United States. Whatever the facts, almost everyone—allies and others—perceives that the Soviets have gained considerable ground on the United States, and the Soviets themselves have behaved in Afghanistan and elsewhere in a way that underscores their confidence in their ability to take unilateral military actions contrary to the interests of the United States and its allies and to do so with relative impunity. When the total strength of the United States and its allies is measured against that of the Soviet Union and its allies, however, and with China as a potential Soviet adversary in any major war, the balance appears less favorable to the Soviet Union. This underscores the absolute necessity for enhanced solidarity among the Western allies.

MILITARY REGIONALISM

During the thirty years since 1950, when the United States began building up its military strength in a serious way to meet the Soviet threat, European members of NATO and Japan, while undertaking significant defense programs of their own, have limited their efforts almost without exception to their own immediate regions. The United States accepted major responsibility for providing a counterweight to the Soviet strategic forces. The United States also accepted the political and economic realities that constrained its allies to limit their contributions in magnitude, in kind, and in geographic disposition. Although the economic interests of the major European NATO allies and Japan were global in scope, most of them accepted only limited military responsibilities; there was a view in Washington that growth in the economic power of Western Europe and Japan was in itself one effective way to contain the expansion of Soviet strategic influence.

LIMITS OF ALLIANCES

There are no formal or informal tripartite security arrangements linking the United States with both Japan and NATO. The United States maintains separate and independent security links with Western Europe through the North Atlantic Treaty on the one hand and with Japan through the United States–Japan Treaty of Mutual Cooperation and Security on the other. But these two alliances have not often generated military cooperation in times of crisis outside the treaty areas: Britain and France took unilateral action in the Suez crisis of 1956, and Japan remained uninvolved in the fighting by Americans in Korea and Vietnam.

There are deep historical, economic, and geographic reasons for this. After the devastation of World War II, the European nations and Japan struggled simply to survive. With the onset of Communist aggression, the United States was the only power in the world that could rapidly rebuild its military forces to contain the Soviet Union. Europe and Japan had different priorities. NATO was born in 1949, and the gradual rearmament of West Germany was subsequently accepted. The Soviet Union did not appear a major Pacific threat at that time. The shares of national resources of the European nations and Japan that have been devoted to defense now appear to be substantially less than would have been expected in a system of more equal and less limited alliances.

Perhaps most important, these "alliances" were not initially conceived as genuinely reciprocal security arrangements. On the contrary, they were primarily U.S. guarantees of the security of those other nations, undertaken in the interest both of the United States and those nations to prevent their piecemeal intimidation and drift into the Soviet sphere. Neither the North Atlantic Treaty nor the Japanese treaty, as conceived, really envisioned a partnership in which these allied nations might have to contribute to larger global security interests. Most of the other NATO nations and Japan saw themselves initially not so much as partners, but rather as holders of an American insurance policy—with remarkably reasonable annual premiums. Viewed from this perspective, it is not so surprising that there has been little evidence of "allied solidarity" concerning Suez, Korea, Vietnam, or even the Middle East: These had nothing to do with the original "policy coverage."

Japan emerged from U.S. occupation in 1952 with a constitution containing an article (IX) that states in part: "land, sea and air forces, as well as other war potential, will never be maintained. The right of belligerency of the state will not be recognized." Under pressure from the United States during the Korean War, the Japanese established a 75,000 man national police reserve. which developed into a 250,000 man Self-Defense Force, but they have consistently interpreted Article IX as prohibiting the dispatch of troops overseas. In 1976, the Japanese government decided that for the present, defense expenditures in each fiscal year should not exceed 1 percent of GNP. Japan's defense budget has thus been lowest in proportion to GNP of any major power in the world. In addition, successive prime ministers of Japan have adhered to three nonnuclear principles—Japan will not manufacture nuclear weapons, will not maintain such weapons on its territory, and will not permit them to be introduced into its territory.

It should be noted that successive U.S. administrations have not spoken to the issue of Japanese armament with a consistent or unified voice. Some U.S. officials have argued that a military resurgence in Japan would create consternation throughout Asia and might upset the political balance within Japan. Others have argued for a rapid build-up, with special emphasis on sea and air protection. The U.S. government has never—even to this day—fully resolved these contrasting approaches, although recent U.S. government statements indicate that it now favors a steady and significant build-up of Japan's Self-Defense Forces. Japanese governments have, over the years, in accordance with their perceptions of domestic political attitudes, built up their armed forces far more slowly than their rapid economic growth would have permitted.

The U.S.-Japan Security Treaty, as revised in 1960, gives the United States the right to maintain troops and bases in Japan, but is unequal in the way it would operate in time of attack: The treaty provides that an armed attack against either party on Japanese territory would require each party to act to meet the common danger in accordance with its constitutional provisions and processes. But an attack against U.S. forces anywhere outside the territory of Japan does not require the Japanese to do anything. This arrangement has suited the political climate in Tokyo: The Japanese people emerged from their defeat and occupation with strongly pacifist sentiments, and only in the past several years have government leaders been able to talk openly about the possible need for greater defense efforts. The U.S. withdrawal from Vietnam and the possibility of further pullbacks of U.S. forces from Asia and the Pacific, however, impelled Japanese leaders to think more seriously about their security interests. Until then, the American alliance had given them security at relatively low cost to the Japanese budget, and their own "economic miracle" had provided stability and prosperity at home. There had been no reason to go further than they had.

LACK OF EUROPE-JAPAN LINKS

Since the withdrawal of the French from Indochina, the Dutch from Indonesia, and the British from east of Suez in the late 1940s, 1950s, and 1960s, Europeans have shown little interest in military developments in East Asia and the Pacific. The war fought by the United States in Vietnam concerned them mainly because it drained U.S. military manpower and other resources from what they considered the more important task of defending NATO nations in Europe. Nor did Japan identify its vital security interests with developments in the NATO area. Neither the European NATO nations nor Japan perceived that they have security interests in common; each took for granted that the United States could, should, and would shoulder the burden. The Joint Working Group, after studying the new power relationships and world political situation that have evolved during the decade of the 1970s, believes that the time is at hand for a reexamination of these premises.

SOVIET PACIFIC MILITARY BUILD-UPS

The Joint Working Group noted that the worldwide build-up of Soviet military power included major increases in East Asia and the Pacific during the past decade—a doubling of ground forces (reportedly to forty-six divisions with 450,000 men along the Sino-Soviet border); a large increase in the number of fighter-attack and other aircraft, including backfire bombers, and SS-20 Intermediate range ballistic missiles (IRBMs); the addition of submarines, an antisubmarine warfare (ASW) carrier, and other warships to its naval strength in the area; the construction of permanent military bases on Sakhalin and the southern Kuriles (Etorofu, Kunashiri, and Shikotan—islands claimed by Japan) and the recent stationing there of a division of troops supported by MIG-17s, 130-mm artillery, and assault helicopters; building naval facilities at Petropavlosk on the Kamchatka Peninsula; using former American port facilities at Danang and Cam Ranh Bay, as a result of a 1978 treaty of alliance with Vietnam; and appearing with increasing frequency and duration in the waters around Southeast Asia, particularly around the important Straits of Malacca and in the Indian Ocean—waters crucial to Japan's shipping lanes to Middle East oil.

This build-up was certainly not confined to Asia, but was part of a worldwide strengthening of Soviet military power. It is important to note that the rise in Soviet conventional and theater nuclear strength in Europe was equally impressive. In addition, during the decade of the 1970s, the Soviet effort on strategic nuclear forces was substantially larger than that of the United States. The effect of this effort was to cast doubt on an earlier presumption that the United States and its allies could count on U.S. superiority in nuclear weaponry to deter the Soviets from exploiting superiority in conventional forces.

PERCEPTIONS OF UNITED STATES RETRENCHMENT

During the period of this global build-up of Soviet power, the United States was seen by its major allies in Asia to be withdrawing militarily from that area, giving rise to perceptions of a major shift in the balance of power in the region. These Asian fears that the United States could abandon its strategic role in this part of the world were fed by a series of events, including the announcement of the Nixon Doctrine in 1969, the final withdrawal of American troops from Vietnam in 1972, President (then candidate) Carter's call in 1976 for withdrawal of U.S. ground combat forces from South Korea (later suspended), and the U.S. abrogation of its defense pact with the Republic of China in Taiwan. Given the general mood of isolationism in the United States, many Asians came to fear that America would abandon a major strategic role in the area. And given the domestic economic and political problems within the United States and an impression of faltering leadership both at home and abroad, the reliability and capability of the United States as an ally began to be questioned in Tokyo. At the same time, without an effective alternative, the political acceptability of the alliance to the Japanese increased.

These fears were compounded by the perceptions in Asia of the American "swing" doctrine. With rising turbulence in the Middle East and the perception that the United States was giving priority to the security of Europe over the security of its Asian allies, there was concern that if war were to break out in Europe and/or the Middle East, Asia might not even keep the "one-half war" forces of the so-called "one-and-one-half war" U.S. defense capabilities.

Some of these fears have been allayed in recent months. The United States has moderated the "swing doctrine," and the U.S. forces in Asia and the Pacific are no longer automatically redeployed to NATO. The U.S. position in the Philippines seems assured for some time to come as a result of the new base agreements. The U.S. government has also made clear its intention to keep present troop strength in the Republic of Korea (ROK) and to assist in the modernization of ROK forces. And the rapprochement between the People's Republic of China and the United States, strengthened by the normalization of relations on January 1, 1979, has led to closer governmental relations—despite continuing, though "unofficial," U.S. ties with Taiwan. All of these factors have given the impression that the "Vietnam syndrome" that made Washington uncertain with respect to its undertakings in Asia may be receding.

SOVIET INTENTIONS IN THE PACIFIC

The Joint Working Group devoted considerable attention to the question of why the Soviets were building up their power in Asia and the Pacific. A few members related it mainly to the growing tension between Moscow and Peking and to Soviet fears that China would ally itself with the United States, Japan, and other NATO nations to "encircle" the Soviet Union. The Soviets clearly support Vietnam as a counterweight to the expansion of Chinese power into Southeast Asia. Most members, while acknowledging Soviet concerns over China, believed that there is an additional explanation for Soviet actions. In this view, the Soviets have, at least since the end of World War II, sought to extend their power and influence in the world. The Soviets believe in the historical inevitability of their system prevailing over the West, that they are duty-bound to assist that process, and that the development of military power is a critical means of facilitating this process—along with the exploitation of unrest, tensions, and frustrations in the Third World. They have sought what they conceive to be a favorable change in the "correlation of forces" in the world and, in fact, argue today that they have accomplished such a shift. In any event, the new Soviet naval strength in the western Pacific presents a clear challenge to the previous dominance of the U.S. Seventh Fleet in the area.

IMPLICATIONS OF SOVIET BUILD-UP

What are the implications of this major build-up in East Asia and the Pacific for the United States and Japan? Does the new Soviet strength pose the danger of a direct military attack against Japan? The Joint Working Group, while recognizing that it is impossible to assess Soviet intentions with certitude, concluded that the more probable threat is indirect: Their new power gives the Soviets an ability to apply political pressure on nations in Asia heretofore friendly to the United States and especially on Japan—thus gaining increased influence in Asian and Pacific political affairs. And in the eventuality of U.S.-Soviet hostilities anywhere in the world, this build-up could give the Soviets potential superiority and a chance for decisive victory in East Asia, especially if American forces had been shifted to Europe, the Middle East, or elsewhere.

A clear Soviet military superiority in East Asia and the Pacific would have important implications for the unresolved disputes or potential disputes in the region with respect to Taiwan, the tensions between North and South Korea, and the potential for Vietnamese aggression against its neighbors in Southeast Asia.

ROLE OF THE PEOPLE'S REPUBLIC OF CHINA

Central to all these questions is the posture of the People's Republic of China. Will it continue on its present course toward "rational" economic development and modernization, or will it revert to the chaotic politics of the cultural revolution? Will the Sino-Soviet split continue, or will new leadership in one or both nations see advantages in resolving their disputes? To what extent should the United States, Japan, and other Western nations cooperate with China in its drive to modernize? What are the longer term implications of a modernized China for the security of U.S. allies in Asia, including Japan? To what extent will the next generation of Chinese leaders be able to exert control over China's vast population?

While it was not possible to answer these questions with certainty, most members of the Joint Working Group felt that rational economic planning would continue for the foreseeable future, but that it would be a mistake to base policy solely on the judgment that Sino-Soviet hostility would continue indefinitely. Some members felt that there was a possibility of a reconciliation, as each of the Communist giants might sufficiently overcome their differences in order to give them greater flexibility in tackling serious and unavoidable domestic problems in the decade of the 1980s. There was a strong feeling that one factor that could drive China toward Moscow would be Peking's calculation that the United States and its allies were in fact on the decline and the defensive, lacking the strength and the will to maintain a favorable global balance of power versus the Soviet Union. U.S. and allied credibility and reliability would certainly be crucial to the continuation of China's friendly ties to the West. Meanwhile, the existence of the Sino-Soviet dispute had the beneficial effect for the West of forcing the Soviets to tie down considerable military strength along the Sino-Soviet border, thus limiting its ability to enter trouble spots elsewhere.

The Joint Working Group agreed that an economically strong, modernizing, secure, and peaceful China was in the interests of all and that a weakened, humiliated, hostile, or defeated China would have grave consequences for the security both of the NATO nations and of Japan. It was felt that normal economic relations with Peking were highly desirable. On the other hand, most members of the group did not favor giving outright military aid to the People's Republic of China or entering into security arrangements that could encourage the Chinese to undertake military actions outside its borders. Some members of the group were prepared to offer moderate amounts of arms to the PRC and supported current U.S. moves to make available nonlethal military support equipment and dual use technology. They believed that a military strengthening of China would serve to offset the more immediate threat of the Soviet Union. These members, however, saw clear limits to this aid, as they did not necessarily view the PRC as a permanently friendly power, but only one with which the United States shared a possibly temporary convergence of interests. Others felt that no military equipment should be offered to the Chinese, because they fear that the emergence of a powerful PRC may bring turbulence to East Asia in the long run and that military aid to the PRC may unnecessarily alarm the Soviet Union.

THE EMERGING OIL FACTOR

Other changes in the world of the late 1970s affected the perceptions of Japan, the United States, and other NATO nations about the extent of their common security interests. The overthrow of the Shah and the political turmoil in Iran, the Soviet invasion of Afghanistan, and the growing Soviet capability of cutting off oil supplies from the Middle East became vital concerns to all. Continued access to the Persian Gulf was a matter of critical importance to the industries of Western Europe and Japan.[1] Soviet control of Middle Eastern oil would shift the balance of world power. Denial of access to Middle Eastern oil because of political turmoil in the region would obviously have grave implications for the economies of the allied nations and for economic stability in the world generally.

The new dangers require important changes in strategic thinking in Washington and Tokyo and in the capitals of Europe and provide the background to the policy recommendations that follow. Faced with the seizure of American hostages in Iran, the invasion of Afghanistan, and growing Soviet influence in parts of the Middle East as well as rising political unrest throughout the area, the U.S. government has taken some modest steps to reverse the relative decline in its military power and has called on its allies for support in this effort. The "Carter Doctrine" of January 1980, which declares that the United States will fight if necessary to preserve its access to the Middle East, will require a major build-up of American armed forces—particularly rapid deployment forces—if it is to be credible.[2] The current gap

---

1. Japan depends on oil for 75 percent of all its energy needs. Seventy-three percent of that oil came in 1979 from the Middle East. The European Community (EC) nations import 67 percent of their oil from the Middle East; the U.S. figure is 25 percent.

2. "An attempt by any outside force to gain control of the Persian Gulf region will be regarded as an assault on the vital interests of the United States. It will be repelled by use of any means necessary, including military force." President Jimmy Carter, State of the Union Address, January 23, 1980.

between the doctrine and U.S. ability to implement it is dangerously wide and could invite rather than deter a challenge.

CHANGING JAPANESE ATTITUDES

In Tokyo, meanwhile, a new climate of opinion has been forming, foreshadowing a greater willingness to become more responsibly involved in world affairs. The announcement in 1977 of the "Fukuda Doctrine," by which Japan pledged to double its level of foreign aid, and the completion of that doubling by 1980, as well as Japan's conclusion of a treaty of peace and amity with the PRC in 1978 without waiting for Washington to normalize relations with Peking were signals of the change.

Japanese opposition to the U.S.-Japan Security Treaty and to the Self-Defense Forces has waned. Public opinion favors the treaty (by 63 percent in a recent poll) and supports the retention of the Self-Defense Forces (86 percent)—degrees of support unprecedented in the postwar period. Some prominent Japanese have called for a stronger, autonomous self-defense force, independent of the American alliance, but this option appears to have been rejected for now, and most Japanese leaders appear to favor a larger role for Japan in defending its own security interests—but within the framework of the U.S. alliance. The Liberal Democratic party of Japan, which has strongly endorsed the alliance since the party's formation in 1955, was returned to power by a clear majority in both houses of the Diet in June 1980, and the new Suzuki cabinet that emerged in July signaled that Japan would continue upon the course set by its predecessors. The Suzuki cabinet is reportedly willing to raise the rate of increase for defense expenditures in the 1981 budget and to propose the establishment of a comprehensive national security council to deal with security matters. The government of Japan also announced in the summer of 1980 that its patrol aircraft will carry air-to-air missiles for the first time and that its ships will carry torpedoes.

Japan's continued support for the alliance, however, will depend upon the extent to which U.S. leadership appears strong, decisive, and consistent. Further evidence of vacillation, unreliability, military weakness, or domestic instability will seriously undermine the alliance.

The Japanese have within the past year shown a new willingness to join with others in security efforts. In the winter of 1980, Japan sent two destroyers and eight antisubmarine patrol aircraft with 700 seamen to a "Rimpac" naval training exercise in the central Pacific, along with naval forces from the United States, Canada, Australia, and New Zealand. Such a multinational exercise would have been unthinkable a few years ago. In addition, there is an increasing mutuality of interest and shared potential for cooperation between Japan and Australia in the maritime defense sphere. And the U.S.-Japan Security Treaty is producing new cooperation and coordination of defense efforts under the Guidelines for Defense Cooperation adopted by the two governments in 1978.

In March 1980, a security committee was formed in the Diet—the first such committee in the postwar period. The Japanese have also shown interest in opening talks with members of NATO in addition to the United States. The head of Japan's Defense Agency visited NATO headquarters at his own request during the summer of 1979. In May 1980, an informal dialogue between members of the North Atlantic Assembly (NATO parliamentarians) and members of the Japanese Diet was opened at a meeting in Tokyo. The West German defense minister paid a visit to Tokyo in March 1980. The government of Japan has clearly acknowledged that it can no longer adhere to its long-standing policy of separating politics from economics. Foreign Minister Okita declared on January 23, 1980: "The era of so-called passive foreign policy is ended, and we must now embark upon an activist foreign policy. . . ." He added: "Japan can no longer view international relations as external givens but must perceive them as conditions that Japan itself should participate importantly in creating."

Precisely what all this means in terms of Japan's future security policies is not yet clear, but the Joint Working Group believes that the time may be appropriate for new thinking and new policies with respect to Japan's common security interests with the NATO nations. Neither the NATO nations nor Japan will be able to free themselves from vital dependence on Middle East oil for many years to come. Consequently, it is critically important to them that a credible deterrent force be positioned in the area before access is denied, either by Soviet military power or by local political upheavals. The United States declared its intention to provide a credible military deterrent with the help of others in the Carter Doctrine, but this policy cannot and will not be successful if its sole effect is merely to draw down U.S. forces from either the European or northeast Asian theaters or to reduce the capability to reinforce U.S. forces in those areas. Additional responsibilities will accrue to the Europeans, as indicated below. A sharp drawdown in one theater could tempt the Soviets to take hostile action in that theater.

MULTITHEATER STRATEGY

The Joint Working Group believes that the outbreak of U.S.-Soviet hostilities in any one theater might well spread to the others very quickly and that the best way to reduce the likelihood of war would be to maintain an adequate deterrent balance in each theater. Weakness in either Western Europe or Asia would permit the Soviet Union to shift its military resources in the other direction. By the same token, strength in both regions forces a division of Soviet resources and inhibits a massing of military strength in either the West or Asia. Some of the group members even opined that it is very much to the advantage of Western Europe and Japan, as well as the United States, to keep the Soviet theater forces divided and facing three fronts—the European, the Middle Eastern, and the Asian.

Options to Support Strategy

How can this be accomplished? There would appear to be at least three options. One is for the United States unilaterally to expand its military efforts dramatically and quickly so that it might station significant and effective deterrent forces in the Middle East without drawing down forces that are already committed to East Asia and to Europe. This is not a likely or practical possibility. Such a move would require the immediate imposition of U.S. military conscription (which both major political parties in the 1980 election year deny is required) or dramatically increased peacetime pay scales and benefits and other spending that the Congress might or might not approve. The requisite ships, aircraft, and other combat equipment under the best of circumstances require years of lead time before they can be built, manned, and deployed. It is true that the Congress has in recent months been more inclined to increase defense spending than the White House and that the political climate in the United States is changing. But it is also true that there is a growing feeling among Americans that the allied nations should contribute more to mutual defense. There would be strong, perhaps even acrimonious, demands upon the allies by the United States that would jeopardize the kind of close relationships required by the threat.

A second option would be for the European nations of NATO and for Japan to increase their defense capabilities in their own regions, thereby permitting the United States to deploy forces previously earmarked for the European and East Asian theaters to the Middle East. Even then, however, U.S. forces will be stretched too thinly in the three theaters; U.S. aircraft carriers sent from the Pacific or Mediterranean to the Indian Ocean, for example, leave a gap that only the United States can fill today. Moreover, multilateral defense measures in the Middle Eastern theater would be more politically acceptable and credible in the region than a unilateral U.S. presence.

A third option would be for the United States, the other members of NATO, and Japan immediately to undertake a sufficient strengthening of their defense capabilities to permit the deployment of allied forces to the Middle East to which each would contribute according to their capabilities while continuing to maintain a credible and effective level of forces in their respective theaters. Nations not having the military or political capability of providing combat elements could contribute to the logistic support of such allied forces.

IMPLEMENTATION DIFFICULTIES

There would be serious difficulties in accomplishing this third option. The NATO nations of Europe are by no means agreed on the need for stronger military capabilities in the Middle East. Many Japanese, even within the upper echelons of the ruling Liberal Democratic party, harbor reservations about becoming involved in a concerted strategic posture with the United States and other NATO nations lest Japan be dragged into a conflict originating far from its own shores, in a scenario over which it might exercise no control. And it is by no means clear that American voters, facing serious economic difficulties, are prepared to elect a Congress that will support such commitments and the requisite new spending measures.

REALITIES IN RELATIONSHIPS

Underlying these difficulties are some basic realities about the relationships between the United States, Japan, and NATO. While there is growing recognition that these three great power centers of the non-Communist world share a vital interest in acting together to preserve access to the Middle East and to prevent further Soviet expansion, the United States, Japan, and NATO Europe lack the tradition and the institutional structure for working trilaterally on security matters.

The Europeans and Japanese, having devoted themselves primarily to economic goals, have failed in the postwar period to take the security concerns of the others very seriously and often have failed to agree with the United States on how to meet the threat posed by the Soviet Union. Neither the European NATO nations nor Japan have accepted the mutuality of their security interests as a given. In addition, they are reluctant to take any action that could in their view increase tension between East and West.

There is the further question of who speaks for Europe—and through what organization? NATO is not a supranational organization. Each member state continues to raise its own forces and deployes them as it sees fit, assigning some to NATO (except in the case of France, which assigns none) and reserving others for its own defense purposes. For domestic political reasons, West Germany seeks to preserve its *ostpolitick*. Other organizations, such as the European Community (EC), are not primarily concerned with military security. Even on the economic front, the EC has been unable thus far to negotiate a communitywide agreement with Japan. Moreover, there is considerable sentiment in Britain to get out of the community. The disparate European reactions to President Carter's call for common action against Iran after the seizure of American hostages and their dismay over the abortive rescue attempt of April 24–25, 1980, have further separated the allies. The varying reactions to President Carter's call for various economic sanctions and a boycott of the 1980 Summer Olympics in Moscow indicate further disarray and suggest how hard it will be to forge a new sense of unity on common security interests.

Yet what is the alternative? It should be clear that the new threats of the 1980s cannot and will not be met by the United States alone in the same way that earlier Cold War threats were met—by massive increases in U.S. military spending, new U.S. alliance systems, increases in U.S. military and economic support for allies, and unilateral deployment of additional American forces to forward bases throughout the world.

CHANGING ECONOMIC BALANCE AMONG THE ALLIES

There is no longer a large economic gap among the nations of Western Europe, Japan, and the United States. The per capita GNP of each is now approaching equality, and the German and Japanese economies, while smaller than the American, are widely seen as fundamentally stronger in some respects. The dollar has lost strength as the predominant currency for world trade. American attitudes toward military matters, partly as a result of frustration in Vietnam, have changed; there is a consciousness of the limits of military power and a growing reluctance to go it alone. The United States is ready to do more, but the scale and direction of its efforts will be heavily affected by the willingness of the allies to shoulder a greater share of the defense burden and the perception of that willingness by the U.S. Congress.

CONCLUSIONS

To Enhance Allied Military Capability

There appear to be four separate principles that should guide the collective future military efforts of the allies:

- In view of the continuing momentum of Soviet military build-ups, Soviet political expansionism, and Soviet attraction and utilization of client states, the allies must become substantially more aware of their own essential security requirements. Japan and Europe can no longer put off, nor relegate to the United States alone, the commitment of greater resources to their collective security. There can in fact no longer be individual national security for any of the advanced industrialized nations—only collective security in which all participate according to their capabilities. Economic power, geography, political freedom, and individual motivation all favor the Western developed nations. The allies can only lose control of their own future destiny and progress if they lose sight of what is required to earn those benefits by investing more heavily in their own future security.

- Comprehensive security requirements of the allies cannot readily be segregated as between their political, economic, and military components. National security—and collective security—cannot be assured if any aspect is neglected. Political will and economic responsibility and strength are as important as armored divisions and long-range bombers. Unless the allies learn to coordinate and apply their latent political and economic strengths and resilience to our mutual security problems, military efforts may well be totally wasted —and vice versa. Military force cannot compensate for the collapse of political or economic strength and cohesion. Conversely, the assurance of bases, the supply of resources, economic aid to areas of conflict and potential conflict, enhanced energy independence, and the provision of logistic support all should be counted as significant contributions to collective defense.

- The world is not yet ready to forsake respect for—or to resort to—military force. Regional economic and political stability still requires the existence, in sufficient magnitude, of clearly perceived military force. Less well-disciplined nations cannot be permitted to disrupt the continuing progress and evolution of the world through barbaric and terrorist acts designed to intimidate civilized government or corrode the fabric of accepted international institutions. If and when military actions are required to preserve allied security, the legitimacy of such actions will be substantially enhanced in the eyes of all observers if they carry the weight of international cooperation and shared responsibility. Equally important, the effective application of conventional forces is critically dependent on nonmilitary economic and logistic support. For instance, American industrial mobilization supported allied military actions well before the U.S. entered World War II. Similarly, North Vietnamese successes in Southeast Asia—and Cuban successes in Africa—have been made possible by Soviet commercial sea and airlift capabilities. Likewise, U.S. operations in both Korea and Vietnam were significantly enhanced by the cooperation of the merchant marines of several nonbelligerents—as well as logistic support bases in several Pacific nations friendly to the United States.

• The application of limited and appropriate conventional military force can be seriously inhibited if adversary forces are perceived to have strategic superiority. When dealing with an adversary who has both conventional and strategic nuclear forces, conventional forces for deterrence and for defense will be inadequate if not supported by essential strategic equivalence. In other words, the deterrent value of conventional forces is strongly related to the perceived balance of strategic forces.

Based on these general guidelines, it seems clear that by working together, and contributing in many different ways, the allied powers can adopt the requisite "multitheater strategy" collectively.

To Enhance Allied Political Strength

• The United States should offer a clear and consistent sense of purpose and direction to its allies and to its own people.
• All of the allies should, as partners, find new and creative partnership approaches to coordinating their politics and actions.
• The United States and Japan should find ways—at least as effective as the NATO mechanisms—for coordinating their defense efforts in implementing the 1978 Joint Defense Guidelines. Dialogue on a regular basis at both the political and military levels between Japan and NATO would be valuable.

To Enhance Allied Economic Strength

• We need to find new and more effective ways to assure the soundness and stability and growth of our collective economies and particularly to cure the disease of endemic inflation.
• There is a critical need for an extraordinary international cooperative effort to reduce allied dependence on Middle East oil. Countries that are constrained in the level of their military contributions, such as the Federal Republic of Germany and Japan, should make

a compensatory investment in a massive research and development effort to enhance allied energy independence.

- Also, such countries should make compensatory increases in their contributions from their enormous economic and technological skills. They should increase the flow of capital and technical assistance to nations in areas of conflict or potential conflict—such as Turkey, Pakistan, Egypt, and Thailand.

- The allies should cooperatively increase their stockpiles of oil and other essential raw materials, in order to decrease the economic instabilities associated with possible supply interruptions, and should make extraordinary efforts to conserve energy as well as to develop alternative sources.

POLICY RECOMMENDATIONS

The Joint Working Group of the Atlantic Council of the United States and the Research Institute for Peace and Security of Japan believes that the following recommendations can be effective in defending the common security interests of Japan, the United States, and NATO:

1. Forming a Political Framework for Comprehensive Security

A procedure should be established, within or outside the framework of the present "big seven" economic summit conferences, for high level exchanges of views or consultations among the United States, the other major members of NATO, and Japan on comprehensive security questions of common interest to include (but not be limited to) those set forth below. Such activities would address overall goals and missions, including equitable sharing of the overall costs and responsibilities. Existing institutions would be used to the maximum extent possible in implementing decisions that are reached, but new institutions might be established where necessary.[3]

---

3. Franklin B. Weinstein comments: "I have reservations about the desirability of launching a regular program of multilateral security consultations at the summit level. In my judgment, it would be preferable to begin with less formal consultations at the working

2. Establishing a Credible Middle East Deterrent

To deter the Soviet Union from directly or indirectly expanding its influence in the Middle East or obtaining control of access to Middle Eastern oil supplies, an adequate deterrent force should be established as quickly as possible in that area, capable of a variety of missions on land, on sea, and in the air. The United States is the only country capable of taking the lead in this operation. Other NATO nations and Japan should undertake agreed assignments within the region:

- France, the Federal Republic of Germany, the United Kingdom, and Canada should provide appropriate military assets to the Middle East–Persian Gulf area to enhance allied capability and to demonstrate allied solidarity.
- Other NATO Europe nations and Japan should apply their own civil assets, including airlift and sealift, to support this allied presence in the Middle East–Persian Gulf area. Countries with past operational experience in the Middle East region could provide valuable intelligence and training support for forces in or being deployed to the area.

3. Maintaining Deterrence Elsewhere

As the foregoing will require some drawdown of U.S. forces earmarked for deployment to the European and Asia–Pacific theaters in an emergency, and perhaps even limited temporary reductions in U.S. air and naval forces there in peacetime, other NATO nations and Japan should promptly increase their defense efforts to compensate for the drawdowns of American forces.

---

level. Such consultations are likely to be more effective as a means of exchanging views and less provocative, either to Japanese who question the appropriateness of their participation in such an endeavor, or the Soviets concerned about the possible development of an anti-Soviet united front."

4. Strengthening U.S. Forces

The United States should make greater efforts to maintain a sufficiently strong and credible strategic nuclear posture vis-à-vis the Soviet Union.

The United States should promptly increase the size and quality of its conventional forces in order to maintain with its allies a satisfactory level of deterrence in all three theaters. In doing so, the United States should fulfill its commitments under NATO's Long Term Defense Program.

The United States should immediately proceed to implement its plan to create and maintain substantial strategic petroleum reserves.

5. Demonstrating Continued U.S. Commitment in the Asia-Pacific Area

By word and deed, the United States should avoid any implication that it intends to withdraw from the Asia-Pacific region. By demonstrating that it is and will remain a Pacific power, the United States can ease many of the anxieties of its allies and potential supporters in the region.

6. Restoring U.S. Economic Health

The United States should promptly do whatever is necessary to restore its own economy to health, enhancing its productivity, curbing inflation, correcting balance of payments deficits, and reducing its dependence on oil imports.

7. Increasing Japan's Defense Capabilities

Japan should strengthen and improve its Self-Defense Force. It should stress its air defense, antisubmarine, and mine-laying capabilities. Japan may have to increase its own war reserve stockpiles, thereby decreasing its dependence on U.S. combat-sustaining support.

8. Increasing the Effectiveness of the U.S.-Japan Security Treaty

To the maximum feasible extent, Japan and the United States should, in implementing the 1978 Joint Defense Guidelines, standardize and integrate their intelligence, communications, logistics, weapons, and training systems for the purpose of being prepared to undertake joint operations in the event of an outbreak of hostilities. The United States and Japan should also find new and effective means to coordinate joint operations. Japan should increase the application of its own civil assets—including airlift and sealift—to support the movement of U.S. reinforcements across the Pacific.

9. Increasing Japan's Financial Contribution

Japan should continue to increase its share of the costs for maintaining U.S. troops and bases in Japan, since those troops contribute in an important way to the comprehensive security of Japan and the United States.

10. Enhancing Japan's Contribution to Allied Energy Independence

As a significant component of comprehensive allied security, Japan should devote a major new effort to support research and development of alternate sources of energy.

11. Increasing Japan's Contribution to Middle East Stability

Japan should continue to increase its economic and technical assistance to areas of conflict and potential conflict, especially to key nations in the Middle East.

12. Avoiding Trade Conflicts and Protectionism

Japan, the United States, and the other NATO nations should not permit temporary and inevitable trade frictions to undermine their far more important and lasting interest in working together for the common good. Above all, the kind of protectionism that led to disaster in the 1930s must be avoided. The advanced industrial democracies share a huge stake in maintaining regional and world peace and security for all nations and in preserving stability and growth of the world economy under conditions of orderly trade, investment, and access to raw materials. They share an interest in seeing that representative governments flourish wherever possible. All of these shared interests—and more—dictate that they should place potentially divisive trade issues in the perspective of the larger goals and deal with them accordingly.

13. Affirming U.S. Support for the Republic of Korea

The United States must make it unmistakably clear that it will continue its support for the Republic of Korea and that the United States intends to maintain ground combat forces there.[4]

14. Assisting the People's Republic of China

The allied nations should provide economic and technological assistance but not lethal military equipment in support of the modernization program of the People's Republic of China.

15. Supporting the Association of Southeast Asian Nations (ASEAN)

The ASEAN nations represent an important element in the maintenance of the stability of Southeast Asia and occupy a critically

---

4. Franklin B. Weinstein comments: "I do not agree that the United States should indicate an intention indefinitely to maintain ground combat forces in the Republic of Korea."

important geographic position on the sea lines of communication. The allied nations should continue to support ASEAN and maintain close relations with these friendly nations.

16. Supporting Other Diplomatic and Political Measures[5]

Although these recommendations have focused mainly on common security interests and the strengthening of defense capabilities, this should not be interpreted as in any way detracting from the importance of diplomatic and political measures aimed at reducing areas of potential conflict, especially in the Middle East.

The Joint Working Group strongly recommends that the allied nations energetically pursue such efforts in concert.

---

5. Robert W. Barnett comments: "Beyond the foregoing recommendations, there must be readiness to explore mutually beneficial relations with the USSR, and to negotiate such trustworthy arms control and disarmament arrangements as can lift some of the burden of military spending from the world economy."

2 THE BALANCE OF POWER IN EAST ASIA AND THE WESTERN PACIFIC DURING THE 1980s
An American Perspective
Ralph N. Clough

> *Ralph N. Clough, China specialist, diplomat, and author of many books and articles on the countries of East Asia, depicts in broad brushstrokes the power realities in East Asia and how they might be affected during the 1980s by developments inside and outside the region. After assessing the recent build-up of Soviet power in East Asia and the western Pacific and how it might affect the balance of power between the United States and the Soviet Union, he sifts through the complex relationships among the four major powers—the United States, the USSR, Japan, and China—weighs possible sources of instability, and examines trouble spots, including Korea, Taiwan, and the Indochinese peninsula. This overview sets the stage for subsequent chapters on specific security problems in the region and how they relate to the common security interests of Japan, the United States, and NATO.*

Since World War II, the global balance of power in military terms has been dominated by the confrontation between the superpowers. This condition will continue through the 1980s, as no other nation will acquire strategic nuclear power or conventional arms comparable to those possessed by the United States and the Soviet Union. The primary area of confrontation for their forces and those of their allies will continue to be the NATO–Warsaw Pact region. The armaments of some medium-sized and small powers outside this region probably will continue to increase, however, and sizable regional conflicts, such as that between Iraq and Iran, are likely to occur. Such conflicts may involve the United States and the Soviet Union to some extent, but both will try to avoid being drawn into a direct military confrontation.

Determining which of the two superpowers possesses military superiority over the other is not easy. A simple count of the number of men under arms, the numbers and types of weapons, and the size of the military budgets on each side is highly misleading because of differences in the geographical position of each, in the kinds of security threats each force is designed to meet, and in the importance of alliance relationships and many other factors, including uncertainty as to the shape and size of a strategic nuclear force needed to deter the adversary.

However one may judge the current state of the global military balance, the view is widely accepted in the United States and among U.S. allies that in recent years the Soviet Union has been outspending the United States and acquiring new weapons at a faster rate. The U.S. government increased its military budget in 1980, and the climate of public opinion is more favorable to military spending than it was a few years ago. It is impossible to predict, however, which of the superpowers will be in a stronger position relative to the other by the end of the 1980s, because of the number of variables involved, including technological advances, American attitudes toward defense, the impact of regional conflicts, internal political changes, and shifts in international alignment.

The state of the world economy during the 1980s is also extremely difficult to predict, and basic economic changes could have a greater long-term effect on the global balance of power than changes in stocks of arms. Expert predictions as to the availability and cost of energy in 1990 vary widely, but substantial additional increases in the price of petroleum products seem inevitable. A further sharp rise in the cost of energy would produce widespread and serious repercussions. As Adam Ulam has said, "nothing the U.S.S.R. has done since the war has dealt as devastating a blow to the West as the actions of OPEC."[1]

---

1. Adam Ulam, "U.S.-Soviet Relations: Unhappy Coexistence," *Foreign Affairs* 57, no. 3 ("Extra issue"—1979): 567.

The other major uncertainty in economic forecasting is the future international economic role of the United States. Its dominant economic position in the world since World War II has been weakening as other economies, particularly those of West Germany and Japan, have gained in strength. Some further weakening seems likely during the 1980s, but no substitute for the U.S. dollar as the basic international currency is in sight. The countries of the three principal industrial areas of the non-Communist world face difficult decisions as they seek to check inflation, reduce excessively large surpluses and deficits in the international balance of payments, hold down protectionist pressures, and promote economic growth and the expansion of world trade. A retreat to protectionism, low growth rates, and continued inflation would seriously weaken the ability of the United States and its allies to cooperate in maintaining strong defenses.

THE PLACE OF EAST ASIA IN THE GLOBAL POWER BALANCE

It is paradoxical that East Asia has been a secondary theater for the Soviet Union, but a region where the United States has fought two major wars. The large-scale Soviet military build-up in East Asia did not begin until the 1960s and has been directed principally against China rather than against the United States and its ally, Japan. Because of China's hostility and the inability of the Russians to draw Japan away from its alliance with the United States, Soviet leaders must concern themselves principally with the defense of the Soviet Union's long border in East Asia and the avoidance of conflicts that would seriously drain Soviet military power from the primary front in Europe.

The Soviet military build-up in East Asia is not, however, exclusively for defensive purposes. Given China's weakness in modern weapons, Soviet forces positioned along the Chinese frontier are much stronger than would be needed to cope with a Chinese attack. They also serve as a warning to the Chinese not to proceed too far against countries friendly to the Soviet Union, such as Vietnam, lest they suffer a retaliatory blow. Soviet naval and air forces based at Vladivostok and Petropavlovsk, while perhaps more readily justified as needed defense against the United States, also have the missions of demonstrating Soviet power to the Japanese and of spreading Soviet influence through Southeast Asia and into the Indian Ocean, particularly since the Soviets have gained the use of Danang and Cam Ranh Bay in Vietnam.

In one sense, the Soviet Union is in a stronger position in East Asia than the United States, for a large part of its territory lies within this region and provides domestic locations for military bases, while the United States, with the exception of its territory, Guam, is thousands of miles away. There are also, however, strategic disadvantages to the Soviet position. Siberia and the Soviet Far East are sparsely populated and only tenuously linked by rail to the rest of the Soviet Union. It has thousands of miles of land border to defend. Its East Asian neighbors are militarily weak today, but both Japan and China are potentially powerful nations, capable of threatening Soviet territory at some future time, particularly if they should ever join forces. The United States, on the other hand, has no potentially threatening neighbors close to its borders and no land border of its own to defend in East Asia.

Navigation at the principal Soviet naval bases at Vladivostok and Petropavlovsk is hampered by ice much of the year: Both rely heavily on easily cut sea lines of communication for supply, and Vladivostok has access to the open Pacific only through narrow straits that could be readily mined in time of war. U.S. bases in Japan, Guam, and the Philippines are much better located than Soviet bases for the purpose of deploying naval and air power in the western Pacific. Hence the significance of the Soviet alliance with Vietnam. If the Soviets were to establish major naval and air bases in Vietnam, the reach of their military power would be greatly enhanced.[2]

The two wars fought by the United States in East Asia had radically different effects on the global power balance. The political shock waves created by the Korean War facilitated the strengthening of NATO, the rapid build-up of U.S. forces, the U.S.–Japan Security Treaty, and the beginning of Japan's economic recovery and rearmament. The Vietnam War, on the other hand, drained strength from U.S. units committed to NATO, created strains between the United States and its allies, diminished popular support for U.S. military commitments abroad, and set in motion economic trends that weakened the international position of the United States.

---

2. At the Vienna Summit Meeting in June 1979, Brezhnev reportedly assured President Carter that the Soviet Union would not develop such bases. See *Los Angeles Times*, June 24, 1979.

Although the outcome of the Vietnam War strengthened the power position of the Soviet Union in Southeast Asia through its acquisition of an exclusive alliance with Vietnam, opening the door to the possible establishment of Soviet military bases in that country, it compelled the Soviets in return to assume substantial economic, military, and political burdens. The example of Cuba demonstrates that the Soviets are not loath to accept such burdens in distant places if they produce a significant expansion of Soviet influence. Nevertheless, Vietnam is likely to prove a costly investment, particularly in the light of other burdens assumed in Afghanistan, Africa, and Cuba at the beginning of a decade of increasing economic difficulties within the Soviet Union. Cambodian resistance to the Vietnamese military occupation is likely to continue for years, exacerbating the severe economic problems in Vietnam itself and creating a continuing need for Soviet military and economic assistance. Soviet backing of Vietnamese aggression has made even more remote the prospect of improving relations with China and Soviet hopes for increasing its influence among the ASEAN nations.

Since 1975, the position of the United States in East Asia relative to that of the Soviet Union has improved. The only land border in the region to which U.S. forces are now committed, in Korea, is relatively short, and South Korean forces are capable of doing most of the fighting should North Korea attack. Our principal ally in the region, Japan, which is a vital interest of the United States because of the size of its population and economy and its advanced technology, is protected by a water barrier that facilitates its defense. Soviet policies in East Asia have had the effect of strengthening Japanese support of the U.S.-Japan Security Treaty and diminishing opposition to increasing expenditures on Japan's own defense forces. Moreover, the United States and Japan are in the process of expanding relations with China. The end of the Vietnam War and the shift from a state of confrontation to one of selective cooperation in U.S. relations with the People's Republic of China has freed for other uses U.S. forces in the western Pacific that were formerly tied down in Vietnam or deployed to "contain" China. The recent Philippine bases agreement assures the continued use of those important military strongpoints.

East Asia's contribution to the global power balance in economic terms has been growing rapidly. Japan has become the second largest economy in the non-Communist world. Moreover, the non-Communist portion of the region, including Japan, constitutes the fastest growing area of the world with the exception of the Middle East oil-producing region. U.S. trade with East Asia and the Pacific has for several years exceeded its trade with the European Community (EC), and the gap will probably grow. China, under its new, pragmatic leadership, probably will increase its rate of economic growth and become increasingly linked economically with Japan, the United States, and Western Europe.

Seen from Moscow, the potential long-term threats to Soviet security probably outweigh the prospects for early gains in East Asia that would strengthen the Soviet position in the global balance. Since 1975, overt military conflicts in the region have been limited to conflicts between Communist states. Moscow's two Communist allies, Vietnam and North Korea, are both economic burdens rather than assets. In addition, North Korea inclines more toward China than the Soviet Union, having forthrightly and publicly condemned the Vietnamese invasion of Cambodia. The one bright spot in the picture, Hanoi's choice of Moscow over Peking, is clouded by the burdens and risks of supporting a distant client state. Finally, the military potential of an industrializing China and of a Japan more defense minded than in the past, together with the trend toward greater cooperation among the United States, Japan, and China, must present a disturbing prospect to the Soviet Union.

BIG POWER RELATIONS AND POSSIBLE CHANGES IN 1980s

The two fundamental big power relationships in East Asia at the outset of the 1980s are the U.S.-Japan alliance, which has lasted for nearly thirty years, and Sino-Soviet hostility, which has persisted for nearly twenty. The patterns of behavior that have developed on the basis of these relationships are resistant to change.

The U.S.-Japan alliance has served both countries well and is highly regarded by the people of both countries. Criticism of the treaty has declined to a low level in Japan, and cooperation between U.S. and Japanese military forces is closer than ever before. Uneasiness among the Japanese at the reduction of U.S. forces in the western Pacific, particularly the once planned but now suspended withdrawal of ground combat forces from Korea, combined with the growing strength of the Soviet Pacific fleet have increased pressures in Japan for a greater defense effort. Even though the new interest in defense is unlikely to cause Japan to increase defense spending much above the past ceiling of 1 percent of GNP—barring some dramatic increase in the threat to Japan—the continued growth of Japan's economy will permit sizable annual increases in the defense budget.

The principal problems between the United States and Japan today are economic. The continuing large Japanese surplus in trade with the United States is stimulating protectionist sentiment in this country. Structural differences in the economies of the two countries and the difficulty of managing their economies so as to cope with problems of growth, inflation, and unemployment in each without adversely affecting the other probably ensure that economic difficulties will continue to plague the alliance throughout the 1980s. As indicated above, unusual strains are afflicting the global economy, and the United States and Japan will be able to moderate their bilateral difficulties only in the context of measures also agreed upon by the governments of the other principal non-Communist economies.

While the prognosis for the U.S.-Japan relationship in the short-term future is mixed—good military relations accompanied by economic strains—the prognosis for Sino-Soviet relations is for continuing tension as a result of Vietnam's invasion of Cambodia and China's invasion of Vietnam. Should a full-scale war between the Soviet Union and China result, the United States would face difficult decisions as to whether to give the Chinese material assistance. However, both Peking and Moscow have strong reasons for wishing to avoid a large-scale war. The Chinese deliberately limited their "punishment" of Vietnam in order to avoid compelling the Soviets to do more than rush material aid to the Vietnamese and make threatening statements.

Even though the two big Communist powers probably will continue to avoid a major military clash with each other, rivalry in Southeast Asia will perpetuate the tension between them and keep prospects of reconciliation remote. Moscow had its best recent opportunity to seek better relations with Peking in the months after Mao's death, but proved unwilling to make sufficiently important concessions to China. Now that China has embarked on a policy of rapid modernization through reliance on the West, the Soviets will find it even more difficult to improve relations with the Chinese. The pattern of hostility has become so deeply imbedded in the thinking and policies of each side that reciprocal actions to moderate the hostility are likely to be difficult even when new leaders take over in Peking and Moscow.

The Sino-Japanese peace treaty, signed despite vehement Soviet objections, and the long-term trade agreement between China and Japan have set the stage for much closer relations between these two Asian powers in the 1980s than in the past. China clearly regards Japan as the principal supplier of capital and technology for its modernization program, and Japan sees China as an increasingly important market and a supplier of oil and coal, with the China trade increasing from its present level of 2 percent of Japan's total trade to perhaps as much as 5 percent by 1985. Territorial disputes over the Senkaku Islands and undersea resources on the continental shelf have been set to one side by mutual consent, and agreement has been reached on cooperation in the production of oil off the China coast. Japan's dispute with the Soviet Union over the northern islands and uneasiness at the growing power of the Soviet Pacific fleet produce sympathy among the Japanese for Chinese criticisms of the "polar bear," although Japan does not wish to take sides with China against the Soviet Union. In the long run, Japan and China may become rivals for leadership in Asia, but during the 1980s, the forces causing them to cooperate seem weightier than those that would drive them apart.

Steady and mutually advantageous expansion of economic relations between Japan and China in the 1980s can occur, however, only if China remains politically stable. The most serious threat to stability is the possible failure of Teng Hsiao-p'ing's modernization program to satisfy the rising expectations of the people. Many essential objectives will be difficult to achieve—increasing agricultural production, accumulating the enormous investment capital needed for industrial expansion, making more consumer goods available as incentives for increased productivity, expanding exports to pay for needed technology, and rebuilding the crippled educational system to meet the rising demand for technicians, engineers, and scientists.

Another threat to the modernization program is the drain on resources imposed by the conflict with Vietnam. Even if fighting on the scale of the February–March invasion of 1979 does not resume and the Soviets refrain from intervening militarily, the need to maintain large forces on the China–Vietnam border indefinitely will be a substantial burden. Moreover, if the conflict should flare up again, the prominence given to the role of China's military forces could readily increase pressures for more rapid modernization of the armed forces, thus diverting resources from more productive investment and increasing the difficulty of satisfying demands for consumer goods.

Soviet obduracy on the northern islands issue, harsh treatment of Japanese fishermen, and growing naval activity in the seas around Japan have cooled relations between the two countries. Both would like to see expanded trade based upon the development of Siberian resources with the help of Japanese capital and technology, but negotiations on large-scale projects have moved slowly. Lack of progress on large projects has resulted in part from Japan's desire to invest heavily only if American firms also participate. For many reasons, American capital has not been available for these large projects, and there are few signs that it will be during the 1980s. Past patterns suggest that Japan's supply of capital and technology to China in the 1980s will expand more rapidly than its supply of capital and technology to the Soviet Union, despite Japan's professed desire to conduct an "equidistant diplomacy" with the two Communist powers. Japan will try to remain neutral in Sino-Soviet disputes, especially if these should lead to military conflict.

Normalization of U.S.-PRC diplomatic relations augurs a substantial expansion of trade, cultural, and other relations between these two powers, although at a slower pace than some of the more euphoric current predictions. By 1985, bilateral trade may have reached $3 billion according to administration officials, three times the 1978 level, but it probably cannot attain the 1979 level of U.S. trade with Taiwan—$9 billion—before the late 1980s. Throughout the 1980s, it will be a small fraction of U.S.-Japan trade, which amounted to $35 billion in 1978.

Political relations between the United States and China will be more important and more difficult to manage than economic relations. The triangular U.S.-China-USSR relationship is certain to pose difficulties, for the United States has a vital interest in maintaining a relationship with the Soviet Union that will minimize the risk of a nuclear conflict, while China deprecates any improvement in Moscow-Washington relations. The China-Vietnam conflict demonstrates how difficult it is for the United States to avoid being used—or at least seeming to be used—by one side or the other when hostility between Moscow and Peking intensifies. The Chinese also, while eager for a relationship with the United States that will strengthen China's position vis-à-vis the Soviet Union, will resent being relegated to the status of a "China card," to be played or not played at the pleasure of the United States.

During the 1980s, the United States may have to seriously reconsider its decision not to supply China with advanced weapons. Further strengthening of Soviet armed forces relative to those of the United States or additional Soviet political gains abroad through coups or proxy wars would increase the probability that the United States would wish to improve Chinese defense capability in order to compensate for Soviet advances. On the other hand, a militarily stronger China would not necessarily be in the U.S. interest in all circumstances. Chinese forces could be used in Southeast Asia or against Taiwan in ways contrary to U.S. interests.

DEVELOPMENTS WITHIN THE REGION AFFECTING MAJOR POWERS

Vietnamese determination to dominate Indochina, as evidenced by its military presence in both Laos and Cambodia, will continue to disturb Southeast Asia during the 1980s and affect the major powers. Already China and the Soviet Union have become deeply involved in the region through their support of Cambodia and Vietnam. The prospects look bleak for making all of Southeast Asia a "zone of peace and neutrality," as desired by the ASEAN nations, from which big power military intervention would be excluded. The Chinese pledge to support an anti-Vietnamese guerilla war in Cambodia, the threat of renewed Chinese "punishment" of the Vietnamese if they misbehave, and the probability of increasing Vietnamese dependence on the Soviet Union promise continuing and perhaps intensified projection of Sino-Soviet rivalry into Southeast Asia. Soviet acquisition of a military base in Vietnam would increase the likelihood of Sino-Soviet military clashes in the region. Moreover, if Thailand should be drawn into the struggle, as a result of its territory being used to support a guerilla war in Cambodia and Vietnamese retaliation by armed incursions or by increasing support of the Communist insurgency in Thailand, U.S. interests in the region would be threatened.

In northeastern Asia, the danger of renewed conflict in Korea will continue to pose a threat to U.S. interests in the 1980s. The Korean peninsula is less volatile than Southeast Asia, however. Neither China nor the Soviet Union has shown any signs of willingness to back Kim Il-sung in the use of force against South Korea, and neither is likely to do so as long as the United States maintains its security commitment to South Korea and has forces on the peninsula. By the late 1980s, South Korea probably will be much stronger than North Korea militarily as well as economically, provided the establishment of a successor government to that of Park Chung-hee is successfully managed. Political disorders in the south, or a succession crisis in the north following the death of Kim Il-sung, could increase the danger of war on the peninsula.

Taiwan has weathered well the first year and a half following the shock of U.S. severance of diplomatic relations and the announcement of the early termination of the security treaty. Technical difficulties have hindered the conduct of relations between the United States and Taiwan by unofficial means, but the effects have not been serious. A difficult problem facing Taiwan in the 1980s will be the need to restructure the political system to give greater power to the Taiwanese. Whether this restructuring and the selection of a successor to Chiang Ching-kuo can be accomplished smoothly is uncertain. Political troubles in Taiwan might well attract intervention by the PRC and require a reaction by the United States. Although the use of force by the PRC against Taiwan in the 1980s seems unlikely if the island remains politically stable, differences that already exist between Washington and Peking over the supply of weapons to Taiwan may sharpen, especially with regard to the supply of modern aircraft and other advanced weapons. Other forms of PRC pressure on Taiwan could also create friction between the United States and the PRC. Under some circumstances, the people on Taiwan might declare the island an independent state, which would force on the United States difficult decisions—whether to recognize the new state and whether to help defend it should Peking decide that hope for a peaceful reunification had evaporated.

Economic changes in the region during the 1980s probably will favor the U.S.-Japan axis and states associated with it, provided that there is no severe and prolonged world depression during this period. The Japanese economy seems likely to expand at a moderate rate, somewhat faster than the U.S. economy, while the fast-growing free enterprise economies of the region—South Korea, Taiwan, Hong Kong, and Singapore—assuming no serious political disorders such as those that afflicted South Korea in 1979–1980, probably will maintain a fairly high growth rate at least until the mid-1980s. The prospects for the non-Communist states of Southeast Asia (except for Burma) and for Australia and New Zealand also look reasonably good.

The Soviet Union will pursue the development of Siberia, making some additional natural resources available from this region, but this is an expensive, difficult task, and as indicated above, no large capital assistance can be expected from the United States and Japan. Soviet trade with East Asian countries can be expected to grow some, but it will remain insignificant compared to the trade of the United States and Japan in the region. The two states most closely allied with the Soviet Union—North Korea and Vietnam—probably will continue to be an economic drain rather than an addition to Soviet economic power. Vietnam, in particular, suffers from severe domestic economic problems that are exacerbated by its military occupation of Cambodia, losses suffered in the recent Chinese invasion, and the need to maintain costly defenses against possible future Chinese incursions. Vietnam is thus likely to be an economic burden for the Soviet Union during much of the 1980s.

How China will affect the economic balance in the region is difficult to predict. If the pragmatic policies of Teng Hsiao-p'ing prevail throughout the 1980s and China is relatively successful in managing its difficult problems in economic development, China's economic ties with Japan, the United States, and Western Europe will expand substantially. All parties will benefit from the growing trade. If, however, political turmoil should recur in China or Peking should overextend itself in accepting foreign loans and be unable to repay on time or a Sino-Soviet conflict should break out, China would not be in a position to contribute to the economic health of the region. China seems unlikely, however, to become a significant drain on the resources of the United States and Japan except in the unlikely event of a large-scale war with the Soviet Union in which the United States and Japan chose to back China.

IMPACT ON EAST ASIAN SECURITY OF FACTORS OUTSIDE THE REGION

The recent events in Iran have demonstrated how quickly a sharp reduction in the world supply of oil can affect other regions. Japan's heavy dependence on oil from the Middle East makes it exceptionally vulnerable. South Korea, Taiwan, and most other East Asian countries are similarly dependent on regular supplies of outside oil. Their economies would be hard hit by a global conflict that cut off or greatly reduced the flow of oil to their ports.

The Iranian disturbances have already exerted heavy upward pressure on oil prices. As a result, many countries in East Asia have suffered greater inflation. It will be more difficult for the United States to hold the line on inflation, which in turn will add to economic strains between the United States and Japan. Similar disturbances in other oil-producing countries during the 1980s would further complicate the problem of controlling world inflation and aggravate economic friction between the United States and Japan and other friendly countries in East Asia.

Rapidly rising oil prices and uncertainties about supply will increase Japan's desire to rely more on nuclear power. Consequently, Japan is likely to oppose even more strongly than in the past U.S. urgings that Japan reconsider its program to build nuclear reprocessing facilities and to develop the fast breeder reactor. The South Koreans will be strongly tempted to follow Japan's example. Should the United States abandon its opposition to these nuclear technologies, the risk of nuclear proliferation in the world would increase. On the other hand, continued opposition would cause greater friction with Japan and South Korea.

Because of Japan's dependence on Middle Eastern oil, concern is often expressed about the security of the sea lanes from that region to Japan. These could be most easily interfered with at three places — at the exit from the Persian Gulf, at the Malacca Straits, and in the waters near Japan. The first and second of these chokepoints could be affected by conflicts involving the bordering countries; the third, only by a conflict between Japan and the Soviet Union or Japan and China. Neither of the latter contingencies seems at all likely in the 1980s. Closure of the Malacca Straits could be circumvented by routing tankers via other straits through Indonesia or around Australia. These detours would increase travel time and raise the cost of transporting oil but would be a cheaper and more practicable stratagem than intervening militarily to keep the straits open.

Given the conflicts and uncertainties in the Middle East, the Persian Gulf chokepoint is the one most likely to suffer interference. Since the seizure of power by a revolutionary government in Iran, the United States has deployed ships of the Seventh Fleet into the Indian Ocean more frequently and for longer periods. The Japanese have not objected to the temporary diversion of ships from the Seventh Fleet for this purpose, because maintaining the oil flow out of the Middle East is even more important to Japan than to the United States. If such a diversion should continue indefinitely and on a substantial scale, however, the Japanese might feel more exposed in the presence of the Soviet Pacific fleet—assuming that elements from that fleet were not diverted to the Indian Ocean on a scale comparable to those from the Seventh Fleet. As a consequence, pressures in Japan for increases in Japan's own naval and air power probably would rise.

The Soviet military occupation of Afghanistan has increased apprehension in the United States and among its allies concerning possible threats to the supply of oil from the Middle East, intensifying the concern aroused by events in Iran. The United States has obtained base rights in Kenya, Somalia, and Oman and is developing a quick reaction force to respond to threats in the region. The creation of an American military deterrent force usable on short notice in the Middle East probably will require the transfer of some naval and air units from the Pacific, which will adversely affect the military balance there, unless Japan can be induced to make up the deficiency. On the other hand, Soviet behavior in Afghanistan, by increasing the level of concern among East Asian nations as to Soviet intentions elsewhere, has improved the prospects for greater cooperation among them in security matters in the 1980s.

SECURITY RELATIONSHIP BETWEEN NATO AND EAST ASIA

The military interconnection between the NATO region and East Asia is perceived most keenly by the Soviet Union, the only power that has land borders in both areas. It must divide its ground, air, and sea forces between the two areas. A relative increase or decline in the military threat perceived in one area can be compensated for by shifting forces between areas, so long as there is no simultaneous increase in the threat in both areas. A growing military threat on both fronts would pose the most serious danger to Soviet security.

Although China has no territory in the NATO region, it perceives the linkage between the size of the Soviet military forces in that area and those on China's frontier. Consequently, the Chinese have for years urged Western European and American leaders to strengthen NATO forces. Since the early 1970s, they have also favored an American military presence in the western Pacific and the strengthening of Japanese forces to help counter Soviet expansionism. Relatively weak itself militarily, and fearing Soviet encirclement, China seeks the help of strong, friendly states in both East and West to check "Soviet hegemonism."

The Japanese government no doubt sees the linkage between the NATO and Pacific arenas, but most Japanese commentators tend to disregard it. They do not, like the Chinese, perceive a strengthening of NATO forces as diminishing Soviet capability to deploy forces in East Asia. On the contrary, they tend to regard the two theaters as totally separate, so that a deployment of certain U.S. naval forces from the Pacific to the Atlantic or Mediterranean is seen only as a reduction of U.S. naval capability in the Pacific and not as increasing the Soviet requirement for naval forces on its western front, thus limiting Soviet capability to maintain or reinforce its Pacific fleet. As the Japanese become more defense minded in the 1980s, they will probably come to appreciate more the nature of the global military confrontation between the United States and the Soviet Union and the linkage between the western and eastern fronts. It will be in the interest of the United States to encourage global strategic thinking on the part of the Japanese.

European allies of the United States, confronted primarily by a threat from ground and air forces rather than naval and air forces like the Japanese, seem more sensitive to the military interconnection between the NATO region and East Asia. They recognize the advantages to them of the Sino–Soviet confrontation in diverting a substantial proportion of Soviet military capability to the Chinese frontier. Their interest in supplying modern weapons to China derives from this strategic perception, as well as from commercial motives. If the Warsaw Pact advantage in military forces on the western front should continue or increase in the 1980s, European interest in China as a military counterweight is likely also to increase.

Europeans do not appear to regard the deployment of U.S. forces to the western Pacific, primarily for the defense of Japan, as significantly affecting the level of forces that the United States might otherwise deploy to the European theater. They probably see U.S. naval and air forces in the western Pacific as tying down a roughly equivalent Soviet force. Moreover, units of the U.S. Seventh Fleet have also been deployed to the vicinity of the Persian Gulf and Red Sea, where they serve European as well as U.S. interests in protecting the flow of oil from the Middle East. When U.S. forces engage in relatively large-scale combat in East Asia against a secondary power associated with the Soviet Union, however, as in the Vietnam War, most Europeans are likely to view it as a diversion of U.S. power, reducing that which would otherwise be available to counter Soviet forces. This strategic perception was no doubt one reason, although not the only one, for the unpopularity of the Vietnam War among our NATO allies.

The economic linkage between the NATO region and East Asia is more readily perceived both in Japan and in Western Europe than the military linkage. The major powers are all deeply involved in the world economy, and Japan participates along with the NATO powers in economic summit meetings, the OECD, GATT, and the global financial institutions. All recognize that their security as well as their prosperity depend on the maintenance of the global economic system created after World War II. Just as economic troubles created conditions conducive to the outbreak of that war, so could competitive protectionism, declining world trade, inflation, recession, and unemployment undermine the security of all.

The Japanese feel more exposed to the effects of sweeping economic changes than the NATO countries, for they do not belong to a community of nations like the EC, nor do they have control over large amounts of natural resources like the United States. Since the end of World War II, they have rejected reliance on military power to ensure access to markets and raw materials, relying instead on their security pact with the United States and the workings of the world economic system. An unlikely but conceivable threat to the East Asian balance of power in the 1980s would be economic pressures on Japan so severe as to cause replacement of the moderate and conservative group that has governed Japan since World War II by politicians who would weaken ties with the United States and set Japan on a different course.

3 THE BALANCE OF POWER IN EAST ASIA AND THE WESTERN PACIFIC IN THE 1980s
A Japanese Perspective
Makoto Momoi

Professor Makoto Momoi, a longtime defense analyst who teaches at Japan's National Defense College, argues forcefully that security problems in East Asia and the western Pacific can no longer be seen as regional but must be viewed in a global context. Citing recent challenges to the assumptions once comfortably accepted by Japanese defense experts, Professor Momoi offers three basic approaches that might be adopted by Japan to defense questions and explains how the new concept of "comprehensive national security" can provide a rational basis for future defense planning in Japan.

One of the major purposes of this joint study by the Atlantic Council and the Japan Institute for Peace and Security is to face the realities of contemporary international relations and strategic environments in a global context. No study can succeed if it fails to take account of global perspectives. No longer can we talk about a peninsula in the Far East in regional terms. It was in a global context that James Schlesinger, former U.S. secretary of defense, justified the continued presence of U.S. troops in the Korean peninsula. In his defense posture statement of February 5, 1975, Schlesinger pointed out three reasons why that U.S. military presence in the peninsula would deter other Asian nations from creating problems when war broke out in Europe, why this presence would deter the Soviet

Union from moving its troops west of the Urals, and why the U.S. troops in Korea would deter the Soviets from deploying a second front in Asia.

His view was echoed, though in a slightly different context, by China's Vice-premier Teng Hsiao-p'ing. In an interview with a visiting West German politician, on March 23, 1978, Teng was quoted as saying that it was necessary for China and Japan to collaborate in the East and for Western Europe and the U.S. to collaborate in the West, in order to oppose the Soviet Union. This reflects the Chinese assessment of its strategic environment, in which Peking clearly sees itself not in a regional Pacific-Asian or Sino-Soviet border context but in a global perspective.

The Soviet Union, on the other hand, seems to place a new and stronger emphasis on the Pacific region in a global context: N. Pedrova, commentator in the *New World Note*, stresses a "fundamental change in the global political map." "No longer is the Pacific area a provincial region distant from the center [of the world], because of the globalization of international relations," he asserts.[1]

These and other views of the changing nature of the global stratopolitical map are shared by most of the Japanese who have witnessed in recent years the growing Soviet naval and air presence in the northwestern Pacific. They may not necessarily agree with Vice-premier Teng, who on October 21, 1977, reportedly told an AFP executive that "in order to bury the Soviet Union's world war plan, the whole world, it is hoped, must unite;" but they may buy Pedrova's thesis that the Pacific has become a "focal arena of impending political issues of the contemporary world."

Japanese defense specialists strongly agree with U.S. Secretary of Defense Harold Brown who, in his speech in Los Angeles on February 20, 1978, argued that the United States cannot afford to be weak in Asia while remaining strong in Europe, since U.S. capabilities in the two regions are complementary. A consensus is forming in Japan that a world war may not necessarily be triggered by a military (naval) confrontation in the Pacific but instead might arise in some other part of the world and spread to the region. With the expansion of Soviet naval strength, the Pacific could be an ideal theater for the U.S. and Soviet navies to deploy "naval" (as contrasted to ground) second fronts, if and when a major war breaks out in Europe. A naval

---

1. N. Pedrova, *New World Note* 173 (March 1979).

balance in the Pacific, therefore, contributes to the security of the Atlantic, even if the relationship seems indirect.

REGIONAL PERSPECTIVE

For the past three decades, Japan depended for its own security on U.S. military strength. Japan's underlying sense of security rested on three assumptions: (1) a U.S.-Soviet strategic balance in which Washington was perceived as the superior power; (2) confirmed U.S. commitment and action of the kind that had kept numerous armed conflicts in the world from escalating into major wars; and (3) continued U.S. military presence in the Pacific-Asian region with a relative dominance over other powers.

Today all these assumptions are being challenged: The superpower balance may remain "essentially equivalent" in a purely static analysis but may turn fluid in a dynamic strategic assessment. The Soviet Union may now believe that it is not impossible to contemplate a first strike against the United States, given the increased precision and other improved strategic offensive systems, after which their homeland (including most of their leaders) can expect to survive U.S. retaliatory attacks, thanks to the enhanced strategic defense systems. This, of course, may remain an untested, unproven war plan. One cannot, however, rule out the possibility that the Kremlin leaders, looking at a numerical balance sheet, might gain politico-psychological overconfidence that in turn could be translated into overbearing attitudes in their diplomatic negotiations not only with the United States but with other nations as well. To that extent, the security of these nations might become threatened by Moscow.

Second, the United States has opted for what its allies perceive as selectivity in its security commitment since the announcement of the Nixon Doctrine, while the Soviet Union has acquired capabilities to project its politicomilitary influence to areas distant from Moscow—for example, Africa, the Middle East, and Indochina. Hence, local conflicts may increase in their frequency and even escalate in their intensity as Moscow continues to find new opportunities to exploit local tensions.

Third, in the Pacific-Asian region, U.S. allies perceive, rightly or wrongly, a declining U.S. military presence, if not an erosion of U.S. will. One can of course argue, as did Secretary Brown in his posture statement in 1978, that China can be a strategic counterweight against the Soviet Union. This thesis may be valid only in terms of a mainly land confrontation—for example, along the Sino-Soviet border. It is the Japanese perception that expanded Soviet naval presence is a more serious threat that is not lessened by China's military strength; hence, the "China card" is not a favorite subject in Japan.

Since the three basic security assumptions have been under challenge, Japanese authorities have begun to discuss security affairs in public, with the Soviet Union as a central issue. Early in 1979, the defense minister told the Diet that the Soviet Union could be a "potential threat" if its military presence continues to expand in the Pacific. This was a significant "first," since none of his predecessors had ever singled out the Soviet Union as a threat, and the government of Japan had maintained for domestic consumption that there was no potential enemy, even for defense-planning purposes.

Later, on April 19, 1979, the premier was quoted as having told a *Los Angeles Times* reporter that the Soviet Union could be a "threat" to Japan. Three days later, the Foreign Office established an intramural ad hoc committee on national security. Defense Minister Yamashita reportedly was planning an official visit to South Korea. This, if undertaken, would be another first. Even so, it is doubtful that Japan will undertake a radical change in its basic approaches to national security, mainly because of its self-imposed restrictions and present circumstances.

BASIC JAPANESE APPROACHES

Japanese debates on defense matters remain confused, mainly due to Japan's inexperience in and traditional (postwar) attitudes toward strategic issues. Postwar Japan turned passive in its approaches to strategic affairs. The long continued, almost exclusive reliance on U.S. strategic policies, a unique concept of "exclusively defensive defense" as the basic guideline of defense preparedness, and hence a long-standing policy of not possessing strategic weapons—for example, long-range bombers or any other weapons that might reach targets in territories of other countries—were all contributing factors. These factors did not encourage Japan to develop its own strategic doctrine; rather, its tactical territorial defense programs are heavily dependent on close ties with the United States, particularly in terms of naval and air operations. Japan's major security concern is not so much either maintaining a military balance or writing her own contingency scenario as devising means to avoid conflict or to manage crises. These objectives are not mutually exclusive: Like any other nation, Japan is interested in the military balance in its strategic environment, in scenarios of crises, and in avoiding them. The key question is: What priority should be given to defense based on Japan's own perception of the security environment.

First, there is the question of military balance. Even if Japan is incapable of adding its capabilities to those of others for the purpose of creating an overall balance, Japan pays the keenest attention to the balance of power in the Pacific in general. Numbers do not automatically foretell the outcome of combats; yet they represent the easiest indexes for the public to perceive the existing state of static military situations. For laymen, it is too difficult to perceive dynamic factors in the military balance — quality, logistics, or morale. Static figures are easy to understand; hence the public is impressed when given the figures of 755 ships (1,339,000 tons) in the hands of the Soviet Pacific fleet versus 51 ships (580,000 tons) operated by the U.S. Seventh Fleet. This numerical gap cannot be translated into the possible result of a battle of off-Petropavlovsk. It is perceived in Japan, nonetheless, as an indication that the Soviet Navy has become an increasingly menacing power to be reckoned with in the Pacific.

The perception, if it prevails among the majority of the public, might lead to a wider support for a stepped-up naval build-up that, however, most likely will stop short of a substantial quantitative increase. It may take years, or longer than a decade, before the public will develop faith in a balancing game.

Second, there is the scenario-contingency approach. This emphasizes dynamic aspects of crises; by definition it assumes (at least theoretically) that the U.S. deterrence may collapse, producing either all-out nuclear exchanges and conflicts worldwide or partial mobilization and regional conflict. The Japanese tend to focus their attention on the latter, since for most of them the former is something difficult to envisage in concrete terms.

In thinking about the thinkable (the latter), moreover, the Japanese are psychologically prepared for three worst-case scenarios: (1) circumstances, either external or internal, might keep the United States from committing itself to the direct defense of Japan in time; (2) what the United States can commit might be limited to crisis deployment of its naval and air forces for either tactical deterrent or localization purposes; or (3) if involved in the direct defense of Japan, the United States might stop short of a wholesale counterbase retaliatory offensive for fear of escalation.

For Scenario 1, Japan must acquire the capability of conducting an effective holding operation in order to buy time; and for Scenario 2, it may be forced to program its ground combat ability for prolonged resistance. In Scenario 3, the situation assumes that the war would either spread to Europe or spill over from Europe; hence, in a global context, even a partial counterbase retaliation against the Soviet Union might dissuade the Kremlin from conducting a two-front war. But if the Soviets did move against Japan, the Japanese would face a hard decision—when to make a strategic accommodation. This in turn means that in order to avoid such a hard decision, Japan must devise every possible measure to make it easier for the United States to carry out a counterbase—damage limitation—offensive. Such measures might range from the maintenance of friendly relations with Washington (even at the cost of certain political or trade accommodation in peacetime) to a series of advance and joint plans for strategic coordination.

Third, there is a conflict cause–issue approach. This is the most favored approach in Japan, where the words "comprehensive national security" are popular even though the public risks overemphasizing the meaning of security and underestimating the role of military power. This risk notwithstanding, the approach is gaining momentum among defense and academic circles. Three basic security factors are perceived by the Japanese as elements in "comprehensive national security":

1. Relative international peace that primarily depends on (a) continued U.S.–Soviet détente or a process leading to a reduced risk of a global nuclear exchange, (b) internal politicoeconomic stability of resource-supplying states, and (c) relative safety of sea and air lines of communication.

2. Regional security in Asia that can be best maintained by (a) a balance of politicomilitary influence among intra- and extra-regional states, (b) economic and social stability of regional nations, and (c) minimum gaps in economic and industrial growth among the nations.

3. Japan's own domestic stability, which will continue so long as it maintains (a) relative politicosocial stability or recoverability of a balance if and when it is undermined, (b) its economic growth, and (c) its territorial integrity, secured by both its own efforts and stable and close security ties with the United States.

These three factors (nine subelements) are not mutually exclusive, but should be seen as interdependent. The striking element in this security perception is the relative downgrading of military power. It certainly remains a vital ingredient of Japan's security, but is far from a dominant element.

On the other hand, under this perception, strong emphasis is placed on three policy measures: (1) identifying the causes of conflict, both military and nonmilitary; (2) managing crises under preplanned scenarios and in collaboration with other states concerned; and (3) terminating the conflict before it develops to an unmanageable degree.

CONCLUSION

This chapter was not intended to give value judgments on the Japanese approaches to its national security. The third (conflict cause-issue) approach is more comprehensive than the others; in fact it incorporates—in different degreees—both the military balance and the scenario-contingency approaches. Japan nevertheless most likely will continue to perceive its security environment as a mixture of the three approaches. Each has its particular merit. For intelligence (and public relations) purposes, the military balance scenario is valuable and easily perceivable; for defense planning, the scenario-contingency approach is indispensable. The weakness of both lies in their primarily regional–territorial nature. In this respect, the third approach is global; its defect is the absence of concrete policy proposals. How can Japan contribute to relative international peace and to regional security?

One idea is to allocate a certain percentage (say, 3 to 7 percent) of GNP to the three basic security factors and to permit flexibility to change the percentage of suballocation to the nine subelements in accordance with the degree of need or nature of the crisis at hand.

Such a money-oriented ("buying friendship") policy inevitably has its own built-in limits.

Sooner or later, perhaps by late 1980s when new generations of leaders will be in power throughout the world, Japan will have faced a hard decision—how to go beyond the money-oriented policy in contributing to international peace and regional security. Japan may soon start talking about the regional aspects of its security environments, but it will take some time for it to formulate policies and undertake actions.

In the meantime, the Pacific–Asian region will remain potentially unstable. Most of the regional states enjoy—or suffer from—economic growth of different magnitudes; political systems differ from country to country. Three nuclear powers are directly involved in this region; it is also in this region that three major issues are potentially in dispute—territories, offshore oil deposits, and chokepoints.

These issues could flare up at any time; major regional disputes could escalate quickly if extraregional powers are involved. If the Pacific is to remain the ocean of peace, its security and stability ought to be viewed in a global context, with particular attention to closer connections with the nations of the Atlantic.

4 JAPAN'S FOREIGN POLICY AND AREAS OF COMMON INTEREST, POSSIBLE COOPERATION, AND POTENTIAL FRICTION AMONG JAPAN, THE UNITED STATES, AND OTHER WESTERN COUNTRIES

Seizaburo Sato

Professor Seizaburo Sato of Tokyo University, one of a new generation and style of intellectuals in Japan for whom consideration of current foreign policy and defense policies is no longer regarded as disreputable, documents here the extraordinary changes in Japanese perceptions of the international scene and their own role in it of the past decade. Sato writes that awareness by the Japanese public of growing Soviet military strength in northeast Asia, appreciation of the fact that the era of "Pax Americana" has ended, and the rapprochement between the United States and the People's Republic of China all have created conditions in which Japan, with its growing economic strength and self-confidence, must make a larger contribution to the Western alliance. Remarkably, the perceived weakness of the United States of the past several years has led the Japanese to reaffirm and even increase their support for the U.S.-Japan Security Treaty. Sato believes Japan's foreign policy today stands at a major turning point.

INTRODUCTION

Those Japanese who are interested in world affairs (the group often referred to as "the attentive public") are now increasingly aware that a major change is taking place in Japan's international environment as well as in her international status. Moreover, they are beginning to share a common, though vague, perspective as to the direction in which this change is apparently taking Japan. With respect to the international environment, the prevailing view is that it is going to be harder for the nation than in the past. As for Japan's international status, there is a growing body of opinion that Japan should play a greater role in the world not only in the economic area but in political (and even military) affairs as well.

This is the first time since the end of World War II that the Japanese have become so strongly aware of a crisis in the world community of nations and of her responsibility to it. To be sure, awareness of danger on the international scene grew among the Japanese when the Korean War broke out in 1950; when the U.S. forces bogged down in Vietnam in the late 1960s; when the dollar ceased to be tied to gold, allowing foreign exchange rates to float rather than be fixed in 1971; and when the first oil crisis hit the world in 1973. But in each of these cases, the awareness was accompanied by a sense of helplessness and mistrust of the alliance relationship with the United States. In contrast, the sense of danger that has been growing among the Japanese since the late 1970s, due especially to the second oil crisis touched off by the Iranian revolution and to the Soviet invasion of Afghanistan, is making them aware that they have to ally themselves more closely with the United States and other Western powers and that it is Japan's responsibility to play a more active role in the world than in the past. This trend is clearly reflected in the fact that public support for the Self-Defense Forces and the U.S.-Japan Security Treaty is now markedly on the increase.

This change in the popular view of world affairs is inevitably affecting Japan's foreign policy. As will be explained in more detail later, the Japanese government has become much more articulate in recent years about strengthening the Western alliance, while most opposition groups have been amending, explicitly or implicitly, their old unrealistic stands for "unarmed neutrality" or "dealing with all neighbors equally at arm's length." Viewed in this light, Japan's foreign policy may be said to be at a major turning point now. We will identify below the specific changes that have taken place in Japan's view of the world and in her foreign policy and then consider areas of common interest and potential friction between Japan on one hand and the United States and Europe on the other.

JAPAN'S VIEW OF THE WORLD AND FOREIGN POLICY BEFORE 1970

In the postwar years through the 1950s, the prevailing view of the world in Japan, as elsewhere, was of a world divided between two camps, East and West, different in political organization and ideology and led respectively by the Soviet Union and the United States. This was considered the basic framework of international relations. In the 1960s, with détente beginning between the two superpowers, many Japanese also took it as the new basic trend underlying international relations. In 1964 the UNCTAD organization came into being, and the nations of "the South" united in "Group '77" were increasingly articulate in the world community. Accordingly, the North–South problem emerged as the basis of still another framework for international relations.

Although détente became a steady trend between Washington and Moscow, high East–West tensions continued in Korea and Indochina as did the Washington–Peking rift that had persisted since the Korean War. In the 1950s and 1960s, East Asia was the area where East–West antagonism was most intense. Meanwhile, the influence of the southern countries was still limited, and most Japanese lacked a keen interest in the North–South problem. Indeed, a public opinion survey on foreign policy conducted in August 1978 by the prime minister's office (on a nationwide sample of men and women over twenty) indicated that only 47.2 percent of the respondents had ever heard of "the North–South problem" and that a meager 18.3 percent correctly understood the meaning of the term. Of those who had heard of it, 52.1 percent thought it referred to the rift between North and South Korea, and 14.7 percent believed it had to do with the conflict that had prevailed between North and South Vietnam before their reunification; 3.3 percent even associated it with tension between North and South in the United States in early days of her independence. This means that the majority of Japan's voters had never heard of "the North-South problem" and that two-thirds of those who had heard of it had the impression that it had to do with East-West relations. Thus, neither detente nor the North-South problem could completely supplant the East-West relationship in the minds of the Japanese, in which the three conflicting (or at least not fully coordinated) frameworks for international relations coexisted, often resulting in confused, ambiguous concepts of situations abroad.

This split in the nation's judgment of its environment was closely associated with different values held by different groups of Japanese. Even in the 1950s, when tense East-West relations were predominant on the world scene, three different foreign policy stands were advocated in Japan—one for siding with the West, another for siding with the East, and the third for siding with neither but staying neutral. The first position was held by the conservative party (which has been called the Liberal Democratic Party since 1955) that has been in power almost consistently in postwar years, and the majority of the Japanese consistently supported this policy. The second position was maintained by the Communists and the leftist Socialists, and the third reflected the antiwar sentiment or weariness of war entertained by many Japanese based on their hard experiences during World War II. This, indeed, was the main reason why the idealistic stand of neutralism or "unarmed neutrality" was popular in postwar Japan. The second and third positions essentially conflicted with each other, but had one thing in common—opposition to the first, majority stand. For this reason, they tended to merge and be incorporated into the foreign policy platforms of the reformist parties, which were almost permanently in the opposition.

The détente theory that emerged in the 1960s was willingly accepted by the adherents of the third position. Some of the particularly idealistic backers of this position sympathized with the southern nations and were apt to view international relations in the light of North-South antagonism.

Despite this gap in the nation's judgment and evaluation of its external environment, there was broad agreement among the Japanese until the 1960s that the United States was predominant in the world economically, militarily, and politically, and they had good reason to think so. Although the European Community (EC) nations and Japan were showing economic growth, the U.S. economy was overwhelmingly the most powerful in the world, at least until the mid-1960s. It was not until 1968 that Japan began to show a favorable balance of trade with the United States on a regular basis. In the military area, the United States was superior to the Soviet Union in naval and air strength, though not in ground troops. The islands of Japan could therefore expect to enjoy nearly complete security as long as they remained under the military and economic umbrella of the United States. Until the 1960s, the conservative government of Japan, which identified itself with the first stand, was never very enthusiastic about increasing the nation's armaments, since idealistic arguments for unarmed neutrality had so much influence. This was no wonder, considering the circumstances outlined above.

Predominant in economic power and military strength, the United States naturally had overwhelming political influence. The United States from early postwar years until the 1960s was the world's policeman as well as Santa Claus. This period, then, may well be called one of Pax Americana. In postwar Japan, not only the leftists adhering to the second position but also the idealists and those weary of war were often anti-American because the United States was evidently predominant and, consequently, appeared to them to be the only power in the world likely to take a stiff foreign policy that might lead to war.

JAPAN'S INTERNATIONAL POSITION

For some time after losing the Pacific war, the Japanese generally thought of their country in a highly self-deprecating way. In their own eyes, Japan was a complete loser in World War II—a small, weak, backward country in economic, cultural, and even moral terms. In keeping with this prevailing self-image, the nation then aspired to be readmitted to the world community of nations as a full-fledged member at an early date—a rather modest goal. But the world community was split between East and West, and Japan had three choices of ways of rejoining it—affiliating herself with the West, siding with the East, or taking a neutral position, as we noted above.

The majority of Japanese were in favor of the first alternative and for that purpose chose to make a separate peace with the West and sign a security treaty with the United States to become a Western partner. In opposition to this move, the neutrals and the pro-Easterns joined hands, and the result was a split between the conservatives and the reformists over the issue of the U.S.-Japan Security Treaty. Though bitterly opposed to each other over basic foreign policy issues, however, they shared the objective of having Japan readmitted to the world community and also agreed that they should try to achieve it by taking a modest, "low posture" attitude and following a pacifist foreign policy while seeking reconstruction of the economy at home. This was not surprising, since there was a broad area of agreement among the Japanese as to the basic pattern of international relations and Japan's position in the world.

By the latter 1950s, Japan had overcome the serious economic damage it suffered as a result of her defeat in World War II and, following her recovery of independence in 1952, was admitted to U.N. membership in 1956, thus achieving the goal of rejoining the world community of nations. Reflecting this change, the self-image of the Japanese as a "loser" and "weakling" nation faded, and the Japanese people began to think of Japan as a middle income state rather than a backward country. With their new "middle income" status, the Japanese now generally accepted a new national goal—to join the club of industrial powers. For this purpose, they energetically sought economic growth and wealth. This approach suited the mood of the majority of the Japanese, who had been exhausted by the war and had to give up hope of becoming a military big power after losing the war although they still had nationalistic aspirations. The rapid growth of the Japanese economy in the late 1950s and thereafter was supported by this national ambition.

Another self-image the Japanese had during this period, which partly overlapped the "middle income state" image, was that Japan was a member of the Asian community. Deriving from the prewar concept of a united Asia, this image was linked to the idea of North-South antagonism in international relations and found acceptance particularly among those Japanese opposed to war or favoring unarmed neutrality. Tending to be idealistic, they argued that Japan could play a moral role and hope to influence international relations by identifying herself with the southern nations and speaking for them. This stand, however, was too academic to win the sympathy of the Japanese public in competition with the more pragmatic stand of seeking economic growth first. Especially after Japan achieved the goal of joining the industrial club, and after the southern nations clearly split up due to the oil crisis and increased influence from the

Soviet Union, the concept of Japan as a member of the Asian community and an ally of the South faded in the minds of the Japanese. Considering all this, it is not accidental that, as was noted previously, interest in the North-South problem is very low among the Japanese voters.

CHANGES IN THE 1970s

The End of Pax Americana

In the late 1960s the apparent superiority of the United States began to diminish, and the trend became increasingly clear in the 1970s. The decline of American influence was impressed on the Japanese mind particularly by the following developments:

1. In 1971 the dollar became inconvertible, and foreign exchange rates were allowed to float. As a result, the yen appreciated sharply in relation to the dollar. The Japanese called this series of developments "the Nixon shocks."
2. Japan began to show a favorable balance of trade with the United States regularly year after year. A related problem was a series of cases of friction in U.S.-Japan trade relations, ranging from the textile negotiations in the late 1960s to the more recent arguments over Japanese cars and semiconductors entering the U.S. market.
3. With the first of the oil crises in 1973, the OPEC countries became increasingly demanding. Especially noteworthy was the fact that the United States showed a lack of responsiveness to the new situation in Iran following the revolution.
4. In 1975 U.S. forces withdrew from Vietnam, and subsequently the U.S. military presence in Asia appeared to be on the decline. In Korea especially, U.S. forces were reduced substantially.
5. The Soviets increased their military strength and made it increasingly clear that they would not hesitate to use it, if necessary, to defend or promote their interests. Moreover, the United States was no longer able to take effective action against such Soviet expansionism, as she did at the time of the Cuba crisis. This was clearly demonstrated by the Soviet invasion of Afghanistan.

Japan's Regained Confidence and Awareness of Her External Vulnerability

The decline of U.S. influence in Asia was accompanied by growing Japanese competitiveness in the world market. At the same time Japanese security was becoming increasingly inadequate, in contrast with the situation of the 1960s. The end of Pax Americana made the Japanese confident of their economic success on one hand and aware of their own external vulnerability on the other.

This was well reflected in the reaction of the Japanese public to the oil crises and the Soviet armament increases. The oil crises in 1973 and thereafter invariably caused serious uneasiness among the Japanese, who were more dependent on imported oil for energy than any other major industrial nation. An NHK (Japan Broadcasting Corporation) public opinion survey indicated that even in 1977, when the Japanese economy had absorbed most of the effect of the first oil crisis and the oil shortages were becoming less serious at home as well as abroad, 34 percent of the respondents felt "very insecure" about the nation's energy supply and 51 percent, "a little insecure," while only 9 percent felt "not very insecure" and less than 1 percent, "secure." In a *Yomiuri Shimbun* survey conducted in November 1979, after the emergence of the second oil crisis, 69 percent of the respondents feared that the energy situation might become increasingly critical in the next ten years. However, the Japanese economy had ingeniously overcome the impact of the two oil crises by saving energy and increasing productivity and had succeeded in achieving still higher competitiveness in the world market. At the time of the first oil crisis, Zbigniew Brzezinsky's *The Fragile Blossom* was widely read in Japan. This book stressed Japan's potential weakness. The second oil crisis, in contrast, made successes of such books as Ezra Vogel's *Japan As No. One* and Edwin O. Reischauer's *The Japanese*, both making much of the adaptability, strength, and other praiseworthy qualities of Japanese society—further indication of the change in the Japanese attitude.

The Soviet armament increases also have threatened the Japanese considerably. Previously, the islands of Japan enjoyed almost complete security, provided by the superior nuclear deterrent capabilities and naval and air strength of the United States. After this long period of assured security, the emergence of U.S.–Soviet nuclear parity and the increased Soviet naval and air strength in East Asia have been taken by the Japanese as shocking developments that greatly affect the basis of their security. In a public opinion survey conducted by the *Yomiuri Shimbun* in June 1979, 64 percent of the respondents (or 73 percent of the men), when asked "Do you think the Soviet military activities in East Asia are affecting Japan's security?" answered in the affirmative, while 15 percent thought the nation's security was hardly affected, and less than 3 percent, not at all. It is recalled that in an earlier survey conducted by the *Asahi Shimbun* in 1977, 54 percent of the respondents who were asked, "Do you foresee any possibility of a foreign country resorting to arms to attack or threaten Japan?" answered in the negative, while only 33 percent saw such a possibility. It is evident that the Japanese view of the Soviet Union as a potential threat has undergone a major change in the last two or three years.

The Afghanistan crisis has increased the Japanese wariness of the Soviet Union. Comparison of the results of two *Asahi Shimbun* surveys conducted in December 1978 and March 1980 indicates that the proportion of the Japanese in favor of strengthening the Self-Defense Forces increased from 18 to 25 percent, while the proportion in favor of reducing or abolishing them decreased from 16 to 11 percent. Even among the supporters of the Communist party, which advocates abolition of the Self-Defense Forces, those in favor of strengthening them increased sharply from 8 to 22 percent while those in favor of reducing or abolishing them decreased from 53 to 30 percent. A *Mainichi Shimbun* study conducted during the recent general elections shows that 44 percent of the Japanese want the nation's defense strength to be increased while only 10 percent want it to be reduced or eliminated.

But even with best efforts for saving energy and improving productivity, Japan cannot hope to effectively meet the OPEC challenge single handedly nor to develop sufficient military capabilities of her own to meet the Soviet challenge. Both the oil crisis and the Soviet threat are common problems confronting the Western powers as a whole and evidently cannot be overcome without concerted efforts on their part. This is why the growing awareness of the end of Pax Americana among the Japanese tends to weaken rather than strengthen their inclination to view the new change in the pattern of international relations in terms of "multipolarization."

The multipolarization theory emerged in the late 1960s and prevailed until the late 1970s to explain what was then happening in international relations as a result of French President Charles de Gaulle's new foreign policy, the intensification of the Sino-Soviet dispute, the growing economic power of Western Europe and Japan, and other major developments on the world scene. There is no denying that the decline of U.S. influence in the world tended to encourage the "multipolarization" theory for a while. But as the challenges from the Soviet Union and the OPEC countries grew, the Japanese became increasingly aware that the Western powers had a broad area of common interest and were essentially "in the same boat." By the end of the 1970s, the multipolarization view of international relations had faded in the minds of the Japanese. The process may have been facilitated by the fact that China was now bent on developing friendly ties with the West (particularly with the United States and Japan) with a view to organizing an anti-Soviet alliance.

Recognizing Common Interests with the West and Proceeding Toward a Stronger Western Alliance

The prevalence of the view that, just because Pax Americana is over, Japan must try to ally herself more strongly with the Western powers (especially with the United States) is clearly reflected in the recently changed popular attitude toward the U.S.-Japan Security Treaty. Comparison of the results of *Asahi Shimbun* public opinion surveys conducted in 1974 and 1978 on the question, "Do you believe the U.S. will defend Japan in real earnest in an emergency?" shows that the proportion of respondents answering in the affirmative dropped from 31 to 20 percent, while those answering in the negative increased from 47 to 56 percent. Despite this growing skepticism about the military commitments of the United States, appreciation of the U.S.-Japan Security Treaty markedly increased during these four years. Asked in the same surveys, "Do you think the U.S.-Japan Security Treaty is useful to Japan?" 34 percent of the respondents answered in the affirmative in 1974 whereas 49 percent did in 1978. On the other hand, those answering in the negative decreased from 18 percent in 1974 to 13 percent in 1978.

Public opinion surveys conducted by the prime minister's office indicate the growing support for a policy of cooperation with the

United States even more clearly: Those in favor of maintaining the treaty increased from 44 percent in 1969 to 68 percent in 1978 (the figure for men is still higher, 77 percent), while those calling for repeal of the treaty were reduced by half, from 12 to 6 percent. Asked about the advisability of friendly cooperation between the United States and Japan, 16 percent of the respondents expressed themselves in favor of promoting it in 1969 whereas 41 percent did in 1979. During the same period, those in favor of limiting it to the current level decreased from 56 to 46 percent, and those in favor of reducing it shrank sharply, from 9 to 2 percent. Asked whether or not friendly relations with Western Europe should be promoted, 41 percent of the respondents answered in favor of improving them in 1978 whereas 47 percent did in 1979. Meanwhile, those preferring to limit them to the current level decreased from 38 to 35 percent, and those speaking for reducing them, from 1 to 0 percent. The reason more Japanese were in favor of promoting friendly relations with Western Europe than those with the United States in 1979 was probably that the latter relations were already much closer than the former and considered by most Japanese to be "friendly enough."

There has also been a conspicuous change in the tone of the Japanese press on this subject. Traditionally antigovernment in character, most Japanese newspapers were calling for more friendly relations with the Communist world until recently. But now they speak for the Western alliance as a matter of course. For example, the *Yomiuri Shimbun* had this to say on June 19, 1980: "The Venice summit is aimed at restructuring the alliance. . . . At this opportunity, we should rid ourselves of the notion that [Japan] is big in economic terms but small as a political influence." The *Tokyo Shimbun* declared the same day: "The basic policy of preserving and consolidating the Western alliance is agreeable to Japan too."

The changed attitude of the Japanese voter on international relations has invariably affected the platforms of the political parties as well as the editorial tone of the press. As was noted previously, the main issue between the ruling Liberal Democrats and the opposition was until the 1960s whether or not the U.S.-Japan Security Treaty should be maintained. The opposition parties were all against it. The Democratic Socialists were the first to abandon this stand. By 1970 they had turned agreeable to the treaty on condition that no U.S. forces be kept in Japan, and by 1975 they had become receptive to the existing treaty as such. The Komei party also turned a virtual supporter of the treaty in 1975 and subsequently continued to modify its attitude until it was positively speaking for the pact in 1979. Even the Japan Socialists, who had traditionally held fast to "unarmed neutrality" as a holy tenet, had to say that they would tolerate the treaty at least "for the time being" when they struck a bargain with the Komei party on a joint platform for a possible coalition government. Today, only the Japan Communist party is still explicitly opposed to the U.S.-Japan Security Treaty.

The Japanese government has become much less ambiguous in speech and action about its intention of helping maintain and strengthen the Western alliance and ceased to use such vague terms as "diplomatic amity in all directions." Though skeptical of Washington's lack of consistency in dealing with the problem of the Tehran hostages and the Afghanistan crisis, Tokyo has been explicit in supporting the United States on these issues. With respect to the use of the security treaty with the United States, the Japanese government is making it increasingly clear that the arrangement should help ensure security throughout the world as well as in Japan and her neighborhood. The late Premier Ohira's proposal of Pacific basin cooperation was aimed at promoting general Western cooperation within the framework of the Pacific area and quite contrary to the wartime concept of the Greater East Asia Coprosperity Sphere.

In the long history of mankind, there have been few cases in which many sovereign states equal in status long maintained close, friendly, fruitful relations with one another. Indeed, the Western alliance today may well be called a new, brave venture in man's history. But the members of the alliance are too closely interdependent to break with one another, and the crises they are faced with are so serious that they can hope to overcome them only through close cooperation among them. They cannot afford to fail in this vital attempt.

5 U.S. INTERESTS AND POLICIES IN ASIA AND THE WESTERN PACIFIC IN THE 1980s

Richard L. Sneider

Richard L. Sneider, former U.S. ambassador to the Republic of Korea and former member of the staff of the National Security Council, traces the evolution of U.S. policies toward the nations of Asia and asserts that the United States has legitimate and growing interests in maintaining stability and peace in the region. Weighing the positive and negative developments of the recent past, he analyzes the possible threats to stability—military, political, and economic—and concludes that the United States must continue to play a pivotal role in East Asia. Finally, he proposes a framework and strategy for future U.S. actions in the region.

INTRODUCTION

To many Americans, East Asia during the postwar period has become a wasteland where we have been bogged down in costly assistance programs and even more costly wars. From the fall of China in 1949, followed shortly by the Korean War and climaxed by the Vietnam War, American involvement in East Asia not only has cost well over 100,000 American lives in conflict, but also has drained the country of financial resources and involved major defense commitments. The U.S. role in Asia has been the source of major domestic political conflict and public controversy. There has been a perception in many quarters that U.S. intervention in postwar Asia levied a very high price with apparently little reward and few successes. The one exception is the U.S. partnership with Japan—but even here, Japan's economic success has proven troublesome.

With this record, the inclination of many in the United States to shed the Asian burden and even to turn its back on East Asia is not surprising. The Nixon Doctrine enunciated at Guam in July 1969 was a direct response to this mood; it was an effort to justify a continued involvement in East Asia in terms acceptable to a skeptical and contentious American public. It failed, however. By 1975, the tide for disengagement was overwhelming as Congress, backed by the public, rejected further assistance to South Vietnam and Cambodia.

But as developments since 1975 have demonstrated, America cannot turn its back on Asia without sacrificing vital interests and rejecting its historic and legitimate role as a Pacific power. The United States is not solely an Atlantic power that can isolate itself from East Asia. But the United States is in need of a well-defined role in East Asia and a convincing rationale, if the essential public and congressional consensus on Asian policy is to emerge—and the need is immediate, lest the United States continue what may appear an endless drift in Asia, leading to debilitating uncertainty in both the United States and East Asia. Geography backed by historic experience have dictated inescapable vital national interests in Asia.

BASIC U.S. INTERESTS IN ASIA

Historically, U.S. interests in Asia at their most fundamental level have been, first, to preserve peace and thwart any threat to the United States and, second, to preserve continued U.S. access, economically and otherwise, to the region. America has sought in particular to prevent any one power from dominating the region to the point of constituting a threat to the United States and to its access to the area. Its strategic interests have been served by preserving a balance of power among the major countries in the region in order to prevent any single power from dominating the area and excluding the United States.

U.S. political and economic interests in Asia are derived from these fundamental interests in peace and access to the region. The political interests have historically been to preserve U.S. ability to influence the countries of the region toward these goals. Its economic interests have been to assure access to the raw materials of the region, to the markets of the region, and to the potential for U.S. investment in the region to the end of contributing to the prosperity and growth of the U.S. economy.

U.S. interests in Asia and the Pacific have not varied from the nineteenth century opening of the West and establishment of American power on the Pacific coast. The confusion has come from the means by which America has exercised its power to preserve these interests and from the changing circumstances within the region that have dictated a varying U.S. role within the area. But at no point in history has America turned its back on its Asian interests.

THE U.S. POSTWAR ROLE IN ASIA

The low point of U.S. intervention to protect its interests in Asia was in the period before World War II when the United States was hesitant to move decisively against Japanese plans to dominate the region. The high point came during the war and then during the immediate postwar period when the United States occupied Japan and was the predominant power in the region.

Clearly, the difficulties in defining an American role in East Asia acceptable both to the region and to the U.S. public flow in considerable measure from the drawbacks and failures, whether apparent or real, of these postwar Asian policies. In retrospect, U.S. postwar policy can be divided into two broad phases: (1) from 1945 to about 1969, the period of engagement; (2) from 1969 to the present, the period of gradual, but not total, disengagement.

America's postwar involvement in East Asia at its highest point was virtually total. In the early postwar period, it accepted broad responsibilities in an effort to preserve its vital interests. The United States committed itself either explicitly or implicitly to the defense of virtually every non-Communist nation in East Asia. Its involvement with most countries was almost all-encompassing, embracing not only their external security, but their internal security, their economy, and their politics.

The initial steps to total engagement in Asia were a direct consequence of a perceived need to fill a power vacuum left by the defeat of Japan. Our broadening role stemmed directly from the subsequent confrontation with Communist powers, highlighted by the Korean War and the Taiwan Straits crisis, and from the collapse of the colonial empires of the European metropolitan powers and the emergence of newly independent states that were inherently unstable and inexperienced in self-government. Events forced decisions upon the United States, and new commitments became almost inevitable and justifiable in the light of the immediate crisis.

There was a strong case for America's broad postwar engagement in Asia. As a Pacific power, we had a legitimate interest in seeking a stable, peaceful environment in Asia that would provide security to our western reaches and avoid a repetition of World War II. No other nation had either the deep self-interest or the resources to fill the Asian power vacuum, to occupy Japan, and to contribute to the development and consolidation of the numerous newly independent states of Asia.

The consequence of this total involvement was excessive dependence on the United States and often inadequate efforts to shore up internal weakness on the part of the countries in the region. In the end, our involvement in East Asia led to engagement in the lengthy and costly Vietnam War and a deep sense of disillusion in the United States that the American blood shed in Asia and the vast amounts of money spent should produce so little success.

The seeds for the second phase of Asian policy—partial disengagement—were sown in the failures of the earlier period. While disillusion and pressures for disengagement were widely prevalent in the late 1960s, President Nixon's enunciation of the Guam or Nixon Doctrine in July 1969 marked the official adoption of this policy. Flowing from this was a reduction in the U.S. military role in Vietnam and the withdrawal of a U.S. division from Korea in 1971.

In essence, the Nixon Doctrine placed limitations on the U.S. role in Asia, calling for self-help rather than dependence on the United States; it raised doubts as to U.S. willingness to fulfill defense commitments for nations unwilling to help themselves. As a prod to the Asian nations, there was a deliberate, calculated ambiguity with respect to U.S. preparedness to live up to its commitments. But there was no intention to disavow U.S. interests in Asia—only an effort to reduce the costs.

The reaction in Asia was both positive and negative. The legitimacy of U.S. requests for greater self-help was not contested, and most countries accepted the increased burden on their own resources, although some did so grudgingly. What was confusing was the calculated ambiguity of the doctrine, leading to uncertainty (bordering in some cases on panic) as to how far the disengagement process would go. Congressional actions refusing or reducing U.S. assistance to the region only compounded this uncertainty. By March 1975, when Vietnam and Cambodia fell, the future U.S. role in East Asia was viewed as a question mark. Contingency planning for total U.S. withdrawal from the region was common, with the clear-cut danger that these plans could become a self-fulfilling prophecy.

U.S. INTERESTS IN THE 1980s

The basic issue facing the United States in Asia today is to define and implement a regional policy for the 1980s that avoids the pitfalls of both total engagement and partial disengagement. The policy must be framed in terms of vital U.S. interests in peace and access to the region, which remain constant. But it must also take into account that U.S. interests in Asia are likely to deepen and to become more complex in the decade ahead. Developments within the region and the increasing interdependency of the global economy will increase U.S. economic interests in Asia, but they also underline the need to view regional interests in a global context.

By 1979, American economic interests in East Asia were matching those in Western Europe. The United States conducts about half its trade within the Pacific basin. Since 1965, U.S. trade with Asia and the Pacific has grown at a faster rate than that with the European Community (EC). By 1976, U.S. investment in Asia was about $6 billion. The loan exposure of American banks in the region has been raised substantially in recent years. The anticipated continued economic growth of the countries in the region through the decade of the 1980s—particularly in contrast to the relatively stagnant Western European economies—is likely to necessitate giving an even greater priority to Asian pursuit of U.S. economic interests. Asia will represent a growing market for U.S. industrial products, foodstuffs, and raw materials; an outlet for increasing American direct investment; and a major customer for U.S. financial institutions. America in turn will continue to be the largest and the most important market for the Asian countries in the Pacific basin—not only for Japan, but for the other industrializing countries of the region. Growing Asian–American economic interdependency will make meaningful U.S. involvement in the region even more inescapable.

The framing of an Asian policy for the United States in the 1980s is further complicated, however, by the interrelationship of regional and global interests. Regional policy cannot be considered in isolation, since U.S. interests are both global and regional. The strategic balance in Asia is very much affected by the extent to which Soviet resources are required in the West as the result of U.S. and Western European military strength. Weakness in either Western Europe or Asia permits the Soviet Union to shift its military resources in the other direction. By the same token, strength in both regions forces a division of Soviet resources and prevents a massing of military strength in either the West or Asia.

Economic policies likewise can no longer be regionalized. American economic interests, for example, can no longer be distorted to serve economic relations with either the EC or the Asian area.

Finally, there are global issues that inevitably cut across regional interests and considerations, primarily energy requirements (and more specifically access to Middle East oil resources) and the issue of nonproliferation. Additionally, U.S. interests in the Third World are advanced by the degree to which the Asian countries in concert with the United States can exercise a moderating influence in the North–South debate, in UNCTAD, and in other international fora. Asian policies must therefore be developed that are consistent with U.S. interests not only within the region but on a broader, global basis. Global interests and issues need not lead to a sacrifice of regional interests but may lead to a modification of regional policies.

THE ASIAN FRAMEWORK FOR U.S. POLICY

The objective of U.S. policy in Asia during the 1980s will be to develop a stable power balance that permits the United States to preserve its interests in the region at a cost commensurate with U.S. global interests. The policy will be framed by current and prospective developments in the region, by strength generated within the region, and by threats to stability there.

Positive Developments

As the United States enters the 1980s, there are within Asia both positive developments advantageous to U.S. interests and negative developments that could bring regional instability and threaten U.S. interests. The principal positive development has been the dynamic spurt of national development that began during the 1970s and is likely to continue through the 1980s. In contrast to the early postwar period, when many countries, particularly the newly independent nations, were struggling and insecure, most of the nations of Asia have made major strides toward economic development and stable growth. The economic growth rates of most of the nations of Asia (with the exception of Burma) have been the highest in the world during the past decade. In the 1980s, four of these countries—the Republic of Korea, Taiwan, Singapore, and probably Malaysia—as well as the Crown Colony of Hong Kong, are likely to reach advanced industrial status on a plane with the middle income countries of Western Europe. The economies of Thailand and the Philippines also have relatively improved prospects. Indonesia, while rich in resources, still must develop a more dynamic growth structure.

Along with economic development have come far greater political stability and more effective political leadership. This leadership is technocratically oriented and devoted to the goal of national development and planning. It is supported by an increasing cadre of well-trained technocrats, planners, and economists as well as by a new industrial capitalist class that is dynamic and growth oriented. Economic development is not constrained by an inadequacy of capital, since resources are available not only from the international banking institutions and governments but from private capital resources, since business leaders now see Asia as one of the most promising places for investment. Finally, there is a new mood of optimism and confidence in the region, as well as a growing sense of regional cohesion. No longer do the non-Communist countries of Asia view themselves as in a weak, defenseless position or view the Communist system as "the wave of the future." On the contrary, the mixed economies of East Asia increasingly see themselves as a future model in stark contrast to the stagnancy of the Asian Communist economies.

The second positive development for the non-Communist nations has been the diminution of the Communist threat in comparison to the 1960s and 1970s. Today the major disputes in Asia are between the Communist nations, rather than between the Communist and non-Communist countries. In the few short years since the fall of South Vietnam and Cambodia, the adversary relationships in Asia have changed dramatically. The Sino-Soviet conflict has deepened and broadened. The rivalry between the Soviet Union and the People's Republic of China now has spread to bordering Communist neighbors. The Soviet-Vietnam alliance has served to isolate the People's Republic of China from all but North Korea among its Communist neighbors. Vietnam's thrust into Cambodia to complete its control over the Indochinese peninsula has already resulted in one major Sino-Vietnamese conflict, and during the 1980s, further conflict could break out.

The principal military and economic resources of the Communist states in Asia, with exception of North Korea, are focused on strengthening their relative position within this intra-Communist struggle. Furthermore, each of the Communist countries faces serious economic problems and has demonstrated little capability of escaping stagnancy and low growth without massive inputs of external assistance. Their relative weakness vis-à-vis the non-Communist countries in the region is likely to grow immensely during the 1980s, while differences within the Communist orbit are likely to diminish the potential threat to the non-Communist countries of the region, with two notable exceptions—Vietnam's threat to Thailand and North Korea's aggressiveness toward the South.

Threats to Stability

Strategic Threats. The principal strategic threat to the region stems from the continued growth of Soviet military presence and power in the region. Since the mid-1960s, there has been a very major Soviet military build-up in the Far East. Soviet forces have expanded from twenty divisions and 210 fighter-attack aircraft in 1965 to well over forty divisions and more than 1000 fighter-attack aircraft in 1978. At the same time, the Soviet Pacific Fleet has grown to over seventy-three combatant vessels, exclusive of submarines, and just recently, an antisubmarine warfare carrier has been added.[1] Most of the Soviet

---

1. Department of Defense, *Annual Report* 1980.

build-up has taken place along the Chinese border, where the ground divisions and the bulk of the aircraft are stationed. Smaller Soviet units are stationed on Sakhalin, on Kamchatka peninsula, and on the Kurile Islands off Hokkaido.

The enlarged Soviet naval deployment in the Pacific is of direct concern to U.S. interests. Two trends are apparent in this deployment—first, the modernization of the forces and, second, the emphasis on antisubmarine warfare. The deployment includes not only combat vessels, but approximately one hundred submarines, some of which are deployed in the eastern Pacific and include ballistic missile submarines. The Soviet Far East Fleet also includes well over 300 Soviet aircraft that support its deployments. Soviet fleet activities have increased in the northeast Asia area and particularly in the region around Japan and appear geared to counter American naval power in the region. In addition, Soviet naval power has been very active in the Indian Ocean, running an average of over 7000 ship days, for example, during 1974-1976.

The Soviet naval presence in the Pacific, however, operates under limitations. The principal Soviet naval bases are within easy range of aircraft based in Japan, and the Soviet fleet is confinable if the three major straits providing access to the Pacific are closed. Only the addition of a major base in Vietnam will permit the Soviet fleet to operate effectively from bases outside the Soviet northern waters. Second, Soviet combat vessels lack the fire power and the modern equipment of American naval vessels. Finally, there is evidence that the Soviet Far East Fleet can operate only on a limited basis. Despite the larger number of combat vessels, the ship days of the Soviet fleet in the Pacific Ocean in 1976 were about 5200, in contrast to the U.S. Navy's 19,700 ship days. Concern regarding Soviet fleet activities centers less upon its current capabilities and more upon its potential for expanding naval activity in the 1980s and in particular upon the danger that it will increase its strength relative to U.S. naval deployments in the Pacific. Furthermore, the increasing strength of the Soviet military deployments in Asia relative to the United States, including deployment of the naval backfire aircraft to the region, could threaten the security of key strait passages and provide Moscow with a capability to intervene in regional disputes and to threaten the security of sea lane communications so essential to the region.

The major obstacle to the projection of Soviet military power on the continent of Asia remains the Chinese forces deployed along the

Sino-Soviet frontier. Sino-Soviet rivalry must be expected to persist into the 1980s and with it a continuing strengthening of Soviet forces along the frontier as well as improvement of Soviet logistic capabilities for supporting these forces. The Chinese response will be critical to the maintenance of a military balance in this area. The Chinese are now projecting a continued modernization of their armed forces, including importation of both advanced industrial technology from the West and weapons from Europe in particular. Transfer of military technology to China, however, raises serious objections among the weaker non-Communist states in Asia who continue to nurture fears of Chinese intervention in their countries, particularly through a combination of external pressures, insurgency, and manipulation of the Chinese minorities in Southeast Asia.

The future course of Sino-Soviet rivalry will remain a matter of serious concern into the 1980s. Both the Soviet Union and the People's Republic of China view the actions of the other as an effort to isolate and surround their respective countries. The Soviets fear the development of a U.S.-Japan-China alliance with NATO, and the Chinese worry about Soviet efforts to gain allies all along the Chinese periphery, including its non-Communist neighbors of Iran, Pakistan, and India as well as the Indo-chinese states. Expansion of the Soviet military presence in Vietnam would be particularly alarming to the Chinese. The danger of open Sino-Soviet conflict, therefore, cannot be discarded. On the other hand, a Sino-Soviet reconciliation or even a partial accord would decrease tensions and permit a greater concentration of Soviet as well as Chinese military pressures deployed against the non-Communist countries of the region. The smaller countries of Asia perceive that they cannot ignore these possibilities, although they are slim in the American view.

In the strategic framework, there are two major tension points not directly related to the Sino-Soviet conflict. These are potential thrusts by Vietnam against Thailand and by North Korea against South Korea. A PRC attack on Taiwan is another potential, but less probable, tension area.

The Vietnamese attack against the Pol Pot regime in Cambodia and the installation of a puppet government there has once again raised the specter of a threat against Thai security. Should it attack Thailand, Vietnam has the military potential to overwhelm at least northern Thailand and, in the view of many Southeast Asians, could sweep down to Singapore. Thailand, even with the support of its

Asian allies, has inadequate military capabilities to resist the battle-hardened Vietnamese. The major deterrents against such a Vietnamese attack include the probability of Chinese attacks on Vietnam and the possibility, however unlikely, of direct American intervention. In the short term, the possibility of a Vietnamese attack is also greatly diminished by Vietnam's continued inability to gain full control over Cambodia as well as by the internal weaknesses of its economy and the need to maintain substantial military forces along the Chinese border. In the longer term, however, a firmer structure of deterrence will be required, assuming that Vietnam is able to absorb Cambodia, maintain its control over Laos, and begin to bring order to its economy. The threat to Thailand could also greatly expand with Soviet encouragement and support for a Vietnamese thrust. The U.S. role in this equation will be a critical factor in the 1980s and one of the most difficult problems of U.S. Asian policy.

In Korea, the deterrent equation is more firmly established. It depends principally upon the development of Korean armed forces and the maintainence in Korea of sufficient U.S. military power to discourage a North Korean attack. The decision to suspend the withdrawal of American ground forces from Korea represents a major step in bolstering the deterrent equation. During the 1980s, the relative military strength of the North and the South should undergo a major shift once current plans for the expansion of South Korea's defense industry and force improvement are realized. By the mid-1980s, South Korea should enjoy not only growing economic superiority but a clear superiority in military technology and sufficient military strength to equate with the North. While the North now enjoys a clear superiority of ground, air, and naval forces, it has pronounced weaknesses in its access to more modern military technology and an economy that is virtually static. The principal threat in Korea could come from a conclusion by the North that it has no alternative to aggression once it senses that it will loose its current military superiority. Managing the crossover of North–South military and power relationships will be the crucial factor in assuring an absence of hostilities on the Korean peninsula during the 1980s. Again, the U.S. role in supporting the South will be critical.

The threat to Taiwan seems far less pronounced, given the PRC's preoccupation with the Soviet Union and Vietnam. Furthermore, the necessary military capabilities for a PRC invasion of Taiwan are currently lacking and likely to continue lacking well into the decade ahead as Chinese resources are concentrated in bolstering mainland forces rather than in building up sufficient amphibious forces. Furthermore, the current and future military capabilities of Taiwan would appear adequate to match any development of mainland capabilities for an invasion of the island. A change in Sino-Soviet relationship, however, could have serious implications for the security of Taiwan.

Political Threats. The successful developmental pattern of many of the non-Communist Asian nations and their promising prospects for the future, at least in the short term, should not obscure the problems still faced in the region. The momentum in the new Asia is clearly positive, but the prospects for continued growth and stability are far from consolidated. First, longer term political stability remains a question mark. Most of the regimes in Asia have depended on strong leaders who have proved effective, such as the late President Park of Korea, Prime Minister Lee of Singapore, and President Marcos of the Philippines. But as the case of the assassination of President Park clearly demonstrates, even these leaders can be vulnerable to domestic enemies, and there is no clearly established pattern of succession in these countries. Only in a few of these countries have strong political institutions begun to emerge, and perhaps only Japan has a sufficiently stable political structure to survive political change. While an authoritarian system, no matter how benevolent, suits the present ruling establishments and is accepted by the majority, dependence on strong personal leadership involves inherent vulnerabilities. There is confidence within the region that the new elite establishments will throw up adequate new leadership and that with continued economic growth and experience, stable political institutions, more broadly representative, will emerge. But political stability will remain a question mark until the process of transfer of political power through nonrevolutionary means has been institutionalized.

Second, the growth economies of new Asia remain vulnerable to a variety of potentially adverse developments. Internally, only Korea and Taiwan have achieved a green revolution with relatively equitable income distribution between the urban and rural sectors. Maldistribution between these sectors and within the urban sector remains a constant threat to stability. In the Philippines and Thailand particularly, there are wide gaps between the upper income group and the masses. Furthermore, economic success breeds its own set of new and formidable problems. A country like Korea, for example, must face the question of how to deal with a larger and more vocal labor force upon whose skills and productivity it depends for continued industrialization at a competitive level. The transition to advanced industrial status involves major adjustments to a freer market economy and greater vulnerability to external economic developments, particularly the price and availability of energy sources and economic fluctuations in the United States and Europe. Finally, the very process of growth creates new social tensions, with the emergence of a strong middle class and a labor force exerting pressures for more political leverage within authoritarian establishment structures.

Third, insurgency problems remain in Thailand, Malaysia, the Philippines and Burma. A potential for insurgency also prevails in Indonesia. However, concerns about containing and eventually eliminating insurgency have decreased as a result of the lessened capability for external support from either Peking or Hanoi, their rivalry for leadership over these movements, and the fact that both compete for Southeast Asian official support, forcing a partial disavowal of support for the insurgent movements. The Thais, who have never given the highest priority to stamping out insurgency, are relatively relaxed. Thai leadership appears content to accept a modicum of insurgency, provided that it is contained in the highlands and is not combined with external pressures from Vietnam. But, this may not be the case in the 1980s should Vietnam consolidate its hold over Cambodia.

Fourth, three countries in the region are particularly vulnerable to ethnic, economic, and religious tensions—Indonesia, Malaysia and Taiwan. In Indonesia and Malaysia ethnic, religious, and economic differences divide the majority and ruling Muslim class from the minority Chinese population. The potential for external stimulation and support of the Chinese minorities, including insurgency, and Muslim fears of these possibilities are constant threats to stability. On the other extreme, Muslim religious fundamentalism, should it spread to these countries from Iran, could threaten not only the Chinese minorities, but the sectarian ruling Muslim establishment in both Indonesia and Malaysia as well as lead to Hindu–Moslem conflicts in Indonesia. In Taiwan, there is the potential for conflict between the Taiwanese and the Chinese.

Fifth, there is latent concern about Chinese irredentism. The Chinese have asserted claims to the Spratley, Paracel, and Senkaku islands as well as to the continental shelf extending well into the

China and Yellow seas and to other waters along its long eastern coastline. These claims conflict with those of neighboring countries throughout Asia and have major significance for the development of potential overshore oil resources. While the Chinese may not take military actions to establish control over these islands, their claims and threats inhibit the exploitation of these offshore waters for increasingly necessary energy resources. The destabilizing impact of these territorial issues is likely to increase in the 1980s, particularly if current offshore exploration indicates major oil resources in the North China and Yellow seas.

Finally, the trend toward increased Asian cohesion could be reversed by intraregional disputes among the Asian nations. Regional cooperation is still fragile and partial; historical and latent suspicions, such as between Japan and Korea and the Philippines and Malaysia, inhibit full cooperation. More probable is progress toward enhanced regional cooperation and cohesion, but such a process cannot be taken for granted.

Areas of Economic Tension. The successful pattern of economic growth that is projected to continue well into the 1980s will have its clear rewards, but also some problems. As the scale of the economies of the region grows and they become more sophisticated and industrialized, new sources of economic tension are likely to arise or be intensified. These tensions are likely to be both intraregional and between the Asian region and the nonregional economies, particularly with the developed economies of the United States and the European community. Tensions are most likely to arise from four specific sources. First, the increasingly industrialized nations of Korea and Taiwan are likely to come into growing competition with Japan for markets both within and outside the region. Second, the less advanced countries of the region are likely to find themselves in disputes with the more advanced countries as they seek to protect their infant industries and to gain more favorable terms of trade for their raw materials. Third, the countries of the region are likely to compete with each other for capital and technology, given the fact that both are finite resources. Fourth, and most important, the region is likely to face a variety of protectionist measures in the United States and Western Europe. The closing or partial denial of access to the OECD market could be the most destabilizing development during the 1980s. The thrust of Japan and the newly industrializing of Taiwan and Korea into these markets has already increased protectionist pressures. Should the Asian region find itself even partially excluded from the markets of the advanced nations, the adverse repercussions would not only be economic but would affect the security and stability of the whole region. Continued development of a stable economic and political base in Asia depends upon increased access to the markets, the technology, and the capital resources of the advanced nations.

Other Influences on Asian Stability. Finally, four additional factors will have a profound influence on the prospects for stability and peace in Asia during the 1980s—access to energy; nonproliferation of nuclear weapons; the U.S.–Japanese relationship; and the U.S. role in Asia. During the 1980s, the largest percentage increase in requirements for energy relative to other areas is likely to come from Asia as their economies expand more rapidly and private consumption of energy grows commensurately. The region is dependent on nonregional sources of energy, unless or until a major new source of oil is found in the region. This dependence is particularly pronounced in the industrialized countries of northeast Asia and in Singapore, while the resources of the others are none too plentiful. The region will depend heavily upon continued access to Middle East oil and continued unimpeded use of the sea lanes between the Middle East and Asia. Not only will Japan and Korea, already dependent on the Middle East for almost 90 percent of their energy, be vulnerable to developments in this area, but by the mid-1980s, the vulnerability of other countries will increase. Exploitation of offshore resources is likely to be a growing issue.

Japan, Korea, and Taiwan are already turning to extensive reliance on nuclear energy as well as seeking other sources of energy. This reliance is likely to increase and to put greater pressure on U.S. policies relating to enrichment, reprocessing of nuclear wastes, and breeder reactor technology. Management of Asia's energy requirements will be one of the key factors affecting the stability of the region over the next decade. The importance of this issue needs no underlining.

The growing reliance on nuclear energy in turn will increase the potential for proliferation of nuclear weapons technology in the region. The more advanced industrial nations, particularly Japan, Korea, and Taiwan, already have the scientific talent and industrial capability to develop advanced weapons systems, including nuclear weapons. One of the major challenges of the U.S. security policy during the next decade will be to reduce the attractiveness of developing an independent nuclear capability by enhancing the creditability of the American security commitment and its nuclear umbrella.

The third essential ingredient for any stable power balance in the region is maintenance—in fact, enhancement—of the U.S.-Japanese partnership. This partnership depends first upon maintaining the credibility and reliability of the American commitment to assist in defending the area and to deter nuclear attacks against Japan. The Japanese element in the SALT equation cannot be ignored, and SALT should not be viewed as merely a U.S.-Soviet and NATO issue. Japanese confidence in U.S. strategic capabilities must be maintained as a basis for any partnership. Second, the strength of the partnership depends upon more effective management of U.S.-Japanese economic frictions. Competition and tensions between the U.S. and the Japanese economies are likely to recur during the 1980s, particularly since Japan is likely to move into higher technology exports, directly competitive with one area in which the United States has an industrial advantage. Effective management of these tensions by both countries will be critical and will require a combination of cooperative actions, self-restraint, and agreed ground rules. The alternative would be most destabilizing, not only for the Asian region but for the total global economic and strategic balance.

Finally, the foregoing only emphasizes the pivotal nature of the U.S. role in East Asia over the 1980s. Uncertainty regarding U.S. involvement in Asia and a lack of confidence in the U.S. security commitment to the region, particularly to Korea and Thailand, and the reliability of America as a source of technology, capital, and markets could enhance the underlying and latent factors of instability in the region. On the other hand, a clearly defined U.S. role and policy in the region, backed by adequate military and economic capabilities, could reduce the potential threats to stability and greatly increase the prospects for developing a stable power balance based upon a combination of U.S. and regional resources and strength.

The preservation of vital American interests in Asia is likely to be far less burdensome and costly than at past points in the postwar period. The greater strength of the non-Communist countries of the region and the focus of the Communist countries on intra-Communist differences will require less U.S. resources and lower levels of military deployment. But it will require greater access to U.S. capital, technology, and markets; greater involvement in the region; and new initiatives to reinforce the constancy of the U.S. security commitment to the region. It will also require a change in style—less U.S. demand for special treatment and a greater recognition of the independent status of the countries of the region and of the need for fuller consultations, involving an honest give and take instead of a pro forma exercise. American leaders can also no longer afford to be constantly hopping across the Atlantic to consult with Western European leaders while making only occasional and brief excursions to Asia, largely to the PRC. In formulating East Asian policy during the 1980s, the United States must not constantly be a prisoner of its bipolar past or its defeat in Vietnam, but must be guided by emerging developments in the region. The goals of an increasingly stable power balance in East Asia, regional peace, the reduction of tension, and the furtherance of national development and regional cohesion are within the reach of the United States, provided it pursues a policy of enlightened self-interest.

U.S. MILITARY CAPABILITIES

Since the high point of the Vietnam War, U.S. military capabilities in the Pacific have been steadily drawn down. The hard core of U.S. military posture in the Pacific[2] now consists of:

Ground Divisions
    1 Army division (less one battalion) stationed in Korea
    2/3 Marine division stationed in Okinawa, Japan

Air
    10 fighter-attack squadrons stationed in Japan, Korea, and Okinawa
    1 reconnaissance squadron
    1 Marine air wing in Japan
    About 120 carrier-based aircraft

---

2. Ibid.

Navy
  2 aircraft carriers
  19 surface combatant ships
  6 attack submarines
  11 logistic support ships
  2 amphibious ready groups

Supporting these Pacific forces are ground mobility forces in the continental United States, a ground division and the remainder of the Marine division in Hawaii, air units in the United States, and the Third Fleet, based in the Eastern Pacific. Annual exercises in Korea, as well as the 1976 Panmunjom incident, have demonstrated a capability for a rapid surge of aircraft in the western Pacific. There also are strategic forces based in Guam, including B–52s and nuclear attack submarines.

In peacetime, this force is sufficient, but barely so, to preserve U.S. military power in the region. It provides both a strategic deterrent and tactical air and naval support for the local forces in the region. Its capabilities depend heavily upon the availability of a string of military bases in the Pacific. The base structure has been heavily cut back from the 1960s but is still sufficient. The key facilities are five major air bases in Japan that support the air, naval, and marine aircraft; two major air bases in Korea; Clark Field in the Philippines; two major naval bases at Yokusuka and Subic Bay; bases to support the Second Division in Korea and the Marine division in Okinawa; and assorted logistic support facilities. The principal weakness of this base structure is the long line of supply to Hawaii and beyond to the continental United States. In addition, the bases are vulnerable to enemy attack, as well as to unfriendly local actions. In Japan, this base structure has become increasingly expensive to maintain and has forced some reductions in otherwise essential bases. There is also a lack of adequate surge capabilities in the base structure due to the continued reduction in the Japanese base structure.

During the 1980s the vulnerability of the U.S. military posture could become more pronounced with any expansion of Soviet naval power in the Pacific. Absolute or relative declines in U.S. naval strength in the Pacific will increase the danger of the western Pacific being cut off logistically from the United States as well as endangering the lines of supply for petroleum and other raw materials so essential to the industrialized sector of Asia. Already, use of Seventh

Fleet elements in the Indian Ocean involves potentially risky dispersal of barely adequate naval strength in the Pacific. At the same time, Indian Ocean deployments at increased levels are required to protect the vital pipeline from the Middle East. These trends are likely to continue. This vulnerability will place greater emphasis on the need for local naval forces to supplement U.S. strength—in particular, an increase of Japanese naval capabilities for ASW and the support of efforts to block the three strategic straits required by the Soviet fleet for access to the Pacific. The critical factor, however, will remain in the need to maintain sufficient U.S. naval strength relative to the Soviet fleet to assure control of the seas and the capability of containing the Soviet fleet before it moves out into the Pacific.

THE FRAMEWORK FOR U.S. POLICY

Equally as crucial as U.S. military capabilities will be confidence in American willingness to commit these forces in case of an attack. Since the mid-1970s, the reliability of the United States as an ally has been widely questioned, as a result of our apparent unwillingness to be involved in critical tension points in the region. The announcement of Korean ground force withdrawal only confirmed these doubts and still leaves concerns even though it was later postponed. Vietnamese conquest of Cambodia has increased the uncertainty as a result of America's apparent reluctance to take a positive and involved position despite our commitments to Thailand under the Manila Pact. An American posture of sustained involvement and leadership in Asia is essential for maintaining a balance of power in the region and preserving our interests there. This is the fundamental prerequisite for any Asian policy, and it must be implemented not just through pronouncements but in actions that demonstrate our willingness to accept the risks of involvement and commitment to the security of our allies.

A second fundamental in the American posture toward Asia is the development of a more balanced relationship with our Asian allies. The United States has in recent years given far less attention to the region than to our relations and problems in other areas, except for the relationship with the People's Republic of China and the economic frictions with Japan. The psychological and symbolic aspects of American involvement in the region have largely been ignored.

The fact that President Carter visted only Japan and Korea is a matter of concern. There is a general sense in Asia that the United States, except at a time of crisis, is unwilling to devote sufficient priority at high levels to Asia.

American relations with the region are also plagued with the vestiges of the past, during which all the countries of the region were to a greater or lesser extent clients of the United States. Both the United States and the countries of the region still tend to behave in patterns that were developed during this past client relationship. The Asians too often seek assistance and other supportive actions that are more consistent with a client relationship than with the present situation, and the United States too often behaves like the patron it no longer is. What is needed is a more balanced relationship, a partnership, that is based upon greater reciprocity and mutuality and far greater consultations on problems of mutual concern. On the other hand, the price for sustained American engagement in the region must be a greater willingness on the part of the countries of the region to contribute to the maintenance of the power balance and the preservation of U.S. interests in the region that largely coincide with those of the countries of the region.

CONCLUSION: A PROPOSED U.S. STRATEGY FOR ASIA

To meet the challenge of Asia in the 1980s, a new U.S. strategy is essential. The principal components of this strategy should include the following:

- **National Development and Regional Emphasis.** The focus and priority of U.S. policy in Asia should be to support and bolster the national development and stability of the non-Communist countries of Asia. The success of the developmental process in these nations will have major dividends: It will reduce the burden on the United States to maintain the power balance in the region; it will diminish the vulnerability of these nations to Soviet pressures and their concern regarding efforts to increase Chinese economic and military strength; and it will provide an expanding market for the U.S. economy. Essential to the achievement of these goals will be U.S. actions affording access to the U.S. market; facilitating the flow of American capital, largely from private sources; providing U.S. technology; and treating with understanding the longer term problem of developing stable and more representative political institutions rather than sporadic pronouncements on human rights issues. On the other hand, protectionist policy on the part of the United States or the European community could spell disaster. Liberal U.S. trade policies, however, will require reciprocal actions by the countries of the region, permitting equitable and open access to their markets and reasonable opportunities for foreign investment.

- **Energy.** During the 1980s, the rapidly expanding economies of Asia will require increased energy supplies. The implications for U.S. policy are clear-cut: The sea lanes to the Middle East will need U.S. protection; access to U.S. nuclear energy technology will be critical, as will measures to facilitate solution of the reprocessing and breeder reactor problems; and positive U.S. steps to seek settlement of competing claims to the continental shelf, opening the way for oil exploration, will be needed.

- **Military Posture.** U.S. military capabilities, particularly naval power in the Pacific, must be maintained and, if necessary, strengthened relative to Soviet military capabilities in the Pacific. An important consideration will be to avoid the perception that U.S. military strategy is prepared to sacrifice interests in Asia due to European and NATO commitments, a fallout of the one and a half war war strategy and anticipation that enhanced Indian Ocean deployments will be drawn only for the Seventh Fleet. U.S. military efforts to counteract Soviet capabilities will need to be supplemented by the forces of the countries in the region, particularly by improved Japanese forces, and by measures taken particularly by Japan, but also by the Philippines, to reduce the economic and political burdens of the military bases essential to U.S. operations in the Pacific.

- **Korea and Thailand.** The potential for hostilities in both these countries will require a combination of a strong U.S. military deterrent and negotiating efforts to reduce tensions. In Korea, the maintenance of American military strength will be particularly essential until North Korean economic and technological inferiority force a change in its aggressive posture. For Thailand, the key will be the future status of Cambodia and efforts to reduce and, if possible, eliminate the Vietnamese military presence there.

- **The PRC.** The Asian power balance depends on maintaining sufficient Chinese military strength to deter Soviet pressures or an attack. This objective may require steps to improve and modernize Chinese military capabilities, while minimizing the potential adverse effect of any military assistance to the PRC on Southeast Asia and Taiwan. At the same time, the current preoccupation of U.S. Asian policy with the PRC needs to be reduced in terms both of symbolic steps and of policy actions and to be balanced against the other Asian interests of the United States. Although Chinese strength has significance to U.S. interests, a de facto Sino–U.S.–Japanese alliance at the expense of important U.S. interests elsewhere in Asia is unacceptable. Furthermore, the U.S.-PRC relationship must also place certain obligations on the Chinese, particularly to contribute to the overall stability of the region and to a reduction of tensions in Korea, both of which are in the Chinese interest.

- **Japan.** Critical to any cohesive U.S. strategy for Asia will be strengthening the partnership with Japan. Recent economic frictions, in addition to increased doubts regarding the U.S. security commitment, have strained this relationship. Both the U.S. and Japan need to develop mechanisms and policies for ameliorating economic tensions and for accepting the domestic costs of a more balanced economic relationship. Particularly vital is a less competitive relationship vis-à-vis the PRC, particularly in the development of the Chinese market. They must also look to new areas of defense cooperation that buttress the U.S. military effort in the Pacific to their mutual security interest.

- **Regional Cohesion.** The United States should take an active role in supporting burgeoning regional structures, beginning with ASEAN. The prospects for a broader Pacific basin community are likely to grow in the 1980s, but will need careful nurturing. Such a regional body cannot emerge from an American or Japanese initiative that appears to place the smaller countries of the region in an inferior position, but it will need positive U.S. support once an initiative is taken. It must also be responsive to the needs and style of these countries, particularly the ASEAN nations.

- **Regional-Global Balance.** In the final analysis, the U.S. capability for influencing events in Asia will rest on its inherent economic and military strength and its ability to exercise its power and leadership on a global basis. Maintaining a strategic nuclear balance with the USSR will not depend necessarily on deployment of strategic forces in Asia but will directly affect the U.S. position in Asia. A strong military position in Europe likewise will have a direct impact on Soviet capabilities in Asia. The U.S. role in the global balance thus could be just as vital as local forces deployed in Asia.

On the other hand, emphasis on European interests, to the extent that it draws down military forces essential to Asia or it affords greater weight to European economic interests (as was the case in the Tokyo Round), distorts U.S. interests in Asia. There can be no question of priority for either Asia or Europe. U.S. interests in both are interrelated and deserve equal priority. Our Asian allies must recognize that the nature of the threat in Western Europe requires strong U.S. military forces there—a deployment in their own vital interests. By the same token, our NATO allies must overcome their own insularity and contribute to the strengthening of Asia. The interrelationship works both ways, but the linchpin is the United States. Responsibility for assuring a proper balance between regional and global policies must devolve upon the United States.

6 THE U.S.-JAPAN ALLIANCE
Overview and Outlook

John K. Emmerson
Daniel I. Okimoto

> *Daniel I. Okimoto, assistant professor of political science at Stanford University, and John K. Emmerson, a career diplomat with long service in Japan, examine the factors that underlie the extraordinary alliance between the United States and Japan. Assessing the strengths and weaknesses of the alliance today, the authors point out that the decade of the 1980s may bring new tensions to the relationship in the areas of trade, "burden sharing," and access to Middle Eastern oil. Bilateral competition in electronics, automobiles, semiconductors, and computers will place fresh strains on the alliance; the danger of protectionism will lurk in the background; and a lack of vigorous leadership in Washington could cause additional problems. Yet the alliance "will remain absolutely vital to the national interests of both countries" and to the Asia-Pacific region as a whole, the authors conclude.*

For the United States, the decade of the 1980s opened with dual international crises that were to affect America's relations with friends and allies. The seizure of the American Embassy in Teheran, resulting in the incarceration of its diplomatic personnel as hostages, unified the American people as few events had done before. The sudden Soviet invasion of Afghanistan in the following month evoked the condemnation of all but the Soviet satellites in the United Nations. Japan joined in the overwhelming vote in the General Assembly denouncing the action of the militants in Iran and the aggression of the Soviet Union against Afghanistan.

The locus of these events was the Middle East, but the repercussions were worldwide. Countries in northeast Asia, where the Soviet Union meets China, Japan, and the United States, were affected by the developments. Washington's boycott of Iranian oil and sanctions against the Soviet Union brought Japan, a country totally lacking in oil resources and dependent on foreign trade, directly into the controversy. America's revitalized sense of a Soviet threat led to renewed expectations of a shared defense role for Japan. The crises in the Middle East drew attention to the prospect that the Japanese–American alliance, long considered the linchpin of U.S. policy in East Asia, would suffer tests of strength while acquiring added dimensions of indispensability in the 1980s. What lies ahead for the U.S.–Japan alliance? Are current defense arrangements adequate in the face of altered world conditions?

This chapter seeks to provide an assessment of where the alliance now stands, how it evolved, and what sorts of conflicts might be encountered. The opening part places the alliance in historical perspective and examines in detail the common interests on which it is solidly built. Part two surveys the sources of conflict that have plagued the alliance, and the final part seeks to anticipate the problems and prospects for the future. We believe that the U.S.–Japan alliance is as vital as ever to both countries, even though changes in the world environment threaten to subject it to strain.

THE NATURE OF THE ALLIANCE

The establishment of the U.S.–Japan alliance is a historic demarcation line, dividing post–World War II Asia from its prewar past. For the first half of the twentieth century, big power relations in Asia were continually in turmoil. The major Western powers and Japan were locked in a fierce competition to carve out spheres of influence. China, the largest prize in the imperialist struggle, was fragmented, weak, and vulnerable to foreign penetration. Irresistibly drawn to the vast vacuum created by China's weakness, Japan pushed the boundaries of its empire relentlessly outward, first from Korea to Manchuria, then to North China, and eventually deep into the heart of mainland China. The one country in possession of the requisite power to stop Japan from overrunning Asia attempted to contain Japan's military advance by issuing diplomatic protests and warnings, backed by the application of economic sanctions. For a variety of reasons—mostly having to do with neoisolationist sentiments—the United States was not inclined to deploy forces in the Pacific that might have given teeth to its diplomatic and economic efforts at deterrence. Not surprisingly, the mixture of nonmilitary measures not only failed to halt Japan's military surge across China (much less to roll back Japan's empire to its pre-Manchuria boundaries, as the United States insisted), but by making the costs of compliance (giving up all territorial acquisitions on the Chinese mainland, including Manchuria) seem higher than the calculated risks of desperate action (a surprise attack on Pearl Harbor and a swift thrust into Southeast Asia to seize oil, rubber, and other natural resources), it may even have created circumstances that strengthened the hands of the military expansionists in Japan.[1]

Developments following the end of the war—including especially the establishment of the U.S.-Japan alliance—were instrumental in eliminating several underlying causes of instability in Asia. Colonial governments, from Dutch holdings in Indonesia to the Japanese occupation of Korea, came to an end all over the region. Communist forces unified the mainland under a strong, centralized regime, filling the vacuum that had tempted outside powers to set up their own spheres of influence. Imperial Japan's military machine was completely dismantled under the allied occupation, neutralizing the one indigeneous nation that had the potential industrial and human resources to dominate the region.

At the same time that some of the chronic sources of conflict were being corrected, the foundation of a more stable regional order was carefully laid, the most critical cornerstone of which was the U.S.-Japan alliance. The burying of the Tokyo-Washington hatchet eliminated at one stroke the principal rivalry of the prewar period. Two powerful adversaries, who had fought a long and bitter war, suddenly found themselves bound together by growing linkages of economic, military, and political interdependence. Reacting strongly to the trauma of the war, the two nations followed postwar paths that,

---

1. For an analysis of why U.S. policies made for poor deterrent strategy, see Bruce Russett, "Pearl Harbor: Deterrence Theory" *Journal of Peace Research* 2(1967): 97.

while quite opposite in direction, curiously brought them closer together than ever before. Realizing after the trauma of two world wars that it could ill afford to withdraw again into isolationism, the United States as the world's dominant power moved boldly ahead to construct a postwar system that would protect its national interests and maintain peace. Its most important steps in Asia included the deployment of the Seventh Fleet and the establishment of a mutual security treaty with Japan, both of which served as underpinnings for a formidable naval, air, and ground presence in the region. The significance of such steps is suggested by the fact that a credible structure of deterrence had been missing in the prewar period.

The deterrent structure also provided the Japanese with a strong enough sense of security that they could reverse their expansionist impulses and pull back into a military isolationist stance; assuming an inconspicuous military posture, the Japanese were able to unleash the full force of their energies and skill toward the tasks of economic reconstruction and growth. In this single-minded pursuit the Japanese succeeded spectacularly—beyond anyone's wildest expectations. Over a sustained period of thirty years, Japan's postwar growth rate surpassed that of any other OECD nation. While Japan's economy doubled every seven or eight years, its military capabilities expanded only incrementally, creating what might be called a widening "latent capabilities gap" between its actual and potential level of armament—in terms, that is, of what its industrial infrastructure could be called upon to support under different circumstances and priorities. This "latent capabilities gap," though often taken for granted, has had a significant bearing on the balance of power and the structure of postwar relations in Asia.

Of course, certain ramifications of the U.S.-Japan alliance may have been negative. George Kennan suspects that bilateral negotiations to conclude the military pact may have sent disquieting messages to Moscow and Peking, prompting the two countries to sign their own defense treaty in anticipation of an emergent U.S.-Japan alliance.[2] The two Cold War treaties thereby laid the groundwork for the rigid structure of regional bipolarity that dominated the region until the Sino-Soviet split. Severe tensions gripped the area, particularly during and after the Korean War, and the Cold War pall that settled over Asia chilled relations between the major powers, fore-

---

2. George Kennan, *Memoirs*, 1925-50 (Boston: Little Brown & Co., 1967).

closing for many years any possibility of a less tense, more flexible set of relationships cutting across Cold War cleavages.

While there may have been other opportunity costs associated with the rigid structure of bipolarity,[3] blame for the onset of the Cold War in Asia cannot be laid on the U.S.-Japan military alliance. The Soviet-American competition was global in nature, and there is no way of knowing for certain what might have happened under a different set of circumstances or, indeed, how the lines of causality, linking events to the onset of tensions, ought to be drawn.[4] All we can say with the benefit of hindsight is that the U.S.-Japan alliance has (1) introduced an element of predictability in the region unknown in the prewar period; (2) served as the linchpin of a formidable deterrent against Communist nations; (3) erected an umbrella beneath which a number of Asian nations have been free to develop market economies; (4) allowed enough leeway for both the United States and Japan to establish normal relations eventually with China; (5) laid down an international course for Japan, strikingly divergent from its prewar past; and (6) brought in bountiful bilateral benefits for the United States and Japan at low cost and low risk. Historians in the twenty-first century, looking back on the second half of the twentieth century, are therefore likely to regard the U.S.-Japan alliance as one of the truly seminal developments in postwar Asia, comparable in importance to the unification of the Chinese mainland, the onset of the Cold War, and the Sino-Soviet rift.

Alliance Cohesion

What has held this alliance together when, on the surface, the two nations seem so alien and ill suited? The two nations had already fought a very costly war that had inflamed deep, racist animosities on both sides. Barriers to mutual understanding could hardly seem more imposing, given the contrasts in ecology, power, culture, society, language, and history:

3. See John Dower, "Occupied Japan and the American Lake, 1945-50," in Edward Friedman and Mark Seldon, eds., *America's Asia: Dissenting Essays on Asian-American Relations* (New York: Random House, 1969), pp. 146-206.

4. Yonosuke Nagai and Akira Iriye, eds., *The Origins of the Cold War in Asia* (New York: Columbia University Press, 1977).

Japan	*United States*
Small, island nation	Large, continental nation
Poor in natural resources	Rich in natural resources
Confucianism, Buddhism, Shintoism	Judeo-Christian tradition
Group-oriented society	Individual-centered society
Hierarchical relations	Egalitarian relations
Long historical past	Short historical past
Politicomilitary power	Politicomilitary low posture
Homogeneous	Heterogeneous
Japanese language	English language
Consensual decisions	Majoritarian decisions

Beneath the many differences, there are, of course, underlying similarities—as, for example, the value placed on hard work, thrift, education, and achievement—that make the two cultures more compatible than the listing of contrasts indicates. Nevertheless, the difficulties of mutual understanding across so wide a geographic, linguistic, and cultural divide are enormous—far wider than between the United States and its NATO allies. As an island nation, which closed itself off from the rest of the world for two and a half centuries (from 1600-1867, a critical period in the evolution of modern nation states) and which developed its own very distinctive culture and society, Japan is perhaps something of an anomaly—an economic superstate with no natural allies, at least in the sense that Canada or England are natural allies for the United States. Despite all surface dissimilarities and the genuine difficulties of mutual understanding, the United States is probably Japan's most logical ally. Why?

The U.S.-Japan alliance is successful, because it is based on a solid bedrock of common interests, the most obvious of which include:

- A commitment to market-based economies and the principles of free trade;
- A commitment to representative systems of government;
- Extensive economic linkages—trade, capital flows, and technology transfers;
- Common interests in curbing the power of Communist bloc nations that threaten their own;
- Vested interests in maintaining peace, stability, and the balance of power, both regionally and, to a growing extent, globally; and

- A broad range of specific interests, such as securing stable supplies of energy at acceptable prices.

The list can be extended well beyond those outlined above; suffice it to say here that on the basics, the two nations are closely aligned, because their fundamental interests converge so closely.

Japan's Value to the United States

The importance of the alliance can be analyzed by breaking the mutual benefits down into concrete advantages for each side. Japan is vital to the United States in the following respects:

1. As the third largest GNP in the world whose cooperation is essential for the smooth functioning of the international economic system;
2. As America's second largest trade partner (second only to Canada), which supplies a great many manufactured products at competitive prices while at the same time purchasing large quantities of agricultural goods and other primary commodities;
3. As the dominant economic power in Asia, which is capable of promoting regional growth and stability through trade, aid, investments, training, education, and managerial organization;
4. As the most striking example of an efficiently run and stable democracy in the non-Western world;
5. As a nonthreatening nation capable of playing a useful role in mediating and modulating conflicts in Asia;
6. As a home for military facilities that are essential for the operation of the Seventh Fleet and the forward deployment of U.S. forces in Northeast Asia; and
7. As a potential military power that the United States cannot afford to see turn antagonistic or fall into the hands of hostile powers and whose military assistance and support may become increasingly important to the United States in seeking to offset the Soviet threat.

Japan's value as America's ally has changed over time, as the regional balance and Japan's own position in the world have been transformed. During the 1950s and 1960s, Japan's primary importance was as a military base for the forward deployment of American forces in Asia. Its strategic location—just off the Asiatic continent, at a critical avenue of access to and from the Pacific—made U.S. bases there (including Okinawa) indispensable for carrying out commitments to Korea, Taiwan, and other countries in Asia. Without these bases, the logistics of deploying naval, air, and combat forces would have been substantially more troublesome and costly. In particular, the scope and flexibility of the Seventh Fleet's naval operations—arguably the backbone of America's presence in the Pacific—would have been severely impaired. What bases in Japan offered in terms of logistical facilities for U.S. naval, air, marine, intelligence, and communications activities few, if any, other countries (or combination of countries) could have duplicated.

Since the late 1960s, Japan's value as an economic ally has soared. While the military advantages remain as vital as ever (if not more so today), Japan's growing emergence as an economic superstate has driven up the aggregate value of the alliance to the United States, particularly in the aftermath of the collapse of the Bretton Woods system and the relative decline of America's economic power. The sheer size of Japan's economy means that its weight will be felt in the world, whether in terms of purchasing power, export capabilities, or capital flows. Since political stability is so closely tied to economic variables, Japan is in a position to play a crucial role not only in Asia's drive to industrialize but also in the effective operation of the international economic system.

By contrast, the political value of the alliance has always been less apparent than its military or economic utility. From America's perspective, Japan's political importance has been more symbolic than instrumental—as perhaps the proudest showcase of a stable democracy in the non-Western world. Because the Tokyo government has adhered to a policy of separating politics from economics (*seikei bunri*), Japan has made a tactical habit out of ducking, whenever possible, hard political questions that impinge on its economic maneuverability. But this, too, is changing. Out of the ordeal of "shocks" endured during the 1970s has emerged a new awareness that Japan must start assuming more political responsibility in the world, as befitting an economic superstate and ally of the United States. As the late Prime Minister Masayoshi Ohira remarked in a speech before the National Press Club in Washington, D.C.: "We are also determined to play a more effective political role than in the past, in pursuit of world peace and stability. In particular, as an Asian nation, we wish to fulfill our role and responsibilities by supporting those trends toward stability in Asia, while discouraging tendencies toward instability."[5]

There are already signs of a new political role. The announcement in 1977 of the so-called "Fukuda Doctrine"—by which Japan pledged, among other things, to double its level of foreign aid to Southeast Asia by 1982—is a case in point. Although less heralded, Japan's attempt to serve as an intermediary between Vietnam and the United States in discussions of normalization is another example. Also noteworthy is the fact that Japan did not wait for Washington to conclude a treaty of peace and amity with China. While these acts, either singly or in combination, are in no danger of being considered historic initiatives, they are indicative of a new willingness to take steps not readily apparent in the past. As a nation in possession of considerable economic inducements, Japan may find itself in an increasingly advantageous position to play a constructive role in the region. The benefits for the United States, though still not very consequential, could grow as interactions between nations in Asia become more convoluted.

America's Value to Japan

For Tokyo, the value of the U.S.-Japan alliance is, if anything, even greater than it is for Washington. Japanese leaders believe that they have more at stake than Americans, even if assigning greater weight to one over the other may be misleading because of the alliance's immense value for both sides. What the Japanese derive from the alliance includes:

1. A solid sense of security, something the Japanese never had in the prewar period;
2. Relative regional stability, the result not only of America's commitments and presence but also of the defensive nature of Japan's security posture;

---

5. An address by Prime Minister Ohira Masayoshi, National Press Club, Washington, D.C., May 3, 1979.

3. Reliance on the United States to maintain political stability in critical areas—such as the Middle East—that are closely linked to Japan's own national security;
4. Reliance on the United States to maintain a military balance of power around the world not unfavorable to the interests of the non-Communist bloc;
5. The heaviest traffic of goods and services moving across the high seas in the history of commerce (America is Japan's largest and most vital export market, source of technology, and so forth);
6. Firm leadership in the maintenance of a healthy international economic system; and
7. The framework for a predictable international orientation, one that has helped to stabilize politics at home.

Thanks to its alliance with the United States, Japan has found a secure niche in the international system that is in striking contrast to its prewar isolation and perception of encirclement by hostile powers. One of the happy ironies of modern Japanese history is that in losing the war, Japan finally found the sense of international security that had eluded it for nearly a century—from the time Commodore Perry dropped anchor off Japan's shores in 1853. Japan's thoroughgoing reorientation following its crushing defeat, together with the transformation of the regional order in Asia, have brought the sense of security, prosperity, and access to economic markets and raw materials that military aggression had failed so miserably to secure.

The last point deserves elaboration. Like other market economies, struggling to recover from the ravages of war, Japan benefited enormously from the vigorous international economy that the United States helped to bring into existence. America took the lead, for example, in establishing an orderly monetary system, based on the strength of the dollar, that provided a stable framework for international transactions over several decades. The system of fixed exchange rates worked to Japan's advantage during the 1960s, when the value of the yen was pegged at ¥360 to the dollar. The undervaluation of the yen—which grew increasingly problematic as Japan's economy gathered strength—facilitated Japanese exports abroad. What it provided, in effect, was a form of invisible export subsidy, especially with respect to the U.S. market.

In addition to serving as the world's banker, the United States also spearheaded the drive to reduce tariffs and to roll back informal barriers to the free flow of trade. The creation of a global system of liberalized trade proved especially crucial to a resource-poor country like Japan, whose survival rested on its access to overseas resources and markets. As a result, in part of the global system of free trade, the world economy recorded unprecedented rates of growth from 1946-1968; real growth of world GNP rose at an average of 3.8 percent during this twenty-two year period. Seen from this perspective, Japan's own economic development can be considered merely the most dramatic in a remarkable worldwide boom.[6] Giving proper credit to the international context does not diminish in the slightest the magnitude of Japan's performance, since other countries operating within the same environment have failed to come even close to Japan's record.

During the 1950s and early 1960s, when Japan's economy still had not become the third largest in the world, the United States was willing to tolerate a notable lack of economic reciprocity. Although Japan enjoyed relatively free access to the U.S. market, its own market was protected quite asymmetrically from U.S. penetration by a series of trade and investment barriers, ranging from a high number of import barriers to the Foreign Exchange Control and Trade Law, which strictly restricted American access to the Japanese market (see Table 6-1). The Japanese government justified such protection in terms of the need to regulate its chronic balance of payments problem, to protect infant industries, and to facilitate rapid structural transformation. But as Japan's economy grew so large that these justifications could no longer be invoked convincingly, the Tokyo government was forced by foreign pressures to begin scaling down the high walls of protectionism.

Where formal tariff barriers are concerned, Japan is now down to levels roughly comparable to those of other OECD nations.[7] But getting the Tokyo government to remove the barriers took time and not a little external suasion.

The U.S. economy is also crucial to Japan in a more narrow, bilateral sense. There could not have been an ally better suited to meet

---

6. Ezra Solomon, *The Anxious Economy* (San Francisco: San Francisco Book Co., 1976), p. 13.

7. Edward F. Denison and William K. Chung, *How Japan's Economy Grew So Fast* (Washington, D.C.: The Brookings Institution, 1976), p. 53.

Table 6-1. Japanese Import Quota Restrictions, 1962-1973.

Date	Number of Items Under Quota Restriction	Number of Items Under Residual Restrictions Under the GATT
April 1962	490	—
April 1963	229	n.a.
April 1964	174	136
October 1965	161	122
May 1966	168	126
October 1968	164	121
October 1969	161	118
September 1970	133	90
April 1972	79	33
April 1973	83	32
October 1973	82	31

Source: Lawrence B. Krause and Sueo Sekiguchi, "Japan and the World's Economy," in Hugh Patrick and Henry Rosovsky, eds., *Asia's New Giant* (Washington, D.C.: The Brookings Institution, 1976) p. 426.

Japan's economic needs. Many of the raw materials Japan sought—wheat, soybeans, feedstuff, lumber, mineral fuels, and other commodities—were readily made available by the United States, along with valuable American technology, capital, training and educational opportunities, and countless intangible resources that boosted Japan's economic capabilities enormously. The commercial availability of technology, for example, permitted the Japanese to follow a "leapfrog" strategy of catching up to the standards of advanced Western technology and, indeed, surpassing it through product improvements without incurring the full costs of basic and applied research and development. Technological improvements, utilized through the construction of new plant facilities, have contributed significantly to steep rises in Japan's productivity.[8] More importantly, the United States represented the world's largest and most

8. JETRO, *White Paper on International Trade*: Japan 1978 (Tokyo: JETRO, 1979), pp. 203-209.

diversified market for Japan's exports. During the 1950s and 1960s, the differing levels of development made trade between the two countries naturally complementary. The flow of trade has expanded steadily, to the point where it is now the heaviest across the high seas in the history of human commerce (see Table 6-2). For Japan, the American export market, totaling more than $26 billion in 1979 (more than 25 percent of all Japanese exports), has been positively essential. Much of it is concentrated in the manufactured categories — transport machinery, electrical machinery (television, radios, etc.), and general (internal combustion engines, office machines) and precision (scientific and optical instruments, cameras, etc.) machinery.[9]

Owing to its paucity of raw materials, Japan has had to export in large enough quantities to cover its import bill. The export market is vital for other reasons as well: (1) as a mechanism for pulling the economy out of the doldrums of cyclical recessions; (2) as a way of building economies of scale; (3) as a route for riding the international product cycle; (4) as a means of earning foreign exchange to pay for rises in the price of imported primary commodities; and (5) as a stimulus for capital investments in new plant facilities. As Japan's largest single customer, the United States has figured prominently in all five functions. The composition of the bilateral trade in some respects resembles what some people consider a neomercantilist relationship: The United States ships food and raw materials to Japan in return for manufactured products of high value added. There is no doubt that the exchange of goods gives rise to some problems, particularly in the area of balancing current accounts. But a number of Japanese believe that the structure of the trade places Japan at a power disadvantage vis-à-vis the United States. They feel it makes Japan more dependent on the United States than vice versa.[10] But apart from perceptions of which country is more vulnerable and dependent — a question too complicated to discuss in depth here — few can argue with the proposition that economic relations with the United States, in terms of both exports and imports, are absolutely vital to Japan's prosperity.

Alliance with America is also important for reasons of military security. Japan depends on the United States to maintain military capabilities sufficient to guarantee a global balance of power, which

9. Ibid.
10. This is a view that Kosaka Masataka has expressed in conversation.

Table 6–2. U.S.–Japan Bilateral Trade, Trade, and Current Account Balances 1953–1974 and 1975 First Two Quarters ($U.S. million).

Year	Japanese Commodity Exports to U.S.			Japanese Commodity Imports from U.S.			U.S.–Japan Trade Balance (7)	U.S.–Japan Current Account Balance (8)
	Amount (1)	% of Japan Total Exports (2)	% of U.S. Total Imports (3)	Amount (4)	% of Japan Total Imports (5)	% of U.S. Total Exports (6)		
1953	261.5	18.3	2.4	686.4	31.5		-424.9	330
4	279.0	17.3	2.7	692.7	35.3	4.6	-413.7	76
5	431.9	22.7	3.8	682.5	31.3	4.4	-250.6	264
6	557.9	22.0	4.5	997.8	33.0	5.3	-439.9	132
7	600.5	21.1	4.6	1319.3	37.9	6.4	-718.8	-209
8	666.5	24.0	5.2	986.9	34.8	5.6	-320.4	178
9	1028.7	30.3	6.9	1079.5	31.0	6.2	-50.8	383
60	1148.8	27.2	7.8	1447.2	34.6	7.1	-298.4	50
1	1054.8	25.2	7.3	1837.3	36.1	8.9	-782.5	-480
2	1358.0	28.5	8.4	1573.8	32.1	7.4	-215.8	8
3	1497.8	27.6	8.8	1843.6	30.8	8.0	-345.8	-346
4	1768.1	27.6	9.5	2009.3	29.4	7.7	-241.2	-211

5	2413.8	29.3	11.3	2080.1	29.0	7.7	333.7	365
6	2962.8	30.4	11.7	2363.5	27.9	7.9	599.3	710
7	2998.7	28.8	11.2	2695.0	27.5	8.7	303.7	280
8	4054.4	31.5	12.3	2954.3	27.1	8.7	1100.1	829
9	4888.2	31.0	13.6	3989.7	27.2	9.3	1398.5	1270
70	5875.3	30.7	14.8	4652.0	29.4	10.9	1223.3	857
1	7258.8	31.2	15.9	4054.8	25.3	9.3	3204.0	2750
2	9064.3	30.9	16.4	4941.2	24.9	10.1	4123.1	4782
3	9644.8	25.6	14.0	8311.8	24.2	11.8	1333.0	1631
4	12799.4	23.0	12.8	12682.2	20.4	13.0	117.2	1050
6	15689.5			11809.3	18.4			
7	19716.9			12396.1	(17.5)			
8	24914.0			14790.3				
9	26409.3			20334.3				

Sources: Gary Saxonhouse and Hugh Patrick, "Japan and the United States: Bilateral Tensions and Multilateral Issues in the Economic Relationship," in Donald Hellmann, ed., *China and Japan: A New Balance of Power* (Lexington, Massachusetts: Lexington Books, 1976), pp. 100–101. 1978–1979 figures from JETRO Office, San Francisco, quoting statistics from the Japanese ministry of finance.

Table 6–3. Japan and U.S. Dependency on Imports and Share of Total World Imports of Major Basic Commodities (in percentage).

	Degree of Dependency on Imports		Share of Total World Imports		Sources of World Exports		
	Japan	U.S.	Japan	U.S.	Developed Nations	Developing Nations	Communist Nations
Beef	14.1	5.4	2.8	26.7	65.1	31.4	3.5
Wheat	95.1	0.0	9.4	0.0	88.1	3.6	8.3
Maize	99.5	0.0	16.3	0.1	85.0	14.6	0.4
Wool	100.0	26.9	30.6	2.7	88.0	10.1	1.9
Cotton	100.0	0.0	20.7	0.4	22.7	7.9	5.4
Lumber	50.0	0.2	31.2	12.6	49.1	48.0	1.6
Iron Ore	98.9	34.1	41.1	13.4	55.3	42.7	2.0
Copper (ore and base metal)	89.0	16.0	22.0	9.9	45.4	54.0	0.6
Lead (ore and base metal)	72.0	28.0	8.0	18.4	51.5	47.7	0.8
Zinc (ore and base metal)	63.0	46.0	14.7	25.8	84.2	15.6	0.3
Tin (ore and base metal)	97.8	10.0	18.1	32.3	4.3	95.4	0.3
Nickel (ore and base metal)	100.0	90.0	12.4	29.9	76.3	23.3	0.4
Bauxite	100.0	87.9	12.9	28.7	9.6	88.9	1.5
Manganese	97.6	97.7	31.9	16.4	7.6	87.0	5.3

THE U.S.–JAPAN ALLIANCE: OVERVIEW AND OUTLOOK   103

Chromium	99.1	100.0	28.6	24.0	13.3	⎫ 86.7	n.a.
Tungsten	68.3	39.9	9.0	15.6	0.0	⎭ 100.0	17.9
Phosphoric ore	100.0	0.0	15.0	0.5	n.a.	n.a.	—
Coal	63.6	0.0	25.8	0.0	81.8	0.3	—
Crude oil	99.7	19.2	13.7	13.4	4.8	83.0	12.2
Natural gas	34.9	4.0	1.9	37.9	75.6	22.5	1.9

Note: Dependency is the ratio net imports (imports−exports) to domestic use, while shares of world imports are gross (without deducting exports). Data are in most cases for 1972, but 1971 for lumber, and 1973 for dependency ratios for copper, lead, zinc, tin, and nickel. "World Imports" refer to OECD nation imports for iron ore, copper, lead, bauxite, tin, nickel, manganese, chromium, tungsten, phosphoric ore, and beef.

Sources: Japan: MITI, *White Paper on International Trade 1975* (Tokyo: Japan External Trade Organization, 1975), pp. 24–25, 41–42; UN: *Yearbook of International Trade Statistics 1974* (New York: UN, 1975); *Trade by Commodities: Market Summaries: Exports 1972*, vol.1 (Paris: OECD, 1973); and *Imports 1972*, vol. 1 (Paris: OECD, 1973).

preserves a status quo not unfavorable to the interests of the non-Communist world. This deterrent, which the Japanese believe only the United States is capable of providing, serves to discourage hostile nations from engaging in acts across a wide spectrum of conceivable contingencies—from veiled threats and diplomatic bullying to indirect intervention through third parties in areas of crucial importance and outright initiation of warfare, either through miscalculation or deliberate design. Threats at the upper end of the spectrum must obviously be deterred, and give the potentially cataclysmic consequences of uncontrolled war between military superpowers, the Japanese feel that the most extreme threats are probably the most readily deterred. Hostile acts at the opposite end of the spectrum—such as subtle pressures and the application of low risk, nonmilitary sanctions—cannot be entirely deterred, no matter how much military strength one side has at its disposal; but, since such acts pose the lowest threat, there is less need to worry about hostile gestures at this end of the spectrum.

It is the large, often undefined middle range that is most troublesome—for example, the aiding and abetting of domestic insurrection, logistical support in civil wars, and third party intervention in the Middle East and Africa. Whether and in what ways such threats can be deterred, and at what costs, are difficult questions that are related to the global balance of power and Japan's sense of security. For most of the postwar period, the Japanese have not had to worry excessively about the threat of having the non-Communist camp "salami sliced." Having a clear superiority in power, the United States has had the leeway to engage perhaps more actively than other countries in middle range, risk-taking behavior to prevent the status quo from turning unfavorable or to support changes more favorable to its interests. This situation—and the global balance of power—has changed over time, but for twenty or more years following the end of the war, Japan enjoyed the luxury, which few other nations have known, of living in a relatively benign security environment with a low sense of threat concerning military attack or invasion.

The strong sense of security has been reinforced by the assurance that, in the unlikely event of an attack, the United States is fully committed to come to its defense. Article V of the Mutual Security Treaty (MST) states:

> Each Party recognizes that an armed attack against either Party in the territories under the administration of Japan would be dangerous to its own peace

and safety and declares that it would act to meet the common danger in accordance with its constitutional provisions and processes.

Japan's own defense capabilities are limited. Most Japanese defense analysts believe that Japan would not be able to hold out much longer than ten or fourteen days if a massive attack, followed by physical invasion, were actually carried out. Its air force is susceptible to preemptive attacks, which could destroy most of its fighter planes before they had a chance to scramble, and even if that did not happen, Japan's self-defense capabilities are so limited that Osamu Kaihara, formerly a high-ranking official in the Japan Defense Agency, has calculated that Japan's stockpile of ammunition would be completely depleted within a week if a war broke out.[11] If such assessments of Japan's combat weaknesses are not wildly exaggerated, the logical inference that most Japanese have drawn is that Japan must rely on its military alliance with the United States to deter aggression, to intervene early in case of attack, and to insulate the nation against diplomatic blackmail or political bullying. Unless it believes it can somehow guarantee its security through neutralization, or alternatively, unless it manages to achieve military self-sufficiency, Japan has no choice but to entrust its security to the protective umbrella provided by the U.S.-Japan Security Treaty.

Although mention is not usually made of the subject—perhaps because it falls between the crevices of America's military and economic umbrellas—Japan is also deeply affected by world political developments over which the United States exercises considerable influence. Consider the Middle East as an example. As everyone knows, Japan's economic well-being is closely tied to stability in the Persian Gulf, from which it obtains over 80 percent of the oil that keeps the wheels of its industries churning. The revolution in Iran and the Soviet invasion of Afghanistan have demonstrated dramatically how quickly the status quo can change and how fragile are peace and stability. Even if the events in Iran and Afghanistan represent developments on the upper end of adverse consequences, change

---

11. Kaihara Osamu, *Waga Kuni no Boei ni Tsuite (On Our National Defense)* (Tokyo: Gaiko Chisiki Fukyukai, 1974); and Kaihara Osamo, *Watakushi no Kokubo Hakusho (My Defense White Paper)* (Tokyo: Juju Tsushinsha, 1975). See also Nakamura Ryuhei et al., *Jieitai Tatakawaba (If the Self-Defense Forces Should Fight a War)* (Tokyo: Orient Shobo, 1976).

need not be so dramatic to affect Japan's economy.[12] Political disorder in Iran, from which Japan obtained 13.4 percent of its oil in 1978, placed Japan in a difficult dilemma with respect to the U.S. boycott of Iranian oil. If Japan lost a significant amount of oil, its economy would be forced to make a series of adjustments that, if poorly managed, could be destabilizing. Its growth rates would be curtailed, its import costs would rise, its balance of payments thrown into disequilibrium, its exports faced with protectionist barriers, and its economy forced to endure higher rates of inflation and unemployment.

Events in the Middle East following the OPEC oil embargo, 1973–1974, caused deep concern in Tokyo: The upheaval and continued turmoil in Iran, residual problems of the Camp David Accords, Arab pressures on Saudi Arabia, and the like all call into question the once dominant role played by the United States. As much as any country in the world, Japan is painfully aware of the cruel geopolitical reality that most of the known oil reserves lie in one of the world's least stable regions. Whatever role the United States can play in helping to promote political stability in the Persian Gulf, therefore, is seen as safeguarding what is undoubtedly Japan's most obvious Achilles heel. As no other nation seems capable of playing this role, Japan counts heavily on the United States.

In spite of striking cultural, social, and ecological dissimilarities that make the United States and Japan seem like ill-suited allies, therefore, the historic alliance is based on a solid foundation of common national interests on which an elaborate framework of bilateral cooperation has been built. Both parties derive immeasurable economic, military, and political benefits from the alliance, and it would be hard to imagine how differently history might have worked out if the alliance had not been forged. How would Japan have evolved? What would the structure of regional alignments have looked like? In what ways would America's policies toward Asia have differed? Answers to these questions can only be speculative in nature, and the strain put on one's powers of imagination to come up with historical

---

12. There is a tendency to frame Japan's stakes in the Middle East in the most extreme scenarios. While understandable, such scenarios often fail to convey the full range of less extreme, more profitable contingencies that threaten to damage Japanese interests seriously, even if at the "margins." Japan depends on the United States to play a constructive, stabilizing role in the Middle East.

scenarios as credulous and constructive as that brought about by the reality of the U.S.-Japan alliance is only testimony to its seminal significance in postwar Asia.

SOURCES OF ALLIANCE FRICTION

No alliance in the world, no matter how crucial or close, is ever fully free of frictions. The nature of an international system based on national sovereignty and the inevitability of national differences is such that the occurrence of conflicts must be expected in any transnational coalition. The U.S.-Japan alliance, as its postwar evolution illustrates, is no exception. Analyzing where and why friction arose ought to permit us to understand better the "trouble spots" or "problem areas" of the alliance. Identifying the sources of past conflicts also leads logically to the final section of this chapter—a projection of the problems of and prospects for the alliance.

Divergent Styles

The success of the U.S.-Japan alliance implies that if there are strong national interests in common, cultural dissimilarities can be overcome or at least not allowed to wreck the bilateral relationship. This is not to say, however, that all conflicts arising out of cultural differences or compounded by divergent priorities and styles can be wholly eliminated or controlled. Over the postwar period, a number of instances in which conflicts were either generated or exacerbated by cultural differences can be cited. In the important area of commercial transactions among companies in the private sector, for example, differences in Japanese and American approaches to the role of law—and specifically of contracts—have created all sorts of misunderstandings. American businessmen see contracts as binding, regardless of what changes occur in surrounding circumstances, and want to spell out in minute detail the rights, responsibilities, and expectations of each party. Japanese businessmen, by contrast, place more emphasis on the spirit of the agreement than on the letter of the law and view contracts in a longer context of fluid circumstances that can alter the terms or legal validity; if the circumstances under which a contract was drawn up change, the Japanese tend to feel that its provisions or interpretation ought to be adjusted accordingly.[13] The ingrained American impulse to file suit when there is a conflict of interest strikes the Japanese, whose instincts are to search for a compromise in good faith and settle differences amicably out of court, as alien, harsh, and dysfunctionally costly. Americans, on the other hand, feel that international business cannot be conducted if the Japanese undermine the elements of certainty by refusing to abide by legal contracts.

American and Japanese attitudes toward law are sometimes seen as outcroppings of a more basic difference in values: Americans tend to emphasize universal principles, while the Japanese adhere to more situational ethics. This difference can give rise to conflicts not only on the level of interpersonal relationships and corporate interactions, but also at the governmental and policymaking level. The Japanese and American deadlock over the reprocessing of spent nuclear fuels, 1976–1978, is a case in point. In order to implement a global policy designed to arrest the spread of nuclear weapons, the Carter administration decided to discourage the reprocessing of spent nuclear fuels in order to limit the availability of weapons grade materials, especially in countries where there might be incentives to convert them into nuclear warheads. Although previous American administrations had approved of Japan's plans to operate nuclear reprocessing plants, the Carter administration asked Japan to forego reprocessing as part of a systematic, worldwide effort to contain weapons proliferation. Japan, which is far more anxious about its energy needs, balked, claiming that it has no intention whatsoever of surreptitiously diverting reprocessed fuel for weapons assemblage. Granting exemptions, American officials argued, would undermine the efficacy of a universal principle (nonproliferation) that the United States was trying hard to establish. An eventual compromise was reached, but

---

13. The national differences here are slightly exaggerated in order to highlight the conceptual distinctions. As Dan Henderson points out, "Still, from Tokugawa times at least, there has been a tradition of very full and careful documentation of agreements including extensive uses of third-party witnesses and registries to assure understanding, compliance and proof.... In contemporary Japan sophisticated businesses (e.g., trading companies, banks, and large industrials) are aware of the functional importance of the English-language contracting process in achieving real understanding in the more complex foreign transactions." Dan F. Henderson, *Foreign Enterprise in Japan* (Chapel Hill: University of North Carolina Press, 1973), p. 291.

not before significant anxieties and some resentments had been generated.[14]

Divergent Attitudes: Military Issues

Of all the irritants to afflict the alliance from the 1940s to the end of the 1960s, differences in domestic attitudes toward military issues constituted undoubtedly the most sustained and difficult. The problem arose, basically, out of the strength of domestic opposition in Japan not only to the U.S.-Japan Mutual Security Treaty (MST) but also to the very idea of rearmament. In reaction to the war, strong undercurrents of pacifism and neutrality ran through Japanese society; such sentiments were reflected in the Japan Socialist party's policy platform, calling for the MST's immediate abrogation and the dissolution of the Self-Defense Forces (SDF). Left-wing opposition tended, moreover, to be concentrated in politically active and visible groups—labor unions, intellectuals, student organizations, and the mass media. In 1960, when the MST was submitted to the Diet in revised form, such groups held massive demonstrations to protest its ratification. Security issues remained highly visible and politically volatile throughout the 1960s, as reformist parties often seized upon them to highlight their differences with the ruling conservative party. It was not until the United States returned Okinawa to Japanese administrative control and curtailed its involvement in Vietnam that the emotionally charged nature of military issues became defused. The political mood in Japan has changed so fundamentally since then that MST abrogation is no longer an issue—quite the contrary. What is at the heart of Japanese concerns today is the credibility of the U.S. commitment in the face of changing international circumstances.

On the American side, a recurrent theme of disgruntlement centered on the feeling that Japan was not carrying its fair share of the financial and military burdens under the MST, a criticism that has come to be referred to as the "free ride" hypothesis. Although the proponents of the "free ride" theory have always been individuals, and it has never been the official policy of the U.S. government,

---

14. On the reprocessing issue, see Henry S. Rowen and Ryukichi Imai, *Nuclear Proliferation and Nuclear Energy: Japanese and American Views* (Boulder: Westview, 1979).

these individuals have tended to be politically prominent leaders—Richard Nixon, John Connally, Melvin Laird, and others. Their lineage, indeed, can be traced all the way back to the original set of negotiations between the United States and Japan, when John Foster Dulles, as the chief U.S. representative, wanted Japan to amass a ground force of 350,000 capable of repulsing Soviet invasion.[15] Prime Minister Yoshida Shigeru balked at so high a figure, citing economic and political constraints as compelling reasons for his reluctance. While the United States has refrained from applying pressures on Japan, individual leaders like Dulles and Connolly have been less restrained about voicing their personal displeasure at Japan's failure to upgrade its defense capabilities. Criticism grew particularly vocal around the time that Japan's economy emerged as the third largest in the world. Some critics, in fact, attributed Japan's economic success to the abnormally low defense burden it carried, arguing that its remarkable growth was only made possible by U.S. assumption of the lion's share of the defense burden.

Defense Expenditures and Economic Growth

Is this interpretation accurate? How much of Japan's growth is attributable to its capacity to push the bulk of its defense expenses off onto the shoulders of the United States? There is no doubt, of course, that the U.S. taxpayer relieved what would otherwise have been a heavier tax burden. But admitting this is entirely different from agreeing with the proposition that it was only Japan's light military burden that made its rapid growth possible.

The low military burden–high economic growth rate hypothesis is quantitatively testable, once certain assumptions are made explicit. One estimate has been made, using the following extreme set of assumptions:[16]

1. Japan would have wound up spending as much as *6 to 7 percent* of its GNP, instead of one percent, for national defense.

---

15. Martin Weistein, *Japan's Postwar Defense Policy, 1947-68* (New York: Columbia University Press, 1971), pp. 58-59.
16. Hugh Patrick and Henry Rosovsky, "Japan's Economic Performance," in H. Patrick and H. Rosovsky, eds. *Asia's New Giant* (Washington, D.C.: The Brookings Institution, 1976), p. 45 fn.

2. All such expenditures would have come at the expense of capital investments rather than consumption.
3. The average capital-output ratio would have remained constant.
4. Military expenditures would have had no spillover benefits for the civilian economy.
5. Japan's defense budget would have stayed at roughly six to seven percent, even if the external environment had improved.

The assumptions, clearly extreme, tend to tilt the calculations toward an overestimation of the costs of defense expenditures. It is highly unlikely, for example, that Japan would have allocated 6 or 7 percent of its GNP for defense or that, if it did, all such expenditures would have been made at the expense of capital investments. However, even with such built-in distortions,[17] the figures still yield a rather remarkable conclusion—that Japan's average annual growth rate would have shrunk by only around 2 percent, from 10 to 8 percent, keeping Japan at the top of all OECD nations. Of course, a 2 percent reduction per annum, though relatively minor for any given year, would have a much larger cumulative impact over a period of time. Hence, by 1974, the cumulative costs of high defense expenditures would have reduced the size of the economy by a factor of around 30 percent—not an insignificant slowdown, but by no means crippling. Japan's economy would still have grown faster than almost any other country's in the world. Hence, while recognizing the enormous value of America's overall contribution to Japan's defense, we can discount badly exaggerated "free ride" theories that attribute Japan's record-breaking economic growth to its low defense expenditures.

Unequal Capabilities and Roles

Still another source of friction has been the power gap between the United States and Japan. From the beginning of the postwar period, the United States has viewed itself as a global power—for many years the dominant power—with a commensurate load of responsibilities around the world. Japan, on the other hand, has seen itself small, vulnerable, and weak—a nation so devastated by its earlier attempt

---

17. See Mancur Olson, *The Logic of Collective Action* (Cambridge, Massachusetts: Harvard University Press, 1967).

to carve out an empire that it could never again make any pretensions of attaining status as a world superpower. As the United States sees no diminution of Soviet efforts to expand its power, and as America's own resources are stretched by the competition, it would not be surprising to see the United States turn to its strong allies— NATO nations and Japan—to take up some of the slack in solidifying the collective strength of the non-Communist bloc.

The problem of an equitable apportionment of alliance burdens can be seen in terms of what economists refer to as the "collective goods" theory—the notion that if goods or services are provided freely by a government for everyone's benefit and if those goods or services are not exhaustible (that is, any number can partake without depleting the benefits), the individual beneficiaries can be expected to avoid assuming any more of the costs than is necessary: There is, in other words, a tendency to share in the benefits without offering to shoulder commensurate costs.[18] Although alliance structures depart somewhat from the collective goods model, the analogy is not without parallel where the behavior of dependent allies is concerned. When alliances are threatened by the growing power of adversaries, pressures to redistribute the burden of responding to the challenge are likely to rise, particularly in cases where the "senior" partner feels that it is incurring a disproportionately large share of the burden. From the late 1960s, this trend has become especially notable in the U.S.-Japan alliance, and it has given rise to conflicts that may grow more intense over time.

Economic Competition

We have already observed that where tensions gripped the alliance during its first two decades, these largely arose over questions of military security—and primarily from Japan's side. Leftist opposition to the MST peaked in 1960 with the massive demonstrations that convulsed Tokyo and declined steadily thereafter. With the agreement to return Okinawa to Japan's administrative control and the MST's extension in 1970, Japanese and American leaders began talking optimistically about the onset of a new era of "fine tuning" in the alliance—an era, that is, free from the static of military controversies

18. Ibid.

and one that would require only minor adjustments to bring whatever dissonance arose quickly back into harmony. With the most grating military irritations seemingly behind, the outlook for the U.S.-Japan alliance at the start of the 1970s appeared brighter than ever—headed for a halcyon era free of nagging frictions and conflicts.

As the decade of the 1970s unfolded, however, U.S.-Japan relations ran headlong into a maelstrom of "shocks" and "crises," the likes of which had never before visited the alliance. The 1970s began on a discordant note with protracted negotiations over voluntary restraints of Japanese textile exports to the United States (which began in the late 1960s but carried over into the 1970s); the rancor of the textile dispute sounded an ominous warning of economic frictions to come. It was followed by the "Nixon shocks" in the early 1970s—the announcement of his intention to visit Peking, the slapping of a 10 percent surcharge on certain foreign imports, and the abandonment of the Bretton Woods system of fixed exchange rates. As if the Nixon shocks were not enough, there followed a succession of "aftershocks" that continued through the 1970s—the U.S. soybean embargo (1973); tensions caused by the OPEC oil embargo (1973-1974); the Lockheed scandal (1976); the Korean troop withdrawal announcement (1977); the nuclear reprocessing impasse (1976-1977); and the trade imbalance crisis (1977-1979); and the questions of Japanese cooperation in sanctions against Iran and the Soviet Union; as well as higher defense expenditures to meet the Soviet threat posed by its intervention in Afghanistan (1979-1980). Instead of moving into an era of "fine tuning," free of major conflicts, the U.S.-Japan alliance entered into one of the most stressful periods of its postwar history.

The underlying cause of many of the "shocks" can be traced to transformations in the distribution of power in the international system—the newly found power of OPEC nations, the expansion of Soviet military power, Japan's emergence as the world's third largest GNP, the relative erosion of U.S. economic and military dominance, and so forth. The shocks of the 1970s represented, in this sense, outcroppings of fundamental realignments in the international order, calling for appropriate adjustments on the part of the two allies. This could be seen in the political (normalization with China) as well as in the military arena (termination of the Vietnam War, reduction of U.S. forces in Asia, and the growth of the Soviet presence). But it was perhaps most evident in the economic sphere, where Japan's development brought it directly into competition with the United States and other advanced industrial states, forcing a painful reevaluation of old policies, particularly under worldwide conditions of slower growth and increasingly costly energy supplies.

The U.S.-Japan relationship is no longer one between two highly unequal economies at different points along the path of economic development. Japan has caught up quickly, and though the U.S. economy is still the largest in the world by a clear margin, the two are now formidable economic competitors across a broad range of sectors—steel, automobiles, electronics, semiconductors, and computers. Now that vertical complementarity has given way to horizontal competition, it is hardly surprising that tensions have invaded the bilateral alliance, particularly because both economies operate within the framework of open, representative systems of government that allow various interest groups structured leeway to lobby for the enhancement of their own interests vis-à-vis foreign competition. Within such systems, political frictions growing out of economic competition can cause troublesome problems. Conflicts are aggravated when, as in the case of the U.S.-Japan current accounts imbalance (1976-1979), the following sorts of conditions obtain: (1) domestic stagflation; (2) high rates of unemployment in the deficit country; (3) inelastic demands on the supply of energy; (4) weaknesses in one country's currency, especially when it is the world's major currency; (5) powerful political clout on the part of threatened interest groups; (6) weaknesses in the base of support for executive leadership; (7) dissynchronous business cycles; (8) divergent means of recovering from recession; and (9) differences in the fundamental mode of government-business interactions. Such conditions exacerbate conflicts that accompany economic competition, giving rise to the specter of protectionist backlashes which require drawing heavily on the reservoir of good will and trust built up over a long period of time.

The decade of the 1970s witnessed, in short, the intrusion of complex, recurrent problems assaulting the alliance from all directions (not simply confined to the military domain) and largely symptomatic of fundamental changes taking place in the international system. The fallacy of the "fine tuning" forecast was that it focused only on the bilateral relationship to the exclusion of larger global factors at work. The crises of the 1970s demonstrate vividly the need to view the U.S.-Japan alliance in the broad context of world developments. Keeping that in mind, let us survey, in conclusion, the potential problems that appear to lie on the horizon.

PROBLEMS AND PROSPECTS

Outlook

Forecasting what lies ahead for the U.S.-Japan alliance in the 1980s and beyond is difficult, because there are so many hard to gauge variables external to the alliance itself that are likely to impinge on the bilateral relationship. Whether the alliance is harmonious or riddled with tensions will be determined largely by developments within the international system, particularly with respect to the supply and price of crude oil and the evolving balance of power between the Communist and non-Communist nations. The interdependent nature of the international system is such that the future of the U.S.-Japan alliance is more sensitive than ever to perturbations in the environment. A distinction must be drawn, of course, between the concepts of sensitivity and vulnerability, since the two need not be necessarily synonymous;[19] but there can be little question that the U.S.-Japan alliance, like all alliance networks, is going to be affected as much or more by global and regional trends as by developments more specifically bilateral in nature. While not all of the international variables can be laid out here, mention can be made of at least the following factors that are likely to have a seminal bearing on the shape of the U.S.-Japan alliance:

1. Energy availability
   - Price and supply of crude oil
   - OPEC production and supply decisions
   - Expansion and diversification of alternative energy sources
   - Instability in the Middle East, as demonstrated by the revolution in Iran and the invasion of Afghanistan

---

19. International sensitivity here refers to the extent to which a country is affected by external developments; vulnerability goes beyond that to include the country's capacity (or lack thereof) to deal with that sensitivity at minimal costs.

2. Economic growth
   - Aggregate and bilateral growth rates
   - Levels of inflation and unemployment
   - Patterns in the redistribution of wealth
   - Trilateral patterns of savings, investments, and expenditures
   - Adjustments to the international divisions of labor

3. The Politicomilitary balance
   - Global nuclear and conventional balance
   - Regional balance
   - Responses to the expansion of Soviet capabilities
   - Trends in superpower relations—United States, Russia, China, Japan, and Western Europe
   - Political leadership and stability in key regions and countries, countries, especially the Middle East
   - Intracamp rivalries, Communist and non-Communist alike
   - Potential domestic instability arising out of economic difficulties occasioned by an energy shortage
   - Adjustments to the expected changeover in leadership in key Asian states

If, on balance, these factors stay relatively favorable—with few sudden shocks—the alliance should not be visited by strains any greater than those already experienced during the 1970s. If, on the other hand, the external environment is thrown into turmoil, U.S.-Japan relations could be severely tested by the problems that accompany unfavorable developments; the possibility of enhanced alliance solidarity in the face of external adversity cannot be ruled out. But in view of the multiple sources of potential conflict in the international system, it would take an improbable conjunction of circumstances for the U.S.-Japan alliance to make it through the 1980s without serious challenge to its cohesion and powers of adaptability. Over what problems might tensions arise? Without attempting to exhaust the list of conceivable contingencies, let us touch upon three general categories.

Military Burden Sharing

We have already observed how military issues, the primary cause of bilateral tensions during the 1950s and 1960s, subsided during the 1970s, drowned out in part by the cacophony of economic competition. Military frictions, however, might return to haunt the alliance. Events in Iran and Afghanistan, for example, have raised hard questions about the defense burden Japan can or ought to be expected to assume for its own security, if not that of the region and the Western alliance as a whole. Japan's stake in the complicated set of issues raised by Iran and Afghanistan is in many respects as great as that of the United States—security of oil supplies, peace and stability in the Persian Gulf, and a credible response to Soviet aggression, to name but a few. If Japan's own interests are so compelling, some ask, why is it not doing more to contribute to stability in the Middle East? Why is the burden falling so disproportionately on America's shoulders?

In discussing allied contributions, a distinction can be drawn between military and nonmilitary assistance. Where direct military assistance is concerned, the Japanese profess that their hands are tied by domestic political constraints, not the least of which is the question of whether sending Japanese forces abroad, say, to the Persian Gulf is constitutional. If the United States were to ask the Liberal Democratic Party (LDP) government to do that, the political reactions within Japan would be emotional and politically polarizing; it is doubtful the LDP would be willing to take the political heat in even raising the question.

If, on the other hand, the United States asks less of Japan, the response might be more receptive. Would Japan, for example, raise the level of military outlays gradually in order to upgrade its own capacity to defend itself? The question is not an idle one, since the redeployment of American naval forces to the Indian Ocean may mean a weakening of deployments in the Pacific. In what areas might the Japanese make a contribution to the preservation of the balance of power in Asia? Against what threats? With what specific missions in mind? Would it be possible to mobilize a domestic consensus on Japan's role? These are questions that need to be raised, discussed, and hopefully clarified if the question of burden sharing is not to cause serious misunderstandings.

Over the short run (i.e., the next three to five years), it seems unlikely that the Japanese would be willing or able to expand military outlays to the levels desired by some Americans (e.g., defense expenditures on the order of 2–3 percent of GNP). Trying to exert pressure on the Japanese to achieve such levels would seem ill advised. The Japanese government feels it lacks the leeway to double or triple its military expenditures. Its budget in 1979 was heavily financed through the issuance of government bonds, and the huge deficit (more than that of the United States, France, England, and West Germany combined) is not sustainable but must be cut back over the next several years. This means, essentially, that military expenditures will not be raised suddenly to levels of other countries.

Fiscal frugality on defense is, of course, not likely to pass unnoticed in the United States, especially when the United States already allocates more than 5 percent of its GNP for defense and when, over the next five or so years, it is committed to annual increments in its defense budget designed to narrow the gap in Soviet-American spending over the past fifteen years. America's burden may feel especially onerous if inflation runs out of control, or if rates of unemployment reach politically unacceptable levels, or if America fares poorly in trade competition with Japan. We see growing evidence of protectionist sentiments in Congress. Rising levels of Japanese imports—automobiles, steel, consumer electronics, semiconductors, and the like—could trigger a backlash of protectionism that would seriously strain bilateral relations and set back efforts at free trade. Under strained circumstances, the United States might seek to link trade and security issues. American legislators, for example, might call for concessions on trade and investment issues, citing Japan's "free ride" in national defense as justification. Or if problems turn very serious, the Japanese may feel compelled to concede on both fronts—a bilateral trade balance (through voluntary restraints on exports, direct investments in U.S. plant facilities, etc.) and higher defense expenditures.

Fixing on defense expenditures as a percentage of GNP may not be the most constructive way of handling the problem of burden sharing. The tacit 1 percent ceiling is a political device used by both progressive and conservative politicians in Japan to impose limits on military appropriations. It is not the only, or necessarily the most revealing, indicator to use in discussing the distribution of defense burdens. Percentage figures fail, among other things, to reveal or shed light on the following facts: (1) that military expenditure in Japan has increased in real terms on an average of around 8 percent per year over the past twenty or twenty-five years, simply as a result of Japan's phenomenal growth rates, which places Japan among the seven or eight countries spending the most money in absolute terms on national defense; (2) that using slightly different accounting procedures (including the more than half billion dollars spent for Japanese employees on U.S. base facilities or using the NATO formula that covers pensions), Japan's defense budget comes to roughly 1.5 percent of GNP; and (3) that multiple indicators of Japan's overall contribution to international security ought to be taken into account, particularly in the nonmilitary sphere.

The latter point is important if the two allies are to arrive at a common understanding of burden sharing. The Japanese tend to take a much broader view of security than most Americans realize or are willing to tolerate. Security is, in fact, perceived as much or more in terms of access to raw materials, open overseas markets, price stability of primary commodities, exchange rate equilibrium, and so forth as it is in terms of military deployments. If a broad definition of security, such as that taken by most Japanese, is acceptable to the United States, there is room for Japan to make a series of valuable contributions to the Western alliance. Indeed, dating back to the oil crisis, 1973-1974, the Japanese have been moving quietly but decisively in the direction of seeking to make an impact through economic diplomacy. A quick review of their efforts, evaluated against the background of very little effort prior to the oil crisis, suggests the progress that has been made:

- Over $17 billion in direct foreign investments in the Middle East (as of 1980),
- $626 million in economic aid to the Middle East (in 1977),
- $147 million in technical cooperation (in 1977), and
- $130 million to Pakistan (1980).

The decision to extend aid to Pakistan in 1980 at a level more than double that of the previous year is indicative of Japan's willingness to help areas of strategic importance. Japanese assistance to Pakistan, Egypt, and Turkey (three key areas in the region's power balance) might help these states stave off economic collapse and political turmoil—outcomes that, from the West's point of view, would be disastrous. It is difficult to quantify the net impact of other contributions, such as trade, construction of industrial facilities, transfer of technology, dissemination of managerial and marketing know-how, and the like, but in terms of promoting economic growth and regional security, such economic contributions may have been as constructive as anything the Japanese might have done in the way of military assistance.

Skeptics might argue, of course, that the Japanese effort is still inadequate and even disappointing. But "inadequate" and "disappointing" relative to what? Relative to the staggering array of problems in the Middle East? Yes. Japanese contributions fall far short of what is needed. Relative to what Japan's economy is capable of providing? Perhaps, though the fact of political feasibility must always be taken into account. But the net effort is not trivial relative to what the Japanese have done in the past or to what most other allied countries are doing. Looked at in logarithmic terms, Japan's recent performance in the nonmilitary areas of assistance is encouraging and constructive. It may not be enough, however, to mitigate, much less eliminate, American criticisms of Japan's low defense expenditures. But the significance of Japanese efforts should not be slighted. Indeed, if the theory of comparative advantage is applied to the area of international security (broadly defined), Japan's main contribution (though perhaps not its only contribution) may lie in the area of nonmilitary assistance—commercial, technical, managerial, and the like.

Such contributions, no matter how valuable or timely, will probably not be enough, however, to deflect criticisms of Japan's military posture if there is no evidence of change. The circumstances that permitted Japan to relegate defense responsibilities to the "back burner," as it were, have probably passed. The time is clearly at hand when it must undertake a wide-ranging review of its security stakes and the threats to them, its capabilities and responsibilities, and the costs and benefits of various options. External pressures to strengthen military capabilities appear to be on the rise. Allies like the United States will probably expect, if not explicitly call for, Japan to accept more of the burdens of its own defense, particularly if U.S. forces have to be redeployed from the Pacific. Over the next five or more years, the Japanese may be called upon, at the very least, to bring their current defense capabilities up to combat effectiveness. This would take time and money, but since it would not be so likely to open a Pandora's box in the eyes of the Japanese, it may be politically more acceptable than open-ended calls for a bigger defense force. In any case, what is required now is a bilateral clarification of mutual security interests, common threats, and preferred responses to those threats. Letting concrete planning slide is apt to cause misunderstanding in the future. The mood in both countries seems to point to closer mutual consultation and cooperation.

How the U.S.-Japan defense relationship evolves over the next two decades will hinge importantly on such factors as (1) national perceptions of threats, self-interest, and international responsibilities; (2) the allocation of resources to safeguard vital security interests; (3) domestic political incentives and constraints; and (4) developments in the international system. Whatever the outcome, it seems likely that military issues will be returned to a place of high visibility within the alliance during the 1980s and beyond.

Economic Tensions

The crisis in Iran serves to remind us that economic, diplomatic, and political complications can strain U.S.-Japan relations when there is inadequate coordination and communication. Some American officials expressed dismay at the "unseemly haste" with which certain Japanese oil companies rushed to purchase Iranian oil after the United States had placed an embargo on it. Japan's purchases not only seemed to undercut American efforts to use economic sanctions to secure the release of the hostages, but also helped to force up the price of oil on the international spot market to well over $40 per barrel. Since the contracted price of oil is often affected by the spot market rates, Japan's massive purchases on the spot market were seen as a catalyst for higher oil prices for all. It was not the kind of reaction American leaders wanted or expected from its ally.

The Japanese, on the other hand, felt misunderstood and unfairly criticized. They felt that the whole hostage crisis could have been avoided if the U.S. had exercised better judgment and that Japan was not properly consulted about any of the sanctions that were unilaterally imposed, such as the oil-purchasing embargo and the freezing of Iranian assets, but was expected nevertheless to cooperate with the United States, regardless of the costs and consequences. They pointed out that Japan is far more dependent on oil from Iran than the United States (somewhere around 13 percent of oil consumption as compared to roughly 4 percent). At the time of the U.S. embargo, Japan had already suffered a significant cutback of oil supplies from U.S. oil majors, estimated at somewhere around one million barrels per day or nearly 16 percent of its total consumption. Iran threatened to cut Japan off from long-term contracts if Japan refused to purchase its oil. Moreover, mixed messages were apparently also signaled from Washington to Tokyo concerning the question of how much oil Japan should feel free to purchase. All this led to misunderstandings on both sides.

The crisis in Iran highlights the importance of undertaking long-term measures to reduce our overall level of dependence on oil from the Persian Gulf through (1) conservation, (2) greater efforts at research and development in alternative sources, (3) conversion to alternative sources of energy, and (4) expansion of stockpiles. In Japan's case, the example of several independent oil refineries promises to increase the security of oil supplies. Kuwait and Gulf Oil have each purchased 25 percent ownership of several Japanese refineries, in return for which they have provided capital and the assurance of increased supplies of oil. Everyone benefits. Kuwait acquires a hold of downstream production facilities, which it has long sought; Gulf Oil gains access to secure supplies; and Japanese refineries are assured of obtaining oil supplies from an OPEC state that owns an interest in its operations.

Notwithstanding such arrangements, the outlook for the 1980s with respect to the availability and price of oil must be considered at best uncertain. While the oil market is loosening, it can be adversely affected in a variety of ways—cutbacks in production, domestic unrest in OPEC countries, another war in the Middle East, and so forth. Some Japanese optimistically believe that Japan is in a better position to handle price fluctuations because it has the capacity to step up its volume of exports to offset the higher costs of imports.[20] Such optimism, however, is based on the assumption that overseas markets will remain open to absorb the larger volume of Japanese exports (since, over the next decade, Japan is going to find it hard to reduce its level of dependence on imported oil to the target figure of

---

20. This view has been expressed by a number of high level bureaucrats, business leaders, and intellectuals in private conversations held during the summer and fall of 1979.

48 percent of its total energy consumption that MITI has apparently set). Whether this assumption is valid will depend to a large extent on the impact oil price hikes and other factors will have on the growth and inflation rates of industrial economies. If growth rates are slowed and inflation rates accelerated significantly, the Japanese may find that there is insufficient demand worldwide to sustain a step-up in exports. Even if it somehow managed to sell abroad in large enough quantities, its exports would be likely to trigger a protectionist backlash, since foreign governments, suffering under the duress of high unemployment, would probably be faced with an upsurge of pressures for protectionism from interest groups threatened by Japanese competition. Either way, the assumption of an open and highly elastic foreign market as a means of coping with oil price hikes is open to question.

While the thankless task of forecasting is best left to specialists, there seems to be a substantial consensus on the high probability of continuing hikes in the price of oil over the next decade. How high the price of crude oil goes will depend on a great many factors, but that it will inevitably rise seems hard to dispute. If the hikes are high, the impact on Japan and the U.S.-Japan alliance could be wide ranging and possibly pernicious. Several questions would be well worth examining:

1. At given price levels, how would the costs of oil affect Japan's economic growth and inflation rates, its international trade and investment patterns, its international orientation, domestic political alignments, and relations with the United States?
2. How would price and supply factors affect the international redistribution of wealth, particularly the North-South problem, and how, in turn, would this affect relations within the industrial bloc?
3. What would economic problems triggered by an energy shortage do to Soviet-American relations and the roles of the USSR and China? How would U.S.-Japan relations be affected?

Many Japanese are deeply worried about a potential clash with the United States over patterns of energy consumption. Specifically, they fear that unless the United States controls its prodigal patterns of consumption in the nonindustrial sector, where the leeway to conserve energy is considerable, pressures placed on aggregate demand will drive world oil prices way up, creating severe tensions for everyone. But such bilateral tensions must be understood as part of a larger problem of global energy supply and demand that is likely to affect the world's economic well-being in the 1980s as much or more than any other variable. The outlook—even given relatively optimistic assumptions—is not very encouraging. If the world is headed for a period of sluggish demand, high inflation and unemployment, and energy uncertainty, all industrial states aligned with the United States are bound to feel the effects of widespread economic, political, and military repercussions. Alliance solidarity will be tested. External adversity will either strain alliances by encouraging unilateralism and short-term national self-interests, or it might have precisely the opposite effect of solidifying ties by raising the incentives for cooperation. Even if the latter should turn out to be the case, the strain of economic problems would still be likely to generate frictions.

Moreover, bilateral competition is bound to continue in such areas as electronics, automobiles, semiconductors, and computers. If one side fares poorly in this competition, the danger of protectionist reactions is always hard politically to cope with, especially if it is part of a larger current account imbalance. Because of its ecological characteristics, Japan has had to live with a chronic balance of payments problem. During the early postwar decades, the problem was one of balance of payments deficits that constrained its growth. From the late 1960s and into the 1970s, the problem turned into one of keeping surpluses from running out of control. We have already noted the severity of tensions that gripped the U.S.-Japan alliance from 1977-1979. While tensions have gradually subsided with the correction of the trade imbalance, many of the underlying "structural" reasons for the crisis are still far from resolved—stiff competition in the knowledge-intensive industries, differential rates of savings and dissavings (the absorption rather than elasticities perspective), dissynchronous business cycles, and so forth.

There can be little doubt that what happens in the economic sphere of the U.S.-Japan relationship deeply affects the nature of the bilateral security alliance, not only directly in terms of mutual trust and good will, but also indirectly in terms of the strains to which the alliance is subject. We have already alluded to the tactic of "linkage politics"—that is, using economic issues to win concessions, say, on defense expenditures or, conversely, utilizing security grievances to wrestle concessions on trade or investment. During the postwar history of U.S.-Japan relations, leaders on both sides have resorted to the linkage technique from time to time. But compared to other bilateral relationships, where it is commonly practiced, the U.S.-Japan alliance has been freer of "linkage pressures" than the extent and importance of the relationship might lead one to anticipate. Until the late 1960s and early 1970s, conflicts tended to stay within their respective sector (military, economic, political, etc.). Should economic frictions intensify, however, at a time when military concerns return to a place of high visibility, the temptation to utilize "linkage pressures" may multiply and compound strains in the alliance. Finding ways of circumventing economic frictions is therefore of paramount importance for the future of the alliance.

In this regard, we believe that one key to the avoidance of conflict is America's capacity to control inflation and to increase its economic productivity, efficiency, competitiveness, and strength. If the United States continues to suffer the corrosive effects of declining competitiveness, the consequences for the U.S.-Japan alliance—not to mention for the U.S. position of world leadership—could not help but be detrimental. It would generate serious economic strains, leading to trade frictions and threats of protectionism, as well as strains on the security side. The revitalization of America's economy would be essential for any attempt to stem the tide of a destructive form of protectionism while at the same time expanding the overall fiscal pie; more money would be available to meet the escalating needs of national defense. From a long-range perspective, therefore, we believe economic revitalization must be given urgent priority by the U.S. government. The future of the U.S.-Japan alliance rests, to a large extent, on the strength and continuing vitality of the U.S. economy. We assume, in saying this, that the Japanese economy will continue to demonstrate the flexibility and resilience that has characterized its past performance.

Political Problems

We have already discussed the ramifications of world developments on the U.S.-Japan alliance. We can anticipate that in the political sphere, Japan's long-standing policy of "omnidirectionality" and "political and military low profile" will become the target of criticism and be characterized as a "free ride." Japan needs to reassess whether world circumstances permit it to continue to play the role of politicomilitary eunuch. Can it respond passively to external events, looking to the Europeans as a standard of reference for its own behavior? Or will it find such passivity and willingness to respond and cooperate only under the duress of pressure a counterproductive and costly way of acting? Are the Japanese fully aware of the criticisms such behavior generates?

As for the United States, it will have to consider what it wants and whether what it wants from its allies is reasonable, given differences in perceptions and objectives and capacities to act. What kind of cooperation does it expect and at what costs? Should we expect complete cooperation when Germany and Japan may feel they have a greater stake in, say, preserving nonhostile ties with the Soviet Union and Iran than the United States? To reiterate a point raised earlier: Both the United States and its allies will have to work out a common framework within which to define interests, pinpoint responsibilities, and identify areas of joint or complementary action.

Nor are political problems confined to the Middle East. There are situations closer to East Asia that are worrisome, as, for example, (1) economic uncertainties, such as those alluded to earlier; (2) low levels of popular support for authoritarian regimes (and hence the dangers of political unrest or revolution); and (3) generational turnovers in political leadership. Looking at the first, we can anticipate that the "spillover effects" of economic stagflation might undermine the foundations of political stability in Asia's most dynamic economies—Taiwan, South Korea, Hong Kong, Singapore—which, coincidentally, have the smallest natural resource base on which to fall back and therefore the highest level of dependence on the import of raw materials and energy. While these countries appear to be among the most politically stable in the region, the possibility of political unrest cannot be counted out in the light of (1) the importance of economic performance in perceptions of political legitimacy; (2) their economic sensitivity to international perturbations; (3) the problems of potential instability created by rapid structural change accompanying economic growth; and (4) the basically authoritarian nature of governance. Japan would be concerned if a neighboring nation like South Korea, which is in the throes of a serious inflationary spiral, were suddenly to experience political turmoil. The assassination of

President Park set off a period of uncertainty. In South Korea, as elsewhere, whoever is in power will have to adjust over the long run to the changing structural realities of an economy that has grown very rapidly over the past fifteen years. Stability will rest to a large extent on the capacity of political leaders and institutions to accommodate growing political demands while steering their economies through difficult straits ahead.[21]

The age of current leaders in such countries as North Korea and the Soviet Union also raises questions about political alignments when a new generation of leaders rises to take the reins of power. Uncertainties in China also leave questions unanswered about the permanence of its currently pragmatic orientation. Obviously, domestic realignments, if accompanied by policy shifts, could create a very different regional order in Asia, which in turn would be likely to affect decisions in Tokyo and Washington. Even if changes introduced by turnovers in leadership proved to be minor, the United States and Japan would have to coordinate rather delicate policies with respect to such matters as technology transfers and Sino-Soviet relations.

Looking more narrowly at the bilateral relationship, we can anticipate potential problems arising out of differences in the domestic context of the two political systems. The two countries are beset in differing degrees with problems of leadership. Over the past fifteen years, the United States has endured what many describe as a paralysis of executive leadership, the symptoms of which include that (1) no one since 1960 has served two full terms in the White House; (2) presidential powers have been increasingly constrained by the assertiveness of the legislative branch; (3) public opinion polls reflect a decline in popular trust in the government; and (4) dissatisfaction with the performance and role of government has increased over time. The Japanese want, expect, and profess to need strong American leadership and express dismay that the United States has not provided as much of it as needed. They feel that bilateral relations are rendered more difficult when strong leadership is not exercised by the United States.

The lack of vigorous leadership in Japan could turn out to be a problem in the bilateral alliance if the United States expects Japan to assume a larger assertive role in the world. Masayoshi Ohira may have

---

21. Samuel Huntington, *Political Order in Changing Societies* (New Haven: Yale University Press, 1969).

represented the last of the old Yoshida school of leaders in Japan — politicians with large and stable factional foundations on which to operate. How much leeway the next generation of political leaders has to move Japan vigorously in new directions remains to be seen. The bureaucracies, traditional strongholds of government power, may be able to provide the leadership that may be required of Japan, but the capacity of the civil service is dependent, to some extent, on a stable and supportive structure of party alignment in Japan. Japan's administrative capabilities are very impressive, judging by past performance, but it remains to be seen whether Japan can adapt to the changing expectations and requirements of a much less favorable international environment.

In sharp contrast to the mood of the 1960s, when Japanese feared the expansion of American military power in Asia and their own possible embroilment in wars instigated by the United States (often referred to as the "magnet theory"), the Japanese are now concerned about America's "separation from Asia," its disengagement from that area of the world. The domestic debate over SALT created the impression in Tokyo that the United States mught be falling behind in the arms race with the Soviet Union. Observing the heat of a presidential political campaign, they may have come to the conclusion that the United States is suffering from a crisis in leadership. Such concerns have perhaps supported the advocates of larger defense expenditures in Japan but there is still no surge of opinion for a heavily armed nation or for an escape from the American nuclear umbrella. Rather, it generated a kind of malaise and frustration that were strengthened by critical comments made by American leaders and spokesmen. However, even the chairman of the Japan Socialist party, while opposing the security treaty and continuing to espouse unarmed neutrality in public, said to Vice-president Mondale in Washington that "for the Japanese people, life without the United States is inconceivable."[22]

In looking ahead to the 1980s, therefore, the U.S.-Japan alliance is faced with the need to adapt to the following problems looming on the horizon:

- The relative erosion of American military, economic, and political power;

22. *Mainichi Shimbun*, November 21, 1979.

- The relative expansion of Soviet power;
- A possible reaggravation of Cold War antagonisms between the USSR and the United States;
- Growing pressures on allies like Japan to assume more of the burdens of alliance;
- A rather gloomy economic outlook for the 1980s, featuring heavy demand pressures on energy supplies, slower growth rates, and inflation and unemployment problems;
- Uncertainties and instabilities of energy supplies from the Persian Gulf;
- The spillover effects of economic stagnancy on political stability, regionally and bilaterally;
- The search for a new modus operandi between the United States and Japan more in keeping with the realities of changes in their power relationship; and
- Differences in domestic politics and problems of effective political leadership.

In spite of these problems, the U.S.-Japan alliance, arguably as critical as any in the world, will remain absolutely vital to the national interests of both countries as well as to the region as a whole. Finding ways of adapting the alliance to the challenges and changing problems of the international environment will be especially important as this historic alliance, separating the postwar from the prewar period, heads into the final two and perhaps most difficult, decades of the second half of the twentieth century.

7 U.S.-JAPAN RELATIONS IN RETROSPECT AND FUTURE CHALLENGES

Fuji Kamiya

Professor Fuji Kamiya of Keio University, a longtime observer of U.S.-Japan relations, traces recent developments between the two nations and points to ever-present potentials for friction in what has been an essentially friendly relationship. Historically, he writes, the most difficult times for the United States and Japan have been when their national power was roughly equal. Because of events during the 1970s, including the "Nixon shocks" and frequent shifts in policy by the Carter administration, the Japanese have become skeptical of American credibility. If the Japanese have been guilty of a "presumptuous sense of reliance" on the United States, the U.S. government must take the blame for ignoring the American responsibility for trade imbalances. The danger is that U.S. demands for more Japanese military contributions will be frustrated and that new trade frictions will be allowed to affect the overall alliance. Professor Kamiya insists that new wisdom will be required in the 1980s if the alliance is to be managed smoothly. The relationship will affect the future of the entire Asia–Pacific area, he concludes.

CRISIS IN EQUAL PARTNERSHIP

Looking at U.S.-Japan relations today in the light of their traditional pattern, one may best characterize them as undergoing a crisis in "equal partnership." A review of relations between the two countries in the past hundred odd years indicates that whenever there is a substantial lack of equality of one sort or another between them — as there was during the period from the last years of the Tokugawa Shogunate to the Russo-Japanese War or during the generation following Japan's defeat in the Pacific War—whenever there is such a clear lack of equality in power, U.S.-Japan relations tend to be smooth and favorable. Then, as the power gap between the two countries narrows, bringing them closer to each other in status in various areas, discordant notes begin to be heard in their relations, as was the case in the 1930s and the early 1940s, with the Pacific War as the climax. From 1970 onward, U.S.-Japan relations have been more conspicuously characterized by growing equality in national power, resulting in an unprecedented growth of friction and tension between the two nations.

Since U.S.-Japan relations began more than a century and a quarter ago, they may be said to have been generally favorable except in the temporary period of the Pacific War. It should be noted, however, that the two nations have never seen their relations develop favorably on the basis of such equality in national power as described above. How to tackle this untried task will be a major problem for them in the 1980s, and whether or not they will succeed in the attempt will have a great deal of bearing not only on their relations but also on the general situation of the Asia-Pacific area and even of the world as a whole. Since the relationship between the United States and Japan is so highly significant both in breadth and depth, their government leaders as well as their peoples need to consider and deal with it with a good deal of circumspection and wisdom.

U.S.-JAPAN RELATIONS IN THE 1970s

Before discussing U.S.-Japan relations in the 1980s, it would be appropriate to look back on the way they were in the 1970s. This may be summarized from various angles, but a major feature of general world politics during the decade was the the Pax Americana prevailing after World War II began to decline in the 1970s.

This was true of both the military and the economic power of the United States, as well as of its ability to control and influence world politics. It is in the context of this relative decline in U.S. power — the other side of the coin being, naturally, the relative rise of Europe and Japan in influence—that U.S.-Japan relations were conducted in the 1970s. Indeed, this general tendency was the main characteristic of the relationship. As the Nixon Doctrine announced in the summer of 1969 began to be implemented in the early 1970s, the United States was no longer able to play the "policeman of the world" role that it had been willing to assume in the 1960s, rushing single-handedly to any new trouble spot in the world. The United States had now to limit its overseas responsibilities and commitments to those deemed essential to its national interest. It is important, first of all, to note this shrinking of the U.S. role.

Second, while reducing its overseas responsibilities and commitments, the United States wanted to keep as much of its traditional voice and influence in world affairs as possible. In other words, the Nixon Doctrine aimed at keeping the international status of the United States essentially unchanged, but at a reduced cost. This idea of "killing two birds with one stone" was perhaps overly optimistic and, consequently, involved in internal contradiction.

While the presidency of the United States shifted from Nixon through Ford to Carter in the 1970s, its foreign policy basically followed this same principle. One approach Washington used for this purpose was improved relations with such adversaries as China and the Soviet Union; another was to seek accommodation with such allies as Western Europe and Japan.

Reviewing the U.S.-Japan relationship as part of such accommodated relations between the United States and its allies, one may note that the late 1960s and early 1970s were marked by textile negotiations and balance of payment arguments. Friction over economic issues was emerging for the first time in postwar relations between the two countries. Indeed, it was about this time that the term "economic war" first appeared in the Japanese media. The "Nixon shocks" of 1971 came under these circumstances. One of them, as everyone knows, was the Washington-Peking rapprochement; the other was President Nixon's new economic policy. These marked a turning point in U.S.-Japan relations.

One serious problem that emerged was a loss of U.S. credibility in Japan. The Nixon shocks were assessed variously at that time, but it was certainly unfortunate that the United States effected the rapprochement with China in a clandestine manner, which mortified Tokyo more than necessary, even to the extent of "shocking" it. It was true that a U.S.-Chinese rapprochement was apparently inevitable—and necessary, too, given the general trend of world politics. In fact, a sympathetic attitude for accepting the development has since been widely accepted by most Japanese. There is no denying, nevertheless, that they have become essentially skeptical of Washington's credibility.

Several years after the Nixon shocks, the United States dropped a previous defense commitment and abandoned South Vietnam (with Saigon falling in 1975). Following this move, the United States appeared to take less interest in Asia, which undoubtedly helped widen the credibility gap in the minds of the Japanese. Although, fortunately, the gap-widening process has not gone very far, this skepticism has affected Japanese attitudes on various issues between the United States and Japan, possibly providing an unfavorably background for them, and the tendency is likely to persist in the 1980s.

U.S. credibility was again reduced when President Carter decided in July 1979 to shelve the idea of withdrawing U.S. ground troops from Korea—an issue that had been pending for years. Moreover, Washington's foreign policy toughened again following the Soviet invasion of Afghanistan at the end of 1979, so that there is now even less possibility of a pullout from Korea in the near future. Only a few years earlier, however, when President Carter was elected in 1976, one of his major foreign policy commitments was to withdraw ground troops from Korea. This, as well as other similar cases that will be mentioned later, indicates that the Carter administration's policy on foreign and military issues has lacked continuity and consistency, and again, Japanese skepticism of U.S. credibility increased.

While the Japanese became more and more doubtful of the United States, the Americans were increasingly dissatisfied with Japan in many ways in the early 1970s. This dissatisfaction, manifest in the four annual foreign policy messages put out during the Nixon-Kissinger period, focused first of all on the trade deficit issue. According to Kissinger's favorite "linkage" theory, Japan should make more drastic concessions to the United States on trade and economic issues, particularly if the existing arrangements are to be maintained in the future, since the United States contributes substantially to Japan's security and defense.

In response, Japan took some emergency measures, including those called for in the Tsurumi-Ingersoll agreement made at the time of the Tanaka-Nixon conference in the summer of 1973. But they did not come close to bringing about a radical, lasting solution to the problem. In this connection, two works, both published in 1972, reflect the U.S. view of Japan at that time—a Department of Commerce report titled *Japan: the Government-Business Relationship* (Washington, D.C.: GPO, 1972) and *The Fragile Blossom: Crisis and Change in Japan* by Zbigniew Brzezinski (New York: Harper & Row, 1972), then a professor at Columbia University and later national security assistant under President Carter. Incidentally, 1972 also saw publication of *The Limits to Growth: A Report for the Club of Rome's Project on the Predicament of Mankind*, edited by Donella Meadows (New York: Universe Books, 1972).

In the late 1970s, U.S.-Japan relations continued without much change in basic appearance and orientation—unless perhaps there was some change for the worse. The United States was increasingly demanding in its dealings with Japan and apparently felt that Japan was not sufficiently responsive to its demands. The resulting frustration caused still more friction between the two countries in the latter part of the decade. Some essential differences were noticeable between this period and the early 1970s, however. Whereas U.S. complaints and demands were mainly in the economic and trade areas during the first half of the decade, in the latter half they more often concerned defense and security issues. This was necessiated not only by the Nixon Doctrine but also by the U.S. need for a reorganization of its strategic preparedness in the Asia-Pacific area following the Vietnam War. Thus, a keen resentment against Japan's "free ride" in the area of security began to mount within both the government and the private sector in the United States.

This did not mean any reduction in the U.S.-Japanese tension over economic and trade issues. On the contrary, the "economic war" between the two countries grew hotter as Japan's annual favorable balance of payments with the United States continued to grow, exceeding $10 billion in 1978. In the early 1970s, by contrast, a trade balance of a few billions a year in Japan's favor had been considered a big problem. This friction over economic and trade issues, if combined directly with that in the defense and security area, would make the future of U.S.-Japan relations extremely insecure. One hesitates to dismiss this possibility completely.

PROBLEMS TO BE ENCOUNTERED IN THE 1980s

On the basis of the above-outlined circumstances in the 1970s, one may now consider some of the problems likely to be encountered in the 1980s. U.S.-Japan relations today have, not surprisingly, both encouraging and discouraging aspects. One the bright side, the relationship between the two countries today, unlike ten years ago, incorporates some safeguards against excessive friction between them. In the early 1970s, one was never free from the fear that the tension over economic and trade issues, if left uncontrolled, might continue to grow until it seriously affected the foundation of the U.S.-Japan security and alliance relationship.

Today, there seems to be a common awareness between the two countries that friction over economic and trade issues should not become so serious as to radically affect their relationship as allies. There seems to be a tacit agreement between them that the former should not be allowed to interfere with the latter. Hence, it may be said that despite increased tension and friction, U.S.-Japan relations today are essentially secure and stable. For example, in March 1979, Senator Sam Nunn led the Pacific Study Group from the Committee on Armed Services of the U.S. Senate and published the so-called "Nunn Report" entitled *U.S.-Japan Security Relationship: The Key to East Asian Security and Stability.* This report expressly states that care should be taken not to let friction in the economic area between the two countries affect their security relationship—a position supported whole-heartedly by the Japanese.

Second, there has been some improvement in Japan's attitude and policy on the security arrangements with the United States. By the fall of 1978, Japan had made two major decisions in this area. One concerned the common guidelines developed for U.S.-Japan defense cooperation, and the other was for paying an increased share of the cost of maintaining the U.S. forces in Japan. These decisions were not only highly important in themselves but also very noteworthy in that they were not separate actions but reflected a general change in the Japanese people's attitude on defense and security. This may be seen from the fact that the opposition parties that used to categorically oppose the government on any defense or security issue began to modify their attitudes in the late 1970s.

More recently, when the Komei party and the Democratic Socialist party made an agreement on a coalition concept in December 1979, the former agreed to follow the latter's policy on the U.S.-Japan Security Treaty and the self-defense forces, thus positively accepting the two pillars of Japan's security system. The Socialist party also met the Komei party more than half way in favor of the latter's new position on the security treaty and the self-defense forces when the two groups worked out a "Socialist-Komei axis" platform in early 1980. The fact that the opposition parties and the people at large as well as the government are becoming more receptive than ever to the idea of strengthening the U.S.-Japan security system is a very encouraging factor when one thinks of U.S.-Japan relations tomorrow.

Third, some public opinion surveys conducted in the United States and Japan in recent years need attention. In October 1978, Potomac Associates, a leading public opinion research institution in the United States, published the results of a study on how much Americans know about Japan and how well they understand the Japanese. In 1979, the Chicago Council on Foreign Relations conducted a survey on U.S. public opinion and foreign policy. On the other side of the Pacific, the *Yomiuri Shimbun* in cooperation with the Gallup Organization carried out a series of simultaneous U.S. and Japanese public opinion polls in September 1978 and in March and October 1979. The *Asahi Shimbun* made similar studies of public opinion here in December 1978 and December 1979. The Public Relations Office of the prime minister's Secretariat has conducted annual public opinion survey on such themes as "The Self-Defense Forces and the Defense Issue" and "Foreign Policy."

These and other studies have indicated that although the current environment of U.S.-Japan relations involves various elements of tension and friction on economic and defense issues, the Japanese public thinks highly of the status quo and remains sufficiently level headed in considering future relations between the two countries. The opinion that Japan's defense and security machinery should stand on two legs—the U.S.-Japan Security Treaty and the Self-Defense Forces—is shared by an overwhelming majority of the Japanese.

Despite the presence of these encouraging factors, there are, on the other hand, a number of discouraging aspects to U.S.-Japan relations today. One of them concerns a presumptuous sense of reliance on the United States still lurking in the minds of the Japanese. The

Americans, for their part, seem to suffer from a lack of self-reflection, as they tend to blame their trade deficits solely on Japan.

If these two factors continue to grow—and to contribute to each other's growth—the U.S.-Japan relationship may become very fragile in the future. Indeed, our immediate environment is not without symptoms of that tendency. One recent example may be found in the storm over the NTT (Nippon Telegraph and Telephone Public Corporation) issue, which was the predominant feature of U.S.-Japan economic relations in early 1979. Looking back on Japan's position on the matter, one may get the impression that Japan essentially lacks willingness to take action voluntarily to solve such a problem unless and until pressure from the other side of the Pacific grows to some extent. It must be admitted that Japan still suffers from a "foreign pressure concessions" syndrome.

At that time the U.S. Congress published the "Jones Report," an investigative report by a task force for the surveillance of trade with Japan, headed by U.S. Representative James Jones (D-Oklahoma) and dispatched from the Trade Subcommittee of the House Ways and Means Committee. Analyzing the trade imbalance between the two countries, the report is often very persuasive in strongly arguing for a more open Japanese market and elimination of Japanese import barriers. At the same time, it completely fails to note the apparently objective fact that the United States is equally at fault in the development of the trade deficits. One important reason why the United States today is unable to export more to Japan is that American labor has fallen in quality, resulting in reduced efficiency in industrial operations, which in its turn has made U.S. goods less competitive. Consequently, the U.S. balance of trade with Japan has become all the more unfavorable. Productivity in all U.S. industries grew at an annual rate of 3 percent on the average in 1957–1967. The rate was reduced by half, to 1.5 percent, on the average in 1967–1977 and finally fell below 1 percent in 1978. This means that productivity is scarcely growing in the U.S. economy today. Nevertheless, the Jones Report gave no attention to this apparently undeniable "American disease."

President Douglas Fraser of the United Automobile Workers, visiting Japan in February 1980, made tough demands concerning Japanese car exports to industrial circles here, with emphasis on proposals for opening Toyota and Nissan plants in the United States. Although his arguments were reasonable in some respects, he often sounded almost intimidating without reflecting on possible faults on the part of the United States that might be responsible for the unusual success of Japanese cars in the U.S. market. Such an attitude may have some immediate effects, but will not produce desirable results in U.S.-Japan relations from the long-range viewpoint.

It should also be realized, however, that there is a presumptuous sense of reliance on the United States in the minds of the Japanese. Putting an end to the vicious circle of the Japanese "reliance mentality" and the American failure to grasp changes in the relative economies of the two countries is an important task that must be tackled in the 1980s. Here, the author would like to touch once again on the matter of public opinion surveys in connection with another discouraging factor in U.S.-Japan relations. Referring to the "Public Opinion Survey on Foreign Policy" conducted by the Public Information Office of the prime minister's secretariat in November 1979, it is noteworthy that, of those asked, "Do you think Japan today is on an equal footing with the United States in diplomatic relations?", 27.9 percent answered in the affirmative and 54.7 percent in the negative, with 17.4 percent saying, "I don't know." Apparently, the majority of the Japanese think the U.S.-Japanese relationship unequal, probably because they have either a "victim complex" or a "protégé complex" vis-à-vis the United States.

The Americans generally seem to feel that Japan has become too powerful economically, while the Japanese generally believe that the United States is still big and strong enough to affect the equality of the U.S.-Japan relationship. It is feared that this gap between the two peoples' views of their partnership may serve as a negative factor when they attempt to settle specific issues between them in the future.

Speaking of gaps, it must be pointed out that a communication gap and an information gap remain to be filled between the United States and Japan. For example, immediately after Washington advocated economic sanctions against Iran following the takeover of the U.S. Embassy in Tehran in November 1979, Japanese trade firms were quick to buy lots of Iranian oil in the spot market, and U.S. Secretary of State Vance bluntly told Japanese Foreign Minister Okita in Paris in December that these acts were "insensitive." As a result, Tokyo was forced to make apologies and explanations to Washington. According to one senior member of the Japanese diplomatic service, that was the biggest blunder in postwar Japanese diplomacy. Indeed, the trouble would probably have been avoided if there had not been a serious failure in communication or exchange of information between the United States and Japan—an area that, though apparently full of communication channels, is still beset with various gaps.

IMMEDIATE TASKS

Several important questions will need attention in U.S.-Japan relations during the 1980s. On the international scene, Christmas 1979 was marked by the Soviet invasion of Afghanistan, and this has led to increased tension between Washington and Moscow. How this incident will affect U.S.-Japan relations is a question that needs close attention now. Looking at the world today, one notes that disputes, tensions, and instabilities tend to occur in strategic peripheral areas of Eurasia, such as Korea, Indochina, Afghanistan, and Iran, where North-South as well as East-West relations are often dangerously close. The current situation in Afghanistan represents one dramatic example of such tension.

An incident of this sort inevitably encourages a review of the U.S.-Japan security relationship, causing Washington to make stronger demands on Japan, especially in the military and security areas. Admittedly, Japan nowadays is generally in a growing mood for responding to such demands, but barriers to their ready acceptance still remain in many specific areas. Although the Japanese are now more concerned about security and defense, there has not necessarily been a radical change in their attitude, held since the end of World War II, in favor of limiting their defense effort to a minimum. In an interview with his new ambassador to the United States, Mr. Okaware, on March 1, 1980, Prime Minister Ohira stated that Japan would proceed steadily step by step in its defense effort, but would find it difficult to sharply increase its defense budget because of financial limitations. Thus, it seems that if the United States is too impatient in pressing its demands, Japan may be unable to respond adequately. That may prove one source of trouble between the two countries in the 1980s.

This is also a problem for the United States as there does not seem to be a consensus as to how much defense effort the United States should demand of Japan. The United States certainly wants Japan to increase its defense contribution, as indicated by the position taken by Secretary of Defense Brown—rather uniquely for a high U.S. official thus far—when he stopped in Japan on his way home from China in January 1980. However, if this U.S. attitude should lead to Japan becoming a full-fledged great military power, that could be a problem and a threat even more serious than that which faces the U.S. policymakers today. This risk will remain as strong in the 1980s as it has been in the past. Thus, although the United States will no doubt continue to urge Japan to contribute more in the defense area, it is actually very difficult to determine how much the United States will want and at what point it will be satisfied. This conflict within the United States is a major problem that will be hard to solve in the 1980s.

With respect to Korea, in 1977, Washington decided without prior consultation with Tokyo to withdraw U.S. ground troops from the Republic of Korea. Although the U.S. government fortunately froze this decision in July 1979, the possibility still remains that the issue shall cause further trouble between Washington and Tokyo in the future. This is because, first, the withdrawal of American troops from Korea had been under contemplation ever since the Nixon Doctrine ten years ago and thus may be a problem that will continue to exist over the years. Second, the virtual reestablishment of military rule in the Republic of Korea in May 1980 has amplified U.S. dissatisfaction and antagonism toward the regime, which may result in strengthening again its desire to withdraw troops. As for China, one critical question will be to what extent the United States will attempt to militarize its relationship with China now that tension has been revived between the United States and the Soviet Union. As Japan at the moment cannot favor the idea of Sino-American military cooperation, the China question might become a source of new friction between Washington and Tokyo, unless the United States pursues this matter with much caution and patience. On the contrary, if the United States rushes too impatiently in this direction, discord may occur between U.S. relations with China on one hand and those with Japan on the other.

In the economic area, one might be concerned with the fact that, contrary to the trend up to 1978, Japan has been suffering from overall unfavorable balances of payments. If Japan attempts to solve the problem in a short period of time instead of dealing with it from a long-range viewpoint and lets its exports to the United States increase sharply as in the past, new frictions may occur between the two countries even after the solution of current issues such as automobiles and electronics.

It must also be pointed out that there are important domestic factors in both countries that tend to make their relationship fragile. In Japan, in spite of the assumption made by many observers that the decades long monopoly of political power by the Liberal Democrats was gradually giving way to a new form of "conservative-reformist coalition" in the 1970s, the LDP won an overwhelming victory in the general election of June 1980. Still, there is no assurance that the party will maintain its absolute majority through the 1980s. There seems to be little possibility of a major radical change in Japan's foreign policy or defense policy even under a possible "coalition" regime in the future. Nevertheless, there is no denying that Japanese politics these days seriously lacks new leadership, a problem to which there will be no quick solution.

In the United States, it is not clear at this writing whether or not the new Reagan government will be more consistent and credible than the preceding administration. All that can be said now is that both Japan and the United States seem to suffer from a common lack of political leadership. It is hoped that this will not present a major hindrance to the successful settlement of conflicts and disputes between the United States and Japan in the future. The danger is that either government, in dealing with an issue between them, may intemperately accuse the other in order to make a scapegoat of it, hoping to cover up some internal weakness.

Thus, U.S.-Japan relations in the 1980s will involve various difficulties in both international and domestic areas. But as was pointed out earlier, the relationship will affect the future of the entire Asia-Pacific area and even the future of global political and economic relations. This should be borne in mind by both countries as they continue to endeavor to maintain and improve the successful relationship with still greater wisdom in the 1980s.

8 JAPAN'S SELF-DEFENSE REQUIREMENTS AND CAPABILITIES

Seiichiro Onishi

> *The building of Japan's self-defense forces has been accompanied by serious political, economic, and legal problems since 1950. Mr. Seiichiro Onishi, former head of Japan's Defense Academy and now secretary general of the Research Institute for Peace and Security in Tokyo, outlines that stormy history, summarizes the current status of each branch of the self-defense forces (SDF), and explains the political and economic difficulties of bringing those forces up to a level that would prepare them to meet current threats. He analyzes the problems that will arise if closer U.S.-Japan cooperation in the defense of Japan is implemented and makes a series of far-reaching proposals for overcoming them.*

The fall of South Vietnam in 1975 initiated a marked change in the attitude of the Japanese public on defense. In the following several years, this change has been accelerated by several important developments bearing directly or indirectly on Japan's security—most decisively by the Soviet invasion of Afghanistan. Meanwhile, the "free ride" charges against Japan's defense policy that began to emerge in the United States in the late 1960s have crystalized into practical requests from Washington for increases in Japan's defense strength. Especially since the recent crises in the Middle East, the United States has been making more urgent requests of Japan as an ally and partner. The Japanese in their present strained financial condition are being pressed for a choice on the defense issue after twenty-five years of inattention.

In this chapter, beginning with a discussion of Article 9 of the Japanese Constitution, I will describe the state of the Self-Defense Forces and their problems from the historical point of view, consider the acceptability of the SDF to the public and to the political parties, refer to U.S.-Japanese cooperation in Japan's defense, and finally suggest some defense tasks, both short and long-range, that need to be tackled in the future.

ARTICLE 9: INTERPRETATION AND PRACTICE

Japan's rearmament began with the stimulus of the Korean War—and largely apart from the people's wishes—only three years after the pacifist constitution came into effect, and subsequent developments in the defense build-up have tended to take place ahead of the new, extended interpretations of the war renunciation clause in Article 9[1] needed to meet them. This evidently has been a major hindrance to the emergence of a national consensus on the defense forces.

On the other hand, public opinion surveys conducted in those days indicate that a substantial portion of the population was in favor of a prodefense amendment to the Constitution. In the general elections for the House of Representatives in 1955, the conservative parties in favor of constitutional amendment failed to command a two-thirds majority, and this situation was repeated in the House of Councillors elections the following year. The movement for constitutional amendment was thus frustrated. The proportion of the population approving of the defense forces and mentioning a need for rearmament as a reason why the Constitution should be amended also decreased.

---

1. Article 9 of the Japanese Constitution states:

Aspiring sincerely to an international peace based on justice and order, the Japanese people forever renounce war as a sovereign right of the nation and the threat of use of force as a means of settling international disputes.

In order to accomplish the aim of the preceding paragraph, land, sea, and air forces, as well as other war potential, will never be maintained. The right of belligerency of the state will not be recognized.

Since then, Japan's defense strength has had to be built up not under any express stipulations of the Constitution but on the theory of a national right of self-defense considered to transcend the Constitution. Arguments over the nation's defense strength have been made not from the strategic viewpoint of whether or not it meets Japan's security requirements in the current international environment but from the legal view of how the national right of self-defense should be defined.

In the course of the development of the SDF, the following principles have gradually been established through official views expressed by the government or resolutions made by the Diet to define the strength level, weapon systems, operational range, rules of operation, and other aspects of the defense forces.

1. No weapons that would present an offensive threat to other countries should be maintained. These include intercontinental ballistic missiles, long-range bombers, and assault aircraft carriers. Most nuclear weapons currently known fall under this category, although theoretically, not all nuclear arms are unconstitutional by definition. With reference to the "three nonnuclear principles" (i.e., Japan will not make, possess, or introduce onto its territory nuclear weapons), it seems to me that the government would be justified in reexamining its conventional policy of prohibiting passage through Japanese waters by vessels carrying nuclear weapons. Nuclear-powered submarines, according to the government view, are exempt from this prohibition.

2. No overseas troop dispatches should be made. In the view of the Japanese government, it is not unconstitutional for SDF units to participate in peace-keeping activities abroad involving no exercise of military power, such as those of U.N. observation teams or in relief activities for major disasters in foreign countries. I believe the government should act more boldly in such areas of activity.

3. The right of self-defense should not be exercised collectively with other countries. Acts of self-defense justifiable in the eyes of international law include both individual and collective exercise of the right of self-defense. Based on the spirit of the Japanese Constitution, however, the right is understood to be exercisable only individually. This view was aired by the government

when the U.S.-Japan Security Treaty was revised in 1960. This principle was considered questionable by military experts in connection with the implementation of the U.S.-Japan Security Treaty. In the spring of 1980, the maritime self-defense forces' participation in the Rimpac maneuver brought the issue into the limelight. However, the Diet debate was settled when the government stated that the joint maneuver was not based on the idea of protecting specific countries through a collective exercise of the right of self-defense but merely aimed at improving the tactical capabilities of the participants.

4. Conscription is barred by the Constitution. While compulsory military service is usually called for in a nation's constitution, there is no such provision in the Japanese Constitution in connection with its Article 9. This principle certainly tends to limit the strength of the Self-Defense Forces. Considering, however, that Britain, with a population about half the size of Japan's, is maintaining a defense force level roughly equivalent to 130 percent of Japan's self-defense forces, it does appear that the latter may yet be increased to some extent even under the present volunteer system.

These constitutional constraints make the basic operating stance of the SDF strategically defensive, compelling them to operate exclusively on the defensive. Generally, operational plans involving no offensive elements are considered unrealistic from a military point of view. Moreover, in the light of the strategic environment in which Japan finds itself today as well as of the recent progress in military technology, it is clearly difficult for Japan to effectively protect itself if it has to stay on the defensive at all times. It needs the security treaty with the United States not just because, generally, such a collective security system is the appropriate choice for a middle class nation like Japan in this nuclear age, but also because the current constitution permits no alternative choice.

The defense concept of the government based on its interpretation of Article 9 tends to lack flexibility and involves irrational elements from a military point of view. Thus, in the course of developing its defense strength, the nation has often witnessed unproductive disputes in the Diet over whether or not specific weapon systems are within the bounds of reasonable capabilities for self-defense.

How have the Self-Defense Forces been regarded by the public in connection with Article 9 of the constitution? Although both the Constitution and the SDF have come to be well established in the minds of the Japanese in recent years, this does not mean that a majority of the people has accepted the government view that the SDF are constitutional. Even in the mid-1970s, when about 80 percent of the Japanese recognized the necessity of the SDF, they were considered constitutional by only about 40 to 45 percent of the population. This gap is apparently reflected in the fact that local popular movements against the construction and use of SDF bases have often developed into lawsuits challenging their constitutionality. Indeed, this trend has caused delays in establishing military installations and also has had the indirect effect of deterring the emergence of a national consensus on the need for defense build-up by encouraging anti-SDF struggles.

However, the situation has improved to some extent since 1976. The courts successively concluded that the SDF had been created and built up by the government as part of its legitimate action in ruling the country and that it was not up to the courts to decide whether or not their presence conflicted with Article 9 of the constitution. The movement against the SDF thus lost its legal ground in the courts and will be much less effective in the future.

It is unlikely, however, that the problem has been solved completely. So long as the legitimacy of national defense and the SDF are based on an interpretation of the constitution rather than on an express stipulation in it, it is doubtful whether or not both the Japanese people and the SDF personnel would deal with a national emergency at the risk of their own lives. Even though the concept of civilian control may play a role as a brake on the misuse of military strength, it will never encourage servicemen and women to stand up in an emergency.

THE JAPANESE SELF-DEFENSE FORCES

Current Strength and Mission

The SDF were built up steadily under four successive defense strength build-up programs covering the period from 1957 to 1976, and now they have grown into a national defense organization that, though modest in scale, is reasonably well equipped and functional as a modern armed force. However, the defense forces have tended to give priority to front line capabilities, while their supply and other logistics support systems have tended to lag behind, and it is feared that they may be rather poor in overall defense capability (see the 1977 Defense White Paper).

Meanwhile, the public has not always been kept informed about the ultimate goals and defense concepts in the course of the implementation of the past defense build-up programs. As a result, when the Fourth Defense Program was announced, the public fearfully wondered how large the SDF would become at that rate of growth. It should also be borne in mind that with the economy lapsing into a low growth phase, it is no longer possible for the government to increase its defense spending as fast as it had been doing in the past. Therefore, the government is seeking to expedite the development of a national consensus on defense by more clearly defining the responsibilities of the SDF and hopes to establish a feasible, realistic defense structure in the foreseeable future. The government will concentrate on maintaining rather than building up the defense strength and will attach more importance to qualitative improvements rather than to quantitative increases in defense strength. This, indeed, was the main aim of the defense program outline released by the government in 1976. To systematically implement the major projects called for in it, the defense agency prepared a mid-term defense estimate in 1979 and began to carry it out in 1980.

The Ground Self-Defense Force (GSDF) is 180,000 strong and is organized around a core of twelve infantry divisions and one mechanized division, for a total of thirteen divisions. Considering the presence of vast foreign ground forces deployed around Japan, the current strength of the GSDF appears to be too modest to meet the needs of territorial defense even if the natural bulwark of the ocean around this country is taken into account. This, coupled with the limited strength of only 39,000 reservists, means that Japan's defense forces lack "depth" in manpower. The reservists probably will not be able to exceed 50,000 so long as the current practice of picking them from among retired GSDF men is maintained.

The GSDF initially had all of its equipment supplied from the U.S. forces, and this fact has tended to hold down its equipment budget, which, moreover, has often been subject to competition from the personnel budget. Obsolescence of equipment does not appear so clearly in the ground defense force as in the maritime and air defense forces. For these reasons, the GSDF has been slow in replacing and modernizing its equipment in general, particularly in armoring its infantry units and making its guns self-propelled, as well as in improving its low level of ammunition reserves.

The Maritime Self-Defense Force (MSDF) consists of a defense fleet including four escort flotillas, two submarine flotillas, five air groups, and two minesweeping flotillas, plus five regional units. It is mainly engaged in antisubmarine and antimine operations in the waters around Japan, which are understood to comprise all waters within 200 to 300 nautical miles of the country's shores and major sea routes within 1000 nautical miles. Compared with the air self-defense force (ASDF), the build-up of the MSDF has not proceeded so rapidly for these reasons:

1. Antisubmarine operations are subject to technical limitations imposed by marine environmental conditions.
2. Since the former Japanese Navy did not have much experience in this field, there has been much controversy about what is the right composition of the antisubmarine forces and which weapons systems they should have.
3. It has taken much time and money to improve their equipment and the training level of their personnel.
4. Unlike the Ground and Air Defense Forces, the Maritime Defense Force has not been subjected to the pressure of important external factors capable of accelerating the improvement of its equipment, which consequently has been rather slow.
5. The MSDF has had trouble maintaining its force level as it has always found it difficult to offer persuasive arguments for specific goals: It is hard to quantitatively determine the amount of work required to effectively protect a nation's vital sea lanes.

The growth of the Soviet Navy in the 1970s has been a threat to Japan's sea defense, and the situation has been made increasingly complex by the addition of aircraft as well as submarines to the Soviet naval strength around Japan. In addition, the reduced presence of the U.S. Seventh Fleet in the western Pacific as a result of the increased tension in the Middle East is compelling the MSDF to assume greater responsibilities in the former area. Although the introduction of P3Cs (reconnaissance aircraft) and the reorganization of the escort flotillas are already under way, one may wonder if these projects do not need reexamination as to their size and timing. It is also urgent for the MSDF to fill the existing gap in the improvement of its equipment, including command, control, and communication systems; marine air defense systems; and torpedo and mine adjustment capabilities. The possible introduction of nuclear-powered submarines will need attention in the future.

The Air Self-Defense Force is organized around a core of ten interceptor squadrons, three support fighter squadrons, and six high altitude SAM units. The ASDF has been urgently required to take over air defense responsibilities from the U.S. forces in Japan and indeed has been receiving a great deal of assistance, both financial and technical, from the latter. As a result, the ASDF has been able to keep its equipment up to date with reasonable success—adopting new fighter models, introducing air defense missiles, and maintaining aircraft control and warning systems.

The ASDF is charged mainly with air defense and ground support responsibilities and leaves it to the U.S. forces in Japan to take offensive action in response to enemy attack. But as this policy is not really adequate for quick response to certain types of emergency, more day-to-day efforts should be made to coordinate U.S. and Japanese operations. The often noted gap in ASDF capabilities for detecting low altitude air intrusions will be largely filled by the deployment of airborne early warning systems and new fighters. It is becoming difficult for it to maintain its high altitude SAMs, as they are growing older and less adequate in performance. The emergence of long-range ASMs, improved electronic countermeasures, and other new factors are making effective air defense operations increasingly difficult. It is important to ensure their successful performance by improving the Electronic Counter Counter Measures (ECCM) capabilities in the warning and surveillance systems. It is also urgent to increase the air defense organization's chances of survival by making air bases and radar sites more resistant.

Because the growth of the Self-Defense Forces has been gradual, a proper balance has been maintained between their personnel and equipment throughout the process of their development, and this at least has been a favorable factor for the steady elevation of their training level. On the other hand, the public attitude toward their training has been deteriorating steadily, and it is feared that the training level and the tactical proficiency of the defense forces may soon cease to improve further. Recent rises in fuel and ammunition costs are likely to accelerate this tendency. Air training space for jet fighters, available sea areas for minesweeping training, ground areas for large-scale troop maneuvers, shooting ranges for large caliber, land range guns—all subject to increasing limitations imposed by new community development programs and environmental protection requirements—may be counted on to deteriorate. The environment for defense-force-training operations will not improve.

The recently reported participation of MSDF units in Rimpac maneuvers, joint maneuvers of U.S. Air Force and Japanese ASDF units, dispatch of GSDF officers to Okinawa witness U.S. Marine landing maneuvers, and other signs of increased interest in U.S. maneuvers on the part of the SDF reflect their desire to overcome their current stalemate in the training area and to achieve a higher level of training.

Status of Arms

The defense forces have been acquiring their equipment in three different ways—receiving some items free from the United States, sharing the cost of others with the United States, and purchasing still others on their own account. These generally correspond to different historical phases of their development. All three services of the defense forces were initially outfitted with equipment granted or loaned from the United States. A cost-sharing formula was used for aircraft in combination with technological licensing agreements. This contributed both financially and technically to the reconstruction of Japan's aircraft industry, which soon became capable of building jet trainers, cargo planes, sea planes, and finally the F-1 ground support fighter. But production of fighter-interceptors and antisubmarine patrol aircraft, the mainstay of air defense and antisubmarine operations, still remains to be built in Japan under licenses from the U.S. because Japanese industry, though now capable of building weapon carriers, is still technically unable to meet the tactical requirements of modern weapon systems in aircraft.

Construction of defense vessels here began in 1953. But Japan has had to rely on the U.S. forces for know-how with antisubmarine weapons, radar, and other shipborn weapons based on latest developments in electronics, since it has accumulated little knowledge in this area. The U.S. Navy has been sympathetic in providing this sort of assistance to the MSDF, allowing the latter to acquire new weapons without difficulty under the foreign military sales system, although in such cases, technology transfers to Japan have generally been a step behind those to the NATO members.

In the area of missiles, where Japan completely lacked accumulated knowledge after the war, research and development have gone through much trial and error. While the development of antitank missiles has been successful, air-to-air missiles made in Japan have been too costly to be practical, and it takes much time to develop short-range ground-to-air missiles.

Progress in electronics has been a vital source of technological innovation in the military sector as well as in the private, contributing especially to the development of weapons systems in performance. Indeed, the major powers have been attaching great importance to electronics in their military research and development programs. In Japan, on the other hand, the defense forces initially laid emphasis on aircraft technology as a means of expediting the growth of an aircraft industry and have tended to invest too little in electronics research. As a result, we are now faced with difficulties in such areas as electronic counter measures (ECMs) and electronic counter counter measures (ECCMs), where release of foreign military technology cannot be expected. The flow of technological know-how in electronics between the military and civilian sectors here seems to be contrary to that of other industrialized countries.

Modernization of equipment is essential to defense strength development, and the defense authorities have been endeavoring to achieve this objective by procuring equipment in the light of available financial resources, cost effectiveness, and the prevailing level of technology in each area. Nevertheless, there have been lags and imbalances in defense equipment modernization, largely because there has not been enough money to be invested in it and but also because the defense authorities have tended to be more interested in weapon carriers than in weapon systems and in strike capabilities rather than in sensing capabilities. This tendency has apparently been reflected in such past faults as the decision to equip the F4E with an improper missile model and the lags noted in the development of torpedoes and antisubmarine underwater sensors.

Successful national production of defense equipment depends on adequate research and development conducted at home. But there has been a gap between principle and practice in this respect, as may be seen from the low proportion of research and development appropriations to the total defense budget.

In this age of quick progress in military technology and quick obsolescence of equipment, a nation aiming to build up modern defense strength by starting from scratch can more reasonably expect to achieve the objective by importing finished equipment from abroad than by launching national production of such equipment, which requires long lead times and much investment in research and development. In the world's more advanced military powers, research and development appropriations are regarded as a necessity for ensuring the procurement of proper equipment tomorrow, and R&D is included in the equipment budget in the broad sense of the term as an item inseparable from current defense equipment. But this approach is often inappropriate for a country underdeveloped in military technology, where projects promising quick results tend to get higher priority in the budget. This tends to make researchers less interested in unique, far-sighted projects. Investment in basic defense research appears even less attractive. Although research and development in the defense area depends considerably on technical resources in the private sector, little cooperation has been offered by researchers in colleges and private institutions, making it unlikely that technological developments in such areas will combine to build up effective defense R&D capabilities. Relatively few trial models of defense equipment have been built, and experiments on them, subject to considerable restrictions, have had only limited feedback for defense research; this has discouraged efforts at improving the reliability of defense equipment.

There has long been controversy over whether defense equipment should be nationally produced or imported. From the viewpoint of national independence in logistics, there is no doubt that national production is preferable. However, weapons produced in Japan have no market outside the defense agency and therefore cannot be expected to come down in cost. For this reason, they have not been favored by the defense program planners and the financial authorities. The current low content of Japanese-made elements in defense equipment production makes one skeptical of Japan's independence in logistics. The active use of highly sophisticated modern weapons in the Middle East wars has revolutionized the conventional pattern of war represented by World War II. Although growing pressure for defense equipment standardization may come through U.S.-Japan consultations on defense cooperation, maintenance of defense production on a reasonable scale and at an appropriate level of sophistication is essential for Japan's defense strength and also necessary for permitting its rapid expansion in an emergency, which is contemplated in the defense program outline. Thus, the question of national production versus imports of defense equipment will remain unsolved for some time.

Readiness

The development of the defense forces has often rested on the notion that it was an ongoing process, yet to be completed, and this has often limited attention to the question of whether or not Japan was ready for defense emergencies. Also, the Japanese public has had an intrinsic inclination to avoid thinking of defense emergencies, and the nation's political leaders have been resting on the assumption that such emergencies can be deterred by the superior military strength of the United States.

As a result, the lack of a state of readiness for an emergency has been disclosed in the following cases:

- In 1965, a hot dispute occurred in the Diet over a "Three Arrow Study" conducted by the defense agency. Although the work had much to do with domestic preparedness for emergencies, public attention focused solely on the possibility of the defense forces getting out of civilian control, while other aspects of it were little heeded.

- In 1972, the mayor of Yokohama resorted to a government ordinance concerning restrictions on vehicles to stop the transfer of tanks from the Sagamihara Depot to Yokohama harbor, as proposed by the U.S. forces in Japan. His attitude reflected the above-noted disinclination of Japanese administrative authorities to incorporate defense requirements into the domestic structure of national life.

- In 1976, a Soviet MIG-25 fighter landed without permission at Hakodate Airport in Hokkaido. The Japanese government dealt with this incident as a case of illegal entrance by a foreign national into Japan in accordance with domestic legislation rather than as one of intrusion by a foreign plane into Japan's territorial air space from the viewpoint of international law. Here again, one can see a reflection of Japan's lack of readiness, both physical and mental, for emergency situations.

- In 1978, Chairman Hiro'omi Kurisu of the joint chiefs of staff caused a sensation in Japan by declaring that any response on the part of the defense forces to surprise attack would exceed their legally sanctioned action, since they were not permitted to do anything under the existing laws until they were explicitly ordered to act in defense. This statement made clear that current legislation on the defense forces and its interpretation by the government were at variance with the essential character of the defense forces—that they should be ready for emergencies at all times.

Thus, looking at Japan's defense posture from the viewpoint of "readiness," one finds much need for improvement within and around the defense forces. The Kurisu statement reminded the defense authorities of the need to increase their preparedness by such means as upgrading their information and communication capabilities, even though the legal aspects of the surprise attack problem still remain under study.

A study of legislation for emergency situations was officially launched by the defense agency in 1977. Since such legislation will concern many matters falling under the jurisdiction of other government agencies, as well as civil rights, a public attitude in favor of national security measures will be essential for its passage. One can hardly expect quick progress toward its realization.

Defense Spending

Japan created the defense forces in 1954, one of the hardest postwar years for the nation's finances. Nevertheless, defense was given a higher priority in the 1954 budget than social security, economic development, promotion of education and science, and other important items. This relatively favorable treatment of defense was limited, however, to the initial phase of defense strength development. By fiscal 1960—the last year of the First Defense Build-up Program and the year in which the U.S.-Japan Security Treaty was revised—defense had lost out to all three other major items in the budget, accounting for less than 10 percent of the government's spending. The figure then continued to decline year after year, until it was down to 5.24 percent in 1980.

Three reasons may be mentioned for this trend. The first is military. The superior military strength of the United States provided security for Japan; by providing military bases to the U.S. forces in its territory, Japan believed it earned the privilege of minimizing its spending on defense. This is what House of Councillors' member Minoru Genda might have had in mind when he spoke of "defending the U.S. bases here" as one of the purposes of the ASDF.

The second reason is domestic and political. Stabilization of the people's living and reconstruction of the national economy had been two imperative needs in postwar Japanese politics.

The third reason concerned Japan's Asian policy. The "pacificist" label was essential for Japan as it was readmitted to the world community of nations. Japan's neighbors, especially in Asia, retained unpleasant memories of the war, tended to suspect that Japan's economic growth might result in increasing its military strength, and wanted assurances that Japan as an economic power would not become a military power.

The defense planners of the Japanese government sometimes took account of the midterm economic program and economic growth trends in estimating the appropriate size of defense spending, but it never occurred to the planners of the midterm economic program to take defense costs into consideration. Every year, as the budget compilation season came around, hard last minute negotiations normally took place at top level meetings of the government and the government party over proposed budget increases on a few major spending items, but these never included defense spending until the question of whether or not it should be kept at 0.9 percent of GNP in the fiscal 1980 budget was finally referred to the top political leadership for decision. For many years, defense costs had been dealt with at the administrative level, and it developed into a political issue only after increasing friction between the United States and Japan in the economic area spread fear among Japanese political leaders a few years ago that it might seriously affect the reliability of the U.S.-Japan security system.

According to public opinion surveys conducted in recent years, those in favor of increasing defense spending increased from 10 percent in 1972 through 20 percent in 1978 and 26 percent in October 1979 to 31 percent in March 1980. This apparently meant that there had been a considerable change from the situation in the 1960s when a majority of the Japanese favored maintaining the status quo on defense. On the other hand, in a public opinion survey conducted by The *Yomiuri Shimbun* in November 1979, 72 percent of those asked to pick two out of a list of nine suggested items for budget-cutting responded, and a very large number of them (44 percent of the entire sample) chose "defense." In another *Yomiuri Shimbun* study, conducted in March 1980, 21 percent of those asked whether or not they would favor an increased personal tax burden for national defense answered in the affirmative and 68 percent in the negative. The financial authorities now consider it imperative to reestablish the finances of the government on a sounder basis: There are powerful pressure groups demanding increased budgets for public works; and the public is strongly concerned about social welfare. Under these circumstances, it does not seem easy to predict how the Japanese will react to their new need for increased defense spending, even though defense is now an increasingly lively issue.

POPULAR ATTITUDES AND POLITICAL SUPPORT

Since the mid-1970s there has been a considerable maturing of national consensus on the mission of the Defense Forces, the significance of the U.S.-Japan Security Treaty, the improvement of the nation's defense strength, and other key defense issues. At the same time, there has been a gradual decline in the resistance, whether active or passive, of the opposition parties (with the exception of the Communists) to the defense policy of the government. In the past, the Japanese, though aware of the necessity of the Defense Forces, have been influenced by the predominance of negative rather than constructive criticism in defense discussions in the Diet and have not been given much incentive to familiarize themselves with the practical details of the nation's defense program, so that the majority of them has passively accepted the defense status quo. Therefore, the recent convergence of the defense stands of the various political parties is noteworthy, as it will have the effect of lessening the gap between their views on defense and those of the public.

According to the results of a recent public opinion survey on defense, the majority of the Japanese have recently come to recognize the legitimacy of the SDF. Nevertheless, there still remain some imbalances and complexities in the public's view of the defense forces. For example, although the attitude of the educational world toward the defense forces has become more supportive, about a quarter of all high schools still refuse to have SDF-recruiting sessions held on their premises. Admission of defense force officers to college graduate schools, once stopped completely following student demonstrations, has not resumed to any great extent. In February 1980, to my surprise, at an air base in Kyushu where the public is generally friendly to the defense forces, a joint maneuver to be conducted by ASDF and U.S. Air Force units faced an intense opposition movement led by the mayor of the local community.

The attitudes of opposition parties toward national defense began to change after the 1975 debacle in South Vietnam. Afterwards, with the 1980 Diet elections drawing near, they proceeded further toward making their stands on security and defense more "realistic" as they attempted to work out ideas for possible coalitions to take power. It is evident that this process was accelerated by the Soviet invasion of Afghanistan. A middle of the road coalition platform agreed upon between the Komei party and the Democratic Socialists calls for "preserving the U.S.-Japan Security Treaty for the time being" and "maintaining the defense forces." Also, the Socialists and the Komei party formally agreed to a plan for a coalition regime from which the Communists would be excluded. This means that the Socialists made concessions toward the Komei party's "realistic" approach. The recent establishment of the special Committee on Security in the House of Representatives, a long-pending issue in the Diet, came about largely because of these changes in the attitudes of the opposition parties, particularly that of the Socialists.

U.S.-JAPAN COOPERATION
IN DEFENSE MATTERS

The establishment of a Subcommittee on Defense Cooperation, agreed upon between Washington and Tokyo in 1976, and the preparation of "Guidelines for U.S.-Japan, Defense Cooperation" by the subcommittee two years later, marked a new epoch in the history of the U.S.-Japan Security Treaty. As the cost of the Vietnam War increasingly strained the Pentagon's finances toward the end of the 1960s, Washington, under the pressure of "free ride" charges made by some Americans against Japan, began to call upon Tokyo to share in the cost of the U.S.-Japan security system by purchasing U.S.-made weapons and paying part of the cost of U.S. forces in Japan.

The Guidelines for U.S.-Japan Defense Cooperation are designed primarily to help the two countries' defense officials develop plans for joint operations and make preparations for their effective execution. Operational responsibilities will be shared according to the Guidelines as follows: "The SDF will conduct defensive operations mainly in the territory of Japan and in sea and air areas adjacent thereto while the U.S. forces will support such SDF operations and carry out operations complementary thereto in areas beyond the capabilities of the SDF." In developing a joint operation plan, Japan's defense forces and the U.S. forces in Japan will evaluate each other's military capabilities and determine their respective operational requirements. Although such evaluations and requirements will vary depending on the scenario of each particular joint operation plan, it may be said that the gap between operational requirements and actual capabilities will generally be small in the case of the U.S. Forces, with their high degree of readiness and great strength, while it will be much larger for the defense forces. Such joint operation plans may even affect the service composition of the defense forces and the defense structure of the nation. Indeed, they may play a constructive role in upgrading Japan's unique defense strength and improving the social basis on which it rests if they help develop the capabilities of the defense forces from the hardware-oriented phase to the operational-readiness-oriented phase.

Today, it is pointless to discuss national defense without referring to regional defense, which in its turn is inseparable from global defense. The United States, an ally of Japan, is seriously concerned about defense on a global scale and views threats to Japan and countermeasures to them in a way that reflects this global outlook. If Washington and Tokyo have different concepts of what will happen in the event of a war, they are likely to find a gap between their operational requirements. This may also mean a gap between their views of priorities in defense strength development. Take, for example, the requirement of blockading the three main straits around Japan in wartime, which was first mentioned as a personal opinion by Senator Gary Hart in the report of the Pacific Study Group to the Senate Committee on the Armed Forces titled *U.S.-Japan Security Relationship: The Key to East Asian Security and Stability* and again taken up for discussion in the U.S. *Annual Report on Defense* 1981.

Senator Hart asserts that these channels may be blockaded with mines, tactical aircraft, and naval units without much difficulty, thus bottling up the Soviet naval forces in the Sea of Japan, whereas Mr. Kaihara is of the opinion that this would be infeasible in practice. According to Kaihara, air and sea control in the straits would be essential for such operations. The strategic importance of the straits would make the fight over such control extremely intense, possibly extending it over much of Japan's territory. In other words, the Japanese might have to pay dearly for that operation in comparison with what the U.S. might expect to gain from it. It is not the kind of approach Japan can readily agree to follow, even though it may be in keeping with Washington's strategic requirements. It is yet to be seen how Washington and Tokyo will be able to resolve the lack of reciprocity between their defense strategies within the framework of their consultations on defense cooperation.

The second major theme found in the guidelines is U.S.-Japanese cooperation in situations elsewhere in the Far East that will seriously affect Japan's security. This theme is based on Article 6 of the security treaty.[2] To deal with situations under Article 6, on the other

---

2. Article 6 states:

For the purpose of contributing to the security of Japan and the maintenance of international peace and security in the Far East, the United States of America is granted the use by its land, air and naval forces of facilities and areas in Japan.

The use of these facilities and areas as well as the status of United States armed forces in Japan shall be governed by a separate agreement, replacing the Administrative Agreement under Article III of the Security Treaty between the United States of America and Japan, signed at Tokyo on February 28, 1952, as amended, and by such other arrangements as may be agreed upon.

hand, Japan's cooperation with the U.S. forces had already been stipulated in the Status of Forces Agreement, and matters concerning their actual application had been taken care of by the U.S.-Japan Joint Committee. Nevertheless, this item was included in the Guidelines on Defense Cooperation because the U.S. wanted some improvement in the way Article 6 had been applied. The main purpose of such work under Article 6 is to discuss ways in which Japan provides the U.S. forces with conveniences, which include, among others, letting the U.S. forces use the SDF bases and enjoy other privileges. This is also necessary for joint operations under Article 5, and in terms of operational requirements, there should be no distinction between such conveniences required under Article 5[3] and those under Article 6.

It is only natural that in interpreting and applying the Status of Forces Agreement, the United States should have been anxious to maximize its freedom of military action, while Japan as an independent nation should have wanted to minimize the privileges granted to the foreign armed forces in its territory. Japan has been making specific facilities and areas available to the U.S. forces and providing them with conveniences in using such facilities as a sort of compensation for the obligation of protecting Japan undertaken by the United States under Article 5, while making little allowance for joint operations with the United States to be conducted under the same article for the defense of Japan.

According to the guidelines, the study of ways of providing conveniences to the U.S. forces in Japan should include letting the U.S. forces share defense forces bases and enjoy other conveniences. On the other hand, defense cooperation under Article 5 should also be implemented in such areas as communications, air traffic control, transportation, repair, and supply—where indeed the two countries' forces will have more and more contacts. Contacts between them will not be limited to combat operations, but will likely call for

---

3. Article 5 states:

Each Party recognizes that an armed attack against either Party in the territories under the administration of Japan would be dangerous to its own peace and safety and declares that it would act to meet the common danger in accordance with its constitutional provisions and processes.

Any such armed attack and all measures taken as a result therefore, shall be immediately reported to the Security Council of the United Nations in accordance with the provisions of Article 51 of the Charter. Such measures shall be terminated when the Security Council has taken the measures necessary to restore and maintain international peace and security.

their coordination within the private sector of Japanese society based on some military requirements shared by the two countries' forces. U.S.-Japan defense cooperation will thus extend beyond the limits of defense administration and will come to involve nonmilitary areas of activity in this country.

CONCLUSION

In concluding, I would like to point out a few objectives that I believe should be sought in the future in matters of national defense.

Immediate Objectives

For the purpose of strengthening the nation's defense, it is of paramount importance to attain with maximum speed the goals set up in the defense program outline with sufficient regard for modernization of equipment and improvement of command communication and logistics support capabilities as well as for the efficient operation and management of units. These goals represent the basic SDF capabilities to be maintained in peacetime and constitute the core of the nation's defense strength, which should be capable of being expanded quickly in the event of an important change in the international situation. Therefore, they should be achieved as minimum requirements for the nation's defense—on our own responsibility and at our own expense, rather than out of regard for the wishes of the United States.

The Midterm Defense Estimate (1980-1984) is the program for achieving these goals, but the trouble is that the program is to be implemented over five years on the basis of equipment delivery contracts still to be signed. Yet while international tension is now expected to rise toward the mid-1980s, the improved SDF organization contemplated in the Midterm Defense Estimate (which itself is considered unsatisfactory by military experts, as it was worked out on the basis of the world situation in the détente period of the early 1970s) will not become operationally effective until the late 1980s. This leisurely pace in the implementation of the program results from the fact that it was determined by financial considerations (specifically, the government policy of not letting annual defense spending exceed 1 percent of GNP) rather than by actual defense needs.

In view of recent developments in international relations, I suggest that priority be given to actual defense needs in seeking the SDF goals and that the implementation of especially urgent items in the Midterm Defense Estimate be accelerated by two years. This would require an increase of about 20 to 25 percent in annual defense spending over the level contemplated in the original program.

Long-Range Objectives

1. Reduce the regular strength of the GSDF and sharply increase reserve strength. The regular forces should be ten divisions of 150,000 men. Of the ten divisions, half should be heavily equipped. The reservists should consist of 50,000 in the regular reserves and 100,000 in volunteer reserves, for a total of 150,000.

2. To permit the antisubmarine forces of the MSDF to be reinforced with vessels of the five regional units in an emergency, the Maritime Safety Agency should be made capable of taking over more coastal defense duties from them in emergencies, and the organization and equipment of the agency should be improved for the purpose of combined operations with the MSDF.

3. The communication and logistical systems of the SDF should be improved, to permit the sharing of air bases by units of the SDF and the U.S. forces in Japan and the military use of civilian airfields in an emergency.

4. The existing intermediate commands of the Ground, Maritime, and Air Self-Defense Forces should be abolished. Rather, a regional joint command should be created in each of the three sectors — northern, middle, and western.

5. Legal steps should be taken to enable SDF units to cooperate in U.N. peace-keeping activities in transportation, communications, and other areas permissible under the Japanese constitution.

6. Establish decisionmaking mechanisms at the political and administrative levels to ensure effective action in an emergency.

7. To overcome various security vulnerabilities found in Japan today, introduce the concepts of civil defense, economic defense, and psychological defense in various systems of social life in Japan.

9 SOVIET POLICY IN EAST ASIA
Gaston J. Sigur

Dr. Gaston J. Sigur, director of the Institute for Sino-Soviet Studies of George Washington University, asserts that Soviet policy toward East Asia rests on a mixture of fear and strength. The Soviets fear the formation of a tripartite alliance of the United States, Japan, and China—a development that could lead to a serious threat from a newly strengthened China on the one hand. On the other hand, their steady build-up of military power in the Asia-Pacific region during the 1970s has improved the "correlation of forces" vis-à-vis the United States and has emboldened the Soviets to the point of exercising their voice anywhere on the globe. Dr. Sigur concludes that the Soviet Union will continue to do everything it can to subvert U.S. interests in East Asia, but that a military confrontation between the two superpowers can be avoided so long as U.S. nuclear and conventional war deterrent and resolve remain undiminished.

In order to discuss Soviet Asian policy realistically, it is first necessary to establish the proper perspective with a few broad observations about the Soviet international position. The Soviet Union is a power motivated both by revolutionary ideology and by national self-interest. On occasion one motive may take precedence over the other, but more often, Soviet policy, as implemented from the Kremlin, is a mixture of the two. Ideology and national self-interest are not necessarily mutually exclusive. They can come together, and from this union can emerge a coherent course of action in any given situation.

The Soviet Union is now a global power, whose leaders think in global terms. Soviet spokesmen more and more present the view that the Soviet Union has the right—and the duty—to exercise its influence anywhere on the globe. In practice, this means, for example, providing support to national liberation forces—support that can be economic, political, and military. Because of Soviet weakness in the political and economic spheres, more often than not it is increasingly in the military area that we are witnessing Soviet intervention and action. The extension of the so-called Brezhnev Doctrine beyond Eastern Europe to Afghanistan in late 1979 is a vivid illustration of Soviet willingness to use military force and of the growth of Soviet confidence as Soviet power has multiplied relative to the West. Soviet leaders have made it clear that the world has been witnessing, in the past several years, a change in what they refer to as the correlation of forces favorable to the Soviet bloc. In particular, the strategic balance is being altered and U.S. will eroded. As a result, U.S. nuclear guarantees are becoming suspect.

As the Soviet Union pursues a more active and interventionist policy abroad, it has not deviated from a long-held posture that its major adversary is the United States and secondarily those powers—Western Europe and Japan—allied with the United States. The United States, Western Europe, and Japan bring together economic, political, and military strengths that, if cooperatively utilized, could cause the Soviet Union to exercise a greater degree of caution in its new global role. Therefore, as we examine Soviet Asian policy, we should do so in the context of a USSR weak economically, but increasingly powerful militarily, a nation desiring and taking steps to achieve global influence and fully aware that any goals it may set to expand its influence are capable of being frustrated in most instances only by the United States or by the United States in concert with its allies, NATO and Japan.

SOVIET POLICY TOWARD JAPAN

The Soviet Union professes to look upon Japan as a pliant and willing ally of the United States. In Moscow's eyes, Japan's foreign policy is basically set in Washington. Japan does as Washington directs. The U.S.-Japan Security Treaty, according to the Soviets, is a military alliance designed to threaten the Soviet Union and to enhance U.S. and Japanese influence in Asia and the Pacific.

More than this, the United States is assisting at the rebirth of Japanese militarism. Soviet propaganda outlets attack what they say is a renaissance of the militarism of the 1930s in Japan. Japan is on the move and is in the process of bolstering its great economic power with commensurate military strength, according to Moscow. In the Soviet view, the United States, wittingly or witlessly, is a partner in this dangerous policy.

In modern history, Japan and Russia have exhibited little trust and friendship for each other. Since the inception of the Soviet regime, this attitude of distrust in the relations between the two countries has been particularly evident. After the Pacific war, the Soviet Union officially continued to see Japan as a future danger to peace. The Sino-Soviet Treaty of 1950 specifically singled out Japan as a potential enemy, albeit allied with another power—namely, the United States. The USSR refused to sign the Treaty of San Francisco in 1951, ending the war with Japan, but in 1956 the Soviet Union and Japan bilaterally agreed to the termination of a state of war and the resumption of diplomatic relations between them. Since that time, though a treaty of peace has not yet been concluded, Japanese-Soviet ties have been correct and proper, but not close. The Soviet Union has viewed Japan as a staunch ally of the United States and, hence, a major competitor. This has been particularly the case during the past decade or so as Japan's economic power has reached maximum proportions.

As stated earlier, one of the most salient features of Soviet foreign policy around the globe is its reliance upon military power. This is especially visible in Asia, where Soviet political and economic strength is transparently weak. Perhaps this explains, in part at least, Soviet policy toward Japan. Western observers have great trouble in understanding why the USSR assumes such a belligerent tone in its dealings with the Japanese. The Soviet explanation may be that since Japan is so closely allied to the United States, Moscow cannot challenge this alliance and Japan's adherence to it with any hope of success and that, therefore, the only way to present a credible Soviet policy to Japan is to exhibit great military strength on the chance that Japanese leaders will become sufficiently intimidated to respond favorably to Soviet initiatives in the economic and political realms and to question even more deeply the U.S. security commitment to Japan. This policy of intimidation would have little prospect of success, of course, if the Japanese believe that the United States retains its capability to provide Japan with the necessary security guarantees.

The northern islands issue perhaps best illustrates Soviet intransigence in dealings with the Japanese. At Yalta it was agreed that the Kurile Islands were to be handed over to the Soviet Union. The question is, Just what are the Kurile Islands? The Soviet Union maintains that they are all of the islands north of Hokkaido, while the Japanese claim that Habomai, Shikotan, Kunashiri, and Etorofu are not part of the Kurile chain. This issue is an emotion-laden one in Japan, and all Japanese political parties have given support, in varying degrees, to the Japanese position that the four islands are an integral part of the Japanese mainland. The Soviet Union, while allowing that it might return Habomai and Shikotan to Japanese jurisdiction, is adamant that Etorofu and Kunashiri are Soviet territory. Some Soviets say that these islands are not particularly significant to them strategically, but that if they bow to Japanese claims, then the Chinese will use this to strengthen their demands for territorial readjustment with Moscow and even post–World War II territorial settlements in Europe may be subject to reexamination. The Soviets also express concern that either Japan or the United States would place military bases on the islands if Japan reassumed sovereignty over them.

The adamant position taken by the Soviets on the northern islands issue puzzles many political analysts, who reason that if the strategic benefit to the Soviet Union of possessing these islands is not considered by them to be overwhelming, then the Soviets would reap major political gains in their relations with Tokyo by offering to return the islands to Japanese sovereignty. However, this reasoning fails to appreciate the fundamental fact that Soviet policy is to an increasing degree based on military strength. By building up its Pacific fleet and its military might in the East Asian and Pacific area generally, the Soviet Union is warning the Japanese that Tokyo should expect no give from Moscow on the northern territories issue and should be prepared for a tough Moscow stance on any matter under negotiation. The Soviet Union has taken a further step to convince Japan of this attitude by sending increasing numbers of military personnel and materiel to the disputed islands. These personnel will strengthen the Soviet capacity to use the islands principally, it would seem, for surveillance of sea traffic through the Kunashiri Channel on the way from or to the Sea of Okhotsk. Additionally, of course, it will secure the islands that guard the Soviet Pacific fleet's access to the ocean from bases in the Maritime Provinces.

In the economic area, the Soviet Union has exerted considerable effort to get the Japanese to assist with the development of Siberia. The Soviets have been particularly anxious to have the Japanese help with energy resource development in this region. While Japan has agreed to assist with some exploration for gas and oil, the major Tyumen oil project, to be furthered with Japanese aid, has not proceeded. The reasons for Japanese unwillingness to move ahead have been based on a number of things, including strategic implication, uncertainty as to how much oil Japan would actually receive from the Soviets, technical problems, and doubts about economic gains.

The Soviets know that Japan and the United States consult with one another regarding support of economic projects in Siberia. While Moscow is not happy about this, it realizes that Siberia is a region of great strategic importance and that both Japan and the United States will exercise great caution before lending assistance to enterprises that might enhance Soviet strategic capabilities.

The Soviet Union is also much aware that Japan is a free enterprise society and that Japanese industries will cooperate in furthering economic programs that will lead to a profit. With this reasoning, the Soviet Union continues to press Japanese business to make even larger contributions to Siberian development in all fields. Japan's heavy concern with profit was perhaps best exemplified by the selling of an 80,000 ton floating dock to the Soviets for use in Vladivostok. This action would seem to go against the Japanese policy of opposition to the Soviet naval build-up in the Pacific.

Fishing negotiations are a significant element in Soviet-Japanese relations. These seldom take place smoothly, and Soviet seizure of Japanese ships that allegedly break the rules laid down in Soviet-Japanese fishing agreements is a regular occurrence. While the Soviet attitude in the fishing negotiations ranges from very tough to conciliatory, the Soviet Union can always use the fishery issue to try to put pressure on Japan in other areas if it so wishes.

Soviet policy toward Japan since 1956 has consistently aimed to neutralize Japan economically and militarily; to gain economic aid from Japan; and eventually, to draw Japan closer to the Soviet Union economically, politically, and ideologically. The 1978 draft agreement presented for Japanese consideration by Foreign Minister Andrei Gromyko contains terms that, if accepted by Tokyo, would lead to the end of the U.S.-Japan Security Treaty and to a political and economic accommodation between Japan and the Soviet Union. The Soviet Union, it appears, sees no real chance at this time to break or seriously weaken the U.S.-Japanese alliance through political or economic means. The Soviet Union seems to be placing its hopes upon its military build-up in the Pacific and the Asian area, which is at least partially designed to put pressure upon Japan and to show the Japanese that for them to depend upon U.S. military might for their protection is a will-o-the-wisp.

SOVIET POLICY TOWARD CHINA

The Soviet Union and the People's Republic of China have been in formal alliance since 1950. In the spring of 1979, China informed the USSR that the treaty of alliance was to end within one year's time. This action was simply the official recognition of the true state of relations between Moscow and Peking that had begun to deteriorate in the late 1950s.

Soviet officials maintain that Moscow's break with Peking took place in 1958, when Mao Tse-tung became angered at the failure of the Soviet Union to support fully and with all necessary weapons, including nuclear, the Chinese Politburo decision to attempt a military takeover of the offshore islands of Quemoy and Matsu and of Taiwan itself. There are other reasons, of course, for the breakdown of Soviet-Chinese friendship, but there is little reason to doubt that Moscow did not feel itself strong enough in 1958 to challenge the United States over the Taiwan issue. Perhaps the Soviet Union also felt that to risk war with the United States over China's desire to conquer Taiwan would be the wrong challenge, at the wrong time, and over the wrong issue. In any event, Soviet and Chinese relations have steadily gone downhill in recent years, and today the two great Communist powers confront one another along their long common border and around the world.

In ideological terms, Soviet propaganda organs ceaselessly attack the Chinese for having abandoned the principles of Marxism-Leninism. The Soviets claim that Maoist thought, upon which Chinese communism still claims to be based, is not Marxist at all, but rather a kind of Chinese nationalism clothed in pseudo-Marxist terminology. It would be a mistake not to take seriously the doctrinal broadsides by the Russians against the Chinese. Among Communists, this sort of argument is very serious indeed and is an important element in the Sino-Soviet confrontation.

More concrete and understandable to the non-Marxist are the territorial disputes between the two countries. It would be a mistake, however, to overestimate these disputes, which could be settled rather easily, given the will on both sides to do so. After all, during the years immediately following the Chinese Communist victory in China, the Soviets and the Chinese signed a treaty of alliance and cooperated in every conceivable way without reference to any substantive territorial issues existing between the two countries. Only after difficulties in relations arose in other areas was the matter of territory raised by Peking.

The Soviet Union also accuses the Chinese of imperialism, of hegemonism, and of having a desire to conquer the world. The Soviets state that Mao Tse-tung had a virulent hatred of the Russians and that this position is maintained by Teng Hsiao-p'ing. The Soviets seem to fear the Chinese. They are not concerned about their military power being a direct threat to Soviet territory at this time, but they presumably are afraid of a future powerful China.

Of great immediate concern are Chinese activities in other countries. While the Chinese are unable to provide economic assistance to developing countries to the same extent as the Soviets, the Chinese do what they can to work against Soviet interests in these countries. This is particularly annoying to the Soviet Union in those countries that are inclined toward socialism. Moscow sees itself as the cradle of world socialism and the fountain of socialist wisdom. To be challenged by Peking on the matter of socialist orthodoxy in countries with leaders leaning toward or professing Marxism is something that Moscow finds close to intolerable.

The Sino-Soviet confrontation as seen in relations with developing countries in Asia assumes more than an ideological meaning when it involves support by the two communist states to so-called people's liberation movements and to Communist governments already in place, such as in North Korea and Vietnam. Those who head these movements and governments must choose between Moscow and Peking or walk a very fine line indeed. Most important to Moscow, though, is the relationship that is growing between the United States and China. The Soviet Union reserves its severest criticism for what it calls the U.S. effort to build up China.

When the United States made its first moves to improve its relations with China in 1971, the Soviets reacted with restraint. Officially, the Soviet position was that it was only natural that Washington and Peking begin to normalize ties. Unofficially, however, the Soviet Union expressed apprehension about this development and about what they considered to be Washington's temptation to play China against the Soviet Union. As one high-ranking Soviet official put it, the Russians are not fearful of China by itself, but are concerned about China with the United States behind her. Certainly this is in part true; but in fact, other Soviets express grave concern over a strong China with or without American involvement.

Soviet military forces arrayed against China are very great (see Figure 9-1). There are now some forty-four Soviet divisions, about 400,000 men, stationed along the Sino-Soviet frontier. While the numbers of military personnel have not increased in recent years, the weaponry has grown in size and has been qualitatively much improved and modernized. According to the *Asian Security 1979* publication of the Japanese Research Institute for Peace and Security (Tokyo, 1980), SA-6 and SA-9 SAM were added to the border force arsenal in 1977, and SS-20 IRBM are believed to be employed in the Trans-Baikal and Siberian military districts. T-64/72 tanks are said to have been introduced, and Major General Yoshino Inaba of the Japan Self-Defense Force reported in October 1969 that some thirty TU-26 Backfire bombers are now stationed in the Irkutsk region, north of Mongolia and west of Lake Baikal. These Backfire bombers have been added to some 2000 combat aircraft in the Soviet Far East, including 500 air force and navy bombers, 1400 air force and air defense force fighters, and 140 navy patrol aircraft plus transport and support aircraft.

Soviet military capabilities in northeast Asia will be enhanced with the completion of the BAM (Baykal-Amur Main Railway) project. This will be an important complement to the Trans-Siberian Railway. The construction status of BAM, taken from *Asian Security 1979*, is shown in Figure 9-2.

Soviet military might assembled against China in Soviet Asia would not appear to be sufficient to launch a full-scale invasion of China all along the frontier. However, Soviet forces would clearly be able to

Figure 9-1. Soviet Military Deployment in the Far East.

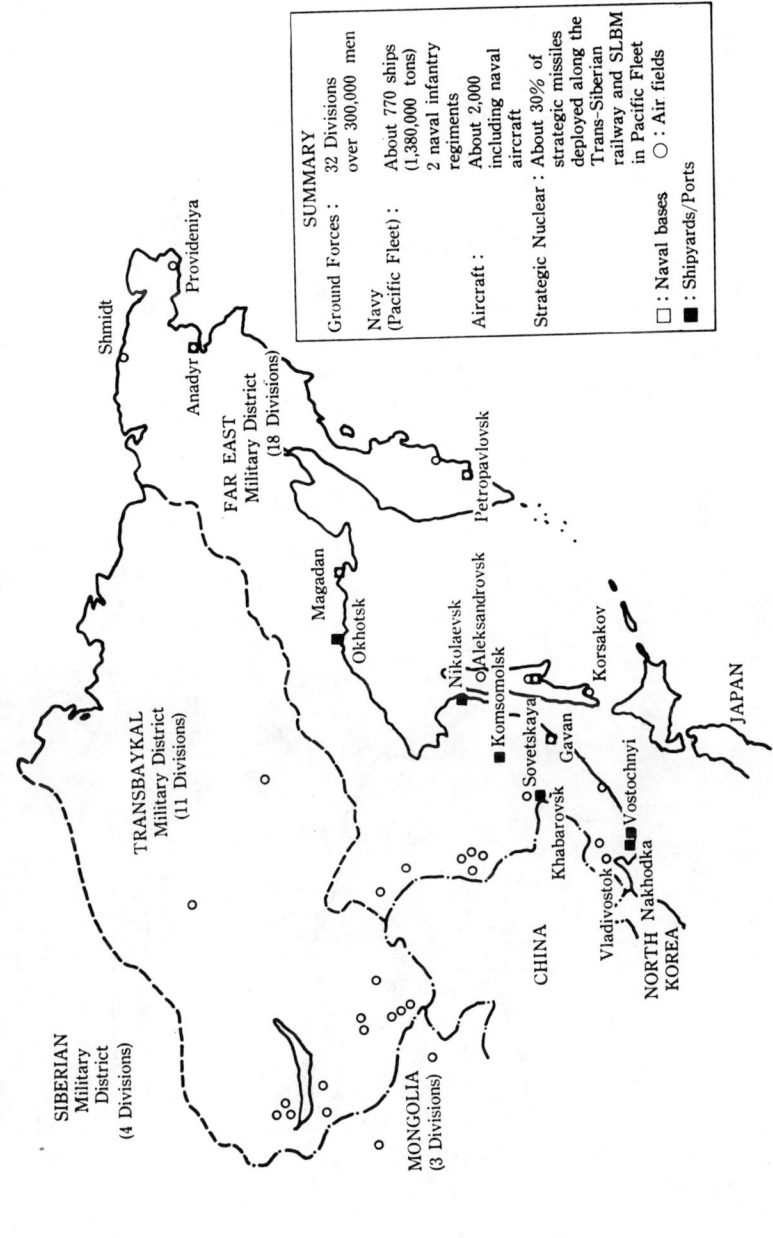

Source: *Asian Security 1979*. Tokyo: Research Institute for Peace and Security.

Figure 9-2. The Baykal-Amur Main Railroad.

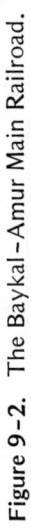

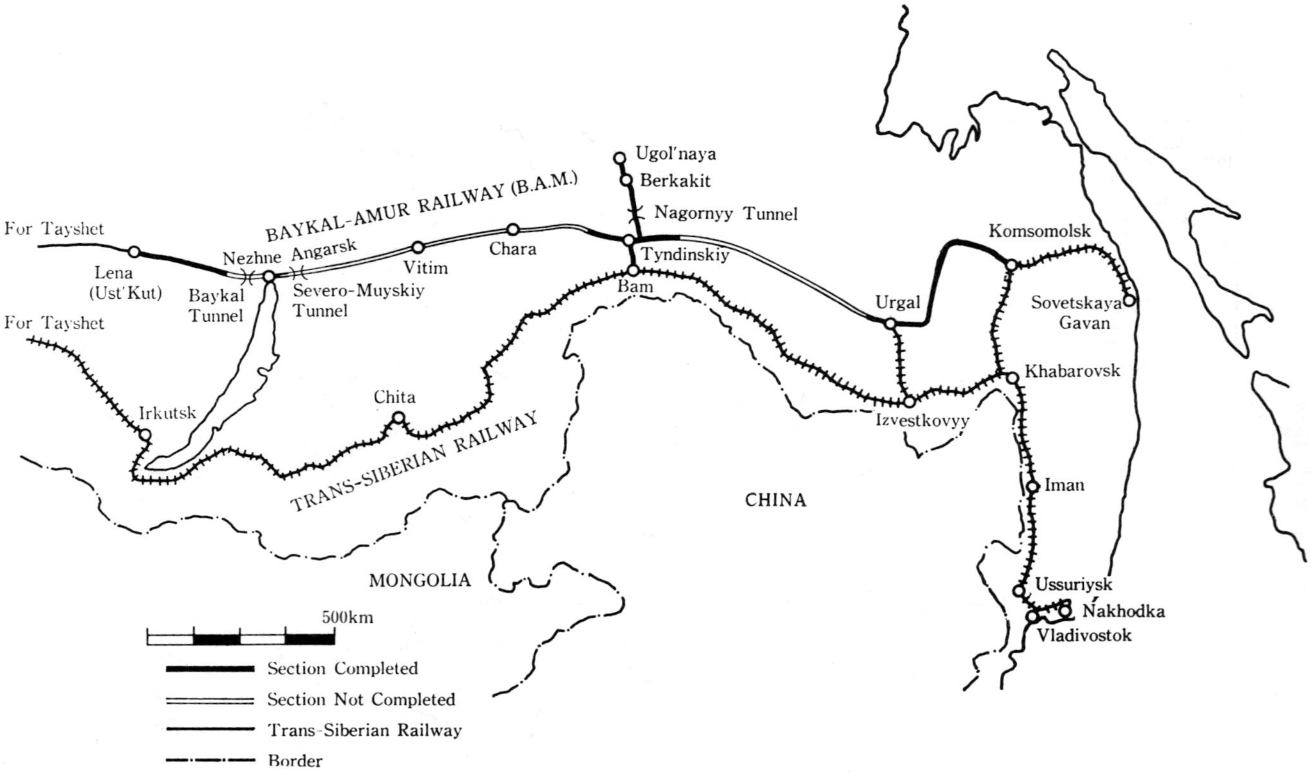

Source: Asian Security 1979. Tokyo: Research Institute for Peace and Security.

defend the Soviet Union against a Chinese attack and could probably successfully occupy part of Manchuria or Sinkiang if this were their mission.

The major purpose of Soviet deployment of forces against China now may be deterrence. The Soviet Union is, in effect, warning the Chinese not to go too far in their anti-Soviet activities and to restrain any tendencies they may have to try once and for all to put an end to Vietnamese military and paramilitary activities in Southeast Asia. Another purpose may be to have Soviet forces positioned to be able to play a role, undetermined and vague at this point, if a politically confused and unstable situation developed in China.

While recognizing that the present Soviet policy toward China is one of antagonism and confrontation, it may not always be this way. Certainly the Soviet Union would like to have a less strained relationship with China and will work to achieve this in the future. Given the differences between the two, any substantive agreements may seem far in the distance. However, it is probable that trade will continue to increase in the coming years and that some territorial arrangements may be reached. It is less likely that Moscow and Peking will be able to settle their ideological conflicts and to sublimate their fundamental dislike and distrust of one another. However, it would be dangerous to conclude that "never the twain shall meet," and Moscow will make every effort to convince Peking, as well as other Asian states, that the United States is weak, vacillating, and untrustworthy and that to rely upon the United States for political, economic, or military backing is not only foolish, but dangerous as well.

SOVIET POLICY TOWARD KOREA

Publicly the Soviet Union fully supports North Korean claims to be the only legitimate government on the Korean peninsula. Moscow professes close friendship with Pyongyang and provides the North Koreans with economic and military assistance, though on a somewhat reduced scale from previous years. The reason for this reduction seems clear: Kim Il-sung has moved his country and its policies closer to China than to the USSR. In February 1980, for instance, at a Communist conference in Sofia, North Korea refused, along with Rumania, to vote in favor of the Soviet-run government in Afghanistan.

This does not mean, however, that Moscow does not exercise influence over Pyongyang. After all, North Korea is still a client state in its relation to the Soviet Union, and in the event of a military conflict on the Korean peninsula, North Korea would need Soviet support and aid. In fact, Moscow's grudging assistance is required now as a needed stimulus to North Korea's ailing economy.

While it is impossible to be certain, Soviet authorities make it clear in private that the Soviet Union counsels Kim Il-sung to think in cautious and prudent terms as he considers his policy toward the Republic of Korea. They say that Moscow has forcefully told the North Korean leader that Russia does not want to see a military conflict in Korea.

Though the Soviet Union has not officially altered its attitude of nonrecognition of the Republic of Korea, it has, nevertheless, in recent years, allowed growing contacts between its citizens and citizens of South Korea. In the summer of 1979, for instance, a number of political scientists participated in the International Political Science Association meeting in Moscow. But despite these signs of moderation, it is unlikely that the USSR will change its policy of fully supporting the Pyongyang line, including the highly significant policy of urging the withdrawal of all American military forces from the Republic of Korea. This, after all, fits with the broad Soviet objective of weakening the U.S. security position in Asia and of undermining the confidence of U.S. allies in American security commitments.

SOVIET POLICY TOWARD SOUTHEAST ASIA

Prior to the complete takeover of Vietnam by North Vietnam in 1975, the Soviet Union was, together with China, a chief military and economic supplier of Hanoi. Without Soviet assistance, Hanoi could never have achieved its surprising victory.

After the war, Vietnam had to choose whether to depend for postwar aid upon Moscow or upon its neighbor and the other great contributor to its victory, Peking. The choice was a comparatively simple one given the historical antagonisms between the Chinese and Vietnamese, the geographical propinquity of China and Vietnam compared to the thousands of miles separating Vietnam from the USSR, and the wherewithal of the Soviet Union relative to that of China.

Vietnam's decision to move closer to the Soviet Union could be discerned in 1975 and 1976 with the large influx of Soviet advisors into the country and the few Chinese advisors to be found in Ho Chi Minh City (Saigon) and elsewhere throughout the country. Cambodia, on the other hand, received almost a surfeit of Chinese personnel, with a noticeable lack of any significant Soviet presence. The stage was being set for a confrontation between Soviet and Chinese surrogate states in Southeast Asia.

It is uncertain just how much influence the Soviet Union has had on the Vietnamese policy of confrontation with China. One thing is clear, however: The Soviet Union gives support to Vietnam and by so doing increases her influence and presence in that country.

In 1978 Vietnam became a member of COMECON, the Soviet economic network, and in December of the same year the Soviet Union and Vietnam signed a treaty of alliance. This treaty seemed in part a reaction to the Sino-Japanese Treaty of Peace and Friendship initialed earlier, but it also set the stage for the Christmas 1978 invasion of Cambodia by Vietnam. In effect, the Soviet Union was warning China not to interfere in Vietnamese attempts to control Cambodia and, eventually, to exercise hegemony over all of Indochina.

China, for her part, refused to accept the Soviet warning in full, and recognizing that lack of any action against Vietnam would be interpreted by other Southeast Asian states as an inability to counter Vietnam and the Soviet Union not only in Indochina but in the area as a whole, China attacked Vietnam border regions in February 1979. Following the Chinese attack, the Soviet policy in support of Vietnam began to emerge clearly.

Soviet officials spread the word that Moscow would not interfere directly in the Sino-Vietnamese conflict unless it appeared that China was attempting to bring down the Hanoi regime or to occupy the entire country. There were intimations that the Soviet Union, if need be, would send pilots to Vietnam to fly in battle formation, as had been done in the Korean War, but that this would be the extent of direct Soviet involvement. Meanwhile, the Soviet Union was rushing all kinds of supplies to the Vietnamese.

The Soviet Union was able to benefit in some ways from the Sino-Vietnamese border fighting. Moscow told the world that the Soviet Union was exercising great restraint by not taking direct action against China, even though, according to Moscow, it would be perfectly within its rights to do so in accordance with the

1978 Soviet-Vietnamese treaty. Also, Moscow said that the Chinese had received a bloody nose from the Vietnamese and that instead of China teaching the Vietnamese a lesson, as Teng Hsiao-p'ing so loudly proclaimed, the facts were just the other way round. Hanoi had beaten back the Chinese attacks, inflicting severe losses on the Chinese army.

Perhaps most importantly from Moscow's viewpoint, the Southeast Asia conflict has strengthened Vietnam's reliance on the Soviet Union. Vietnam must have military and economic support from the USSR to survive and to rebuild. It seems a certainty that the Soviets will demand a price for this support that will require Vietnam to relinquish some of its sovereignty at least on foreign and military security policy. Vietnam, as mentioned earlier, is already tied to Moscow economically through its allegiance to COMECON.

Soviet ships are using Da Nang and Cam Ranh Bay, the two large naval bases of Vietnam built by the United States in the 1960s. The Soviets maintain that their utilization of these ports is at a minimum and that the reason the number of Soviet ships entering Da Nang and Cam Ranh Bay has increased is because of the Chinese threat to Vietnam. They say that if such a threat did not exist, then the Soviets would not need these two great bases. This is a chicken-and-egg argument, given the fact that the Chinese military move against Vietnam was largely a result of Vietnamese action against Cambodia, which began only some thirteen days after the Soviet-Vietnamese treaty of alliance was signed. Whatever the purpose, there is little doubt that ships of the Soviet Pacific Fleet are beginning to dock in Da Nang and Cam Ranh Bay with increasing frequency and that the use of these bases by the Soviet Union gives an added dimension to Soviet naval power in the Pacific and Indian oceans.

The Soviet Union maintains correct, but not particularly cordial, bilateral relations with the ASEAN (Association of Southeast Asian Nations) countries of non-Communist Southeast Asia. Moscow now has formal diplomatic ties with all of these countries, but other relations, including economic, are minimal.

The Soviet attitude toward ASEAN itself changed in 1979. Initially, Moscow strongly condemned the formation of ASEAN. Lately, however, the Soviet Union has indicated that ASEAN is an organization that might be able to contribute to the economic development of its members and is not a threat to any other states in the area. Cooperation, which seemed a possibility between Vietnam and the

ASEAN countries prior to Hanoi's invasion of Cambodia, now is delayed, if not shelved for the foreseeable future. The ASEAN countries, in no uncertain terms, condemned Vietnam's action against Cambodia and have expressed their concern about the refugee matter. On this latter issue, the question of the refugees from both Vietnam and Cambodia, the Soviet Union has shown indifference. It can be assumed, however, that the Soviets supported the Vietnamese expulsion of Chinese residents in Vietnam from that country.

The future policy of the Soviet Union and Vietnam in Southeast Asia has to be a matter of some concern to the non-Communist states in the region and to the United States and Japan. Vietnam may have dreams of achieving a dominant position in the mainland of Southeast Asia, but this will not be easy to accomplish without Soviet support. Both China and the United States would have to be neutralized by Soviet threats of military confrontation to make such a dream realizable.

Thus, to assess Vietnamese intentions in Southeast Asia, once again we must look at the United States and the Soviet Union. If the United States stands firmly behind Thailand, for instance, it is not likely that Vietnam, backed by the Soviet Union, will attempt to extend its influence into that country by force of arms or by conducting flagrant subversive activities.

THE SOVIET COLLECTIVE SECURITY PLAN

In 1969, the president of the Soviet Union, Leonid Brezhnev, unfolded what came to be known as the Soviet Collective Security Plan for Asia. Brezhnev took advantage of U.S. involvement in Vietnam to seize the initiative and make this proposal. The object was to isolate China and eventually to cause a break in U.S. security arrangements in Asia, particularly in the U.S.-Japan Security Treaty. The Soviets pushed this Brezhnev proposal with great vigor for a number of years, but the reaction in most Asian capitals was extremely cool. While the Soviets denied that the plan was designed against China or the U.S. alliances with Asian states, very few Asian leaders took these denials at face value. By the mid-1970s, while the Soviets had not withdrawn the Collective Security Plan, they rarely spoke of it.

However, in meetings between Soviets and Americans in the late 1970s, the Soviet side often referred to the Collective Security proposal and defended it as a serious contribution to the discussion of ways to increase the prospects of peace and stability in Asia. The Soviets also said that they never had any intention of excluding the Chinese from any collective security system and that the United States would not have to abrogate its present security treaties with Asian states if it agreed to a collective security system such as the Soviets have proposed. There is little or no chance that the Soviet Collective Security Plan for Asia will ever be adopted, much less seriously discussed among Asians.

THE SOVIET PACIFIC FLEET

One of the most increasingly powerful instruments of Soviet military power in the Asian area is the Soviet Pacific Fleet. Since 1970, in particular, this fleet has grown in strength and has been a major contributor to the efforts of the Soviet Union to foster its influence in Asia. The main purposes of the Pacific fleet are to help defend the territory of the Soviet Union itself and of Soviet allies in the region, to enhance Soviet prestige and interests in Asia, and to further Soviet political objectives.

While the Soviet Pacific Fleet, in addition to Soviet land power, serves as a deterrent to the Chinese, this naval component of Soviet power is fundamentally designed to counter U.S. and Japanese naval strength in the Pacific, centering, of course, on the U.S. Seventh Fleet, the forward-deployed element of the U.S. Pacific Fleet. What is happening is that the Soviet Union is challenging the Seventh Fleet and is attempting to neutralize the U.S. Navy's ability to secure the commitments of the United States in the Pacific. This is to be accomplished by increasing the numbers of both ships and aircraft assigned to the fleet and by upgrading the quality of the vessels and planes.

Various estimates have been made by official Japanese and American sources regarding the exact strength of the Soviet Pacific Fleet. Japanese numbers, to be found in *Asian Security 1979*, exceed U.S. estimates. This difference in estimates seems to be based, in part at least, on the Japanese count of minor combatants, such as patrol boats and torpedo boats, which would be a great danger to the Japanese coast. But both Japanese and U.S. sources agree that the Soviet naval growth in the Pacific is a matter of grave concern (see Figure 9-3).

Figure 9-3. Outline of Soviet Ships and Military Aircraft Movements Around Japan.

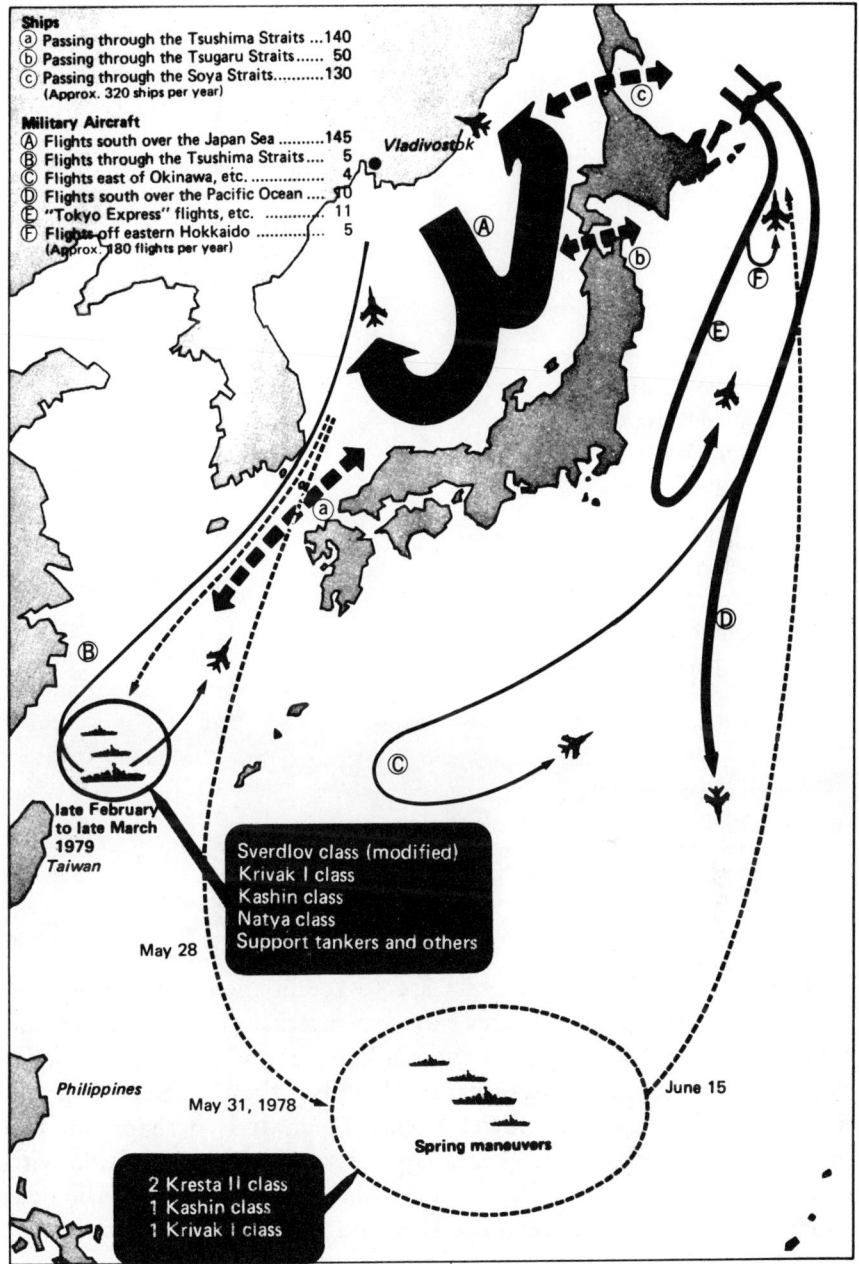

Note: The numbers of the ships and flights denote averages during the past five years.
Source: Defense of Japan 1979. Japan Defense Agency, Tokyo, Japan.

According to the U.S. Navy's unclassified Soviet Naval Order of Battle Estimates of October 1979, the Soviet Pacific Fleet is now a formidable force. These estimates are as follows:

Categories	Official Navy Estimates
Attack Submarines	85
Ballistic Missile Subs (SSBNs)	30
Total Submarines	115
Aircraft Carriers	1
Major Surface Combatants	77
Total Major Combatants	78
Amphibious Ships	20
Patrol Craft	30
Mine Warfare Ships	50
Mine Warfare Craft	45
Total Minor Combatants	145
Underway Replenishment	25
Material Support	20
Fleet Support	35
Other	140
Total Auxiliary Ships	220
Total Ships and Submarines	558
Tactical Aircraft	110
Support Aircraft	70
Anti-Submarine Warfare Aircraft	120
Utility Aircraft	60
Total Naval Aircraft	360

If U.S. commitments in Asia are to retain their credibility, it is critical that the United States move to increase the strength of the Seventh Fleet. The danger to the sea lanes of the Pacific, so crucial to U.S. and Japanese interests, are obvious if the U.S. Seventh Fleet becomes inferior to the Soviet Pacific Fleet. It is perhaps not too much to say that the Soviet strategy for success in competition with the United States in the Pacific and Asian region rests upon the relationship of strength between the U.S. and Soviet fleets.

CONCLUSION

Soviet policy in the Pacific and Asia, increasingly military in nature, epitomizes both Soviet fears and Soviet confidence. On the one hand, the Soviet Union is concerned over the long-term implication for Soviet security of an anti-Soviet, militarily and economically modernized China. Moscow believes that the United States may be doing its best, aided and abetted by Japan, to build up such a China. Above and beyond this, the Soviet Union fears the establishment of a kind of alliance or entente among the United States, China, and Japan that would encircle and threaten the USSR and, at the same time, severely curtail Soviet actions in Asia.

These worries, however, are counterbalanced by Moscow's confidence in its military power. In the global setting, Soviet military power is growing and may indeed surpass that of the United States. The Soviet Union sees itself as a global power with a duty to give assistance to Soviet friends and allies in various areas of the world. The Soviet Union is also looking for weaknesses in the industrialized world's armor and will take advantage of these whenever they may appear. If possible, Moscow will also help to create these weaknesses.

It is probably true, however, that the Soviet Union does not desire a military confrontation with the United States, so long as the U.S. nuclear and conventional war deterrent, in terms both of actual weaponry and of resolve, remains undiminished. If the United States remains strong, it is likely that the Soviet Union will exercise caution in the use of its own military forces and will recommend caution to Vietnam and North Korea. But Moscow, recognizing the United States as its main antagonist, will do everything it can to subvert U.S. interests and to portray the United States as weak and ineffective in its security relations with its Asian and Pacific allies.

10 AN OUTLOOK ON CHINA IN THE 1980s
A Political Turnabout at Home and Improvement of Relations with the USSR

Mineo Nakajima

Experienced observers of the Sino-Soviet conflict cannot agree among themselves over the future of the relationship and the possible implications for defense strategies of the United States and Japan. Professor Mineo Nakajima, an expert on modern China at the Tokyo University of Foreign Studies, believes that China will continue on its current course toward the Four Modernizations under rational economic leadership, but he is not convinced that the intense Sino-Soviet rivalry will continue. In fact, he ventures a prediction that the two huge Asian nations may draw closer together at the party or government level some time in the mid- or late 1980s and cautions that Japan should adopt a "diplomatic strategy flexible enough to withstand possible changes in Sino-Soviet relations."

CHINA'S TURNABOUT AND THE CONTRADICTIONS INVOLVED

Any attempt at the difficult task of making predictions about China in the 1980s should begin with a correct analysis and understanding of the country's situation today. The People's Republic of China, which celebrated its thirtieth anniversary in 1979, is now undergoing a tremendous change. Representing an unprecedented turn away from its foundation on the ideology of Mao Tse-tung thought; this change involves many contradictions as well as favorable possibilities for the future. China today is facing a struggle between its past and present.

I visited China in June of 1979, my third visit to that country. The first was in the fall of 1966, when, just after the beginning of the Cultural Revolution, the Red Guards were running rampant. The second was in early 1975, during the "Anti-Lin Piao, Anti-Confucius" movement, when I traveled by myself from Moscow through Ulan Bator to Peking—crossing the tension-ridden Sino-Soviet border and entering Peking from the West. On my last visit I saw the country after the fall of the Gang of Four. As an observer who had been watching the turbulent situation in China for more than a dozen years, I saw with real amazement the vast change taking place in Chinese society.

In the first place, as I had expected, Maoism was fast becoming a discarded theory, although it was still upheld officially. Unlike the late Premier, Chou En-lai, Mao himself was now only nominally adored by the people, and the nation was finally coming to form a tacit consensus that Mao was a modern "Qin Emperor." This tendency was reflected in the fact that the Fifth National People's Congress at its Second Session gave top priority to democratization of institutions and codification of laws, as well as to the coordination of the "Four Modernizations" program, and declared that no leader is great enough to be above the law. It is noteworthy that the leader of this codification movement was Peng Zhen, who used to be the municipal leader of Peking and was an important target of the Cultural Revolution. In short, all this change was based on the serious conclusion that Chinese society cannot enjoy stability or growth unless socialist construction in China is upgraded from the level of "popular struggles" and institutionalized in the framework of national democratization. Thus, China is trying to institutionalize de-Maoization.

The Cultural Revolution is now being totally repudiated, and it is evident that today the term stands for everything evil. In fact, everything that was overthrown by the Cultural Revolution is being restored and turned around. It is important to note that China today is not only repudiating the Cultural Revolution but rehabilitating practically everyone victimized by Maoism since the mid-1950s. Economic leaders of the early 1950s like Bo Yibo and Bi Muqiao are now coming back as popular figures; and Ding Ling, the famous woman novelist who went down after being branded as an "antiparty writer" in the antirightist movement of 1957, has once again appeared in good condition in a photo in *The People's Daily*. China is beginning to review and even disapprove of the process it has been through since the radical collectivization of farms in the late 1950s. Since the process was led by Mao, it is clear that China is turning against Mao's socialist construction policy.

Second, in considering what China is going to be in the 1980s, it is important to note that its "Four Modernizations" program (for modernizing agriculture, industry, national defense, and technology) involves contradictions. The program underwent substantial amendments (which actually meant reduced goals) in the form of "coordination, reorganization, streamlining, and upgrading" at the last session of the National People's Congress. It had initially been proposed by the realist group led by Chou En-lai and Teng Hsiao-p'ing as a political tool for de-Maoization during Mao's reign. This was not the kind of practical, concrete economic program for quick growth of the Chinese economy that Japanese big business hoped to find in China after the recent rapprochement between the two countries.

Since the Third Plenum of the Eleventh CCP Central Committee, at which Chairman Hua Guofeng and other leaders of the Cultural Revolution right wing criticized themselves, and Vice-Chairman Chen Yun and other old economic leaders were reinstated in important positions, the Four Modernizations program has finally been established as a universal national cause and can no longer remain a political struggle slogan. It is a national program that must be implemented strenuously. Teng Hsiao-p'ing himself—the chief promoter of the policy—seems to have stressed at the Third Plenum of the Central Committee that the Four Modernizations program should not be treated merely as a rosy vision but should be translated into a feasible form.

One problem with this program is that it requires an immense amount of capital (estimated at US$600 billion for the original version of the program), while China's foreign exchange reserves total less than $3 billion. How to raise the needed capital is not the only problem. Having gone through political and social confusion for more than a dozen years, China is still without social systems for effectively controlling the economy—that is, its infrastructure is quite underdeveloped. Improvement of such economic circumstances cannot be done in a day.

Moreover, if the Four Modernizations mean rationalization of operations and mechanization of production in various sectors of the economy, the program will save labor, of which China has plenty. Thus, how to absorb and reassign the nation's vast surplus labor will be a big problem. Both the leadership in Peking and field executives at plants and people's communes are aware of this contradiction inherent in the modernization program.

Some estimate that China's population is already in excess of one billion. The government is hoping to reduce the natural population growth rate from the present 1.2 percent to 0.5 percent by 1985 and to achieve zero growth in population by the end of the century. But this ambitious population control goal seems very difficult to reach. Moreover, Peking's current stoic policy of enforcing stringent birth control and encouraging late marriage will be increasingly hard to maintain in the new "open China," although it has been practicable in the old "closed China." Some people in Chinese society are already beginning to argue that this unusual policy represents an oppression of human rights.

The third social problem in China today concerns the backwash of the Cultural Revolution and the new social pathological symptoms created by the process of change to an "open China." As unfavorable consequences of the Cultural Revolution, it will suffice at this moment to mention the tendency to vagrancy and delinquency of urban youths sent to rural areas for training, the general demoralization and opportunism of the cadres, and the emergence of an extensive group of dropouts represented by the "rural people coming up to town" from the lowest level of agrarian society to demand rehabilitation from false condemnation in the past and to ask for jobs. As many social values are being radically upset, increasing contacts with Japan, the United States, Western Europe, and the rest of the West are causing the Chinese people to show symptoms of "moral subservience to foreigners"—such as the "cult of the West" and "yearnings for Japan"—in reaction to the old prevalence of xenophobia. At the same time, some aspects of "old China" are beginning to reappear in various sectors of Chinese society, which, in fact, was never reformed completely even in Mao's days. China today is faced with the vital task of properly controlling these and other social problems and establishing new standards for its society.

CHINA AT THE POINT OF NO RETURN

Should we now expect that the political and social conflicts inherent in China today are so great that the country is likely to go through another process of political turbulence and swing radically once again from right to left? After the deaths of Mao and Chou, China experienced the ghastly "Tian An Men Square Incident" and the shocking political change in Peking (the downfall of the Gang of Four) in 1976 and has since been undergoing de-Maoization. From the way the country appears today, it does not seem likely that another radical change in domestic or foreign policy will occur soon. In other words, it now seems impossible to reverse the pragmatic trend against the Cultural Revolution—to go back on the policy laid down by the late Chou En-lai, who sought "de-Maoization under Mao" after the failure of the Cultural Revolution. Why?

The most important reason may be found in the objective, historical position in which China today finds itself. After a decade of political turmoil following the Cultural Revolution, the Fourth National People's Congress held its First Session in January 1975, and at this meeting, Chou En-lai delivered a political report—a kind of political legacy in which Chou prescribed China's future in the form of a "Four Modernizations" program aimed at building up modern industrial and economic systems in China. Whatever difficulties are in store for the program, China today has social and national reasons that compel it to proceed, without turning back, in the direction called for by the program. The old cycle of moderation and radicalism, which has been repeated consistently in the process of domestic construction since the foundation of the People's Republic, can no longer be repeated since decisive changes of the early 1970s. This was earlier demonstrated in a paradoxical way by the pay raise demands of the workers participating in the Hangzheu Incident of 1975.

This social development, like the Tian An Men Square Incident with its anti-Maoist implications, is even more significant than such political developments as the Lin Biao Affair in predicting the future of Chinese society. The same necessity makes China want to deal with other countries in a more open, stable way. Unless "Chinese world order" is threatened in peripheral areas along its borders, as in the case of the recent hostilities with Vietnam, resulting in a serious loss of Chinese prestige in the world, it seems that China in the 1980s will have to seek such open relations with the rest of the world while taking meticulous care to maintain the balance of power with other major powers including the Soviet Union.

It should be noted that about 85 percent of China's external trade is already accounted for by trade with Japan, the United States, Western Europe, and other Western areas (Japan alone accounting for about 25 percent). Despite this structural change in Chinese trade, however, there will always be the possibility of China's trading more with the Soviet Union again. Thus oriented, China is beginning to reduce the esoteric nature of its political leadership. Erich Fromm, discussing the significance and functions of ideology in de-Stalinized Soviet society, wrote that what matters in evaluating the foreign policy of the Soviet Union is no longer its ideology but its social, political structure.[1] Similarly, China will soon reach the stage in which its social and political structure rather than ideology will count. Then the Teng Hsiao-p'ing type of leaders, once criticized as realists or "capitalist roaders" (such as Peng Zhen, Chen Yun, and Hu Yaobang, who is younger), will make the right party leadership orthodox and realistic enough for a nonideological type of regime.

Another reason why China cannot reverse its course soon again is the fact that China cannot afford to lose any more time in launching a long-range economic construction program—that is, a full-scale industrialization program. China's awareness of this fact will become keener as it learns more about the outside world. For example, liberation of Taiwan, despite Peking's loud calls for it, is actually not feasible either militarily or socially, and per capita GNP in Taiwan is likely to be, even in a conservative estimate, seven to eight times that of mainland China's in the 1980s.

Indeed, the People's Republic has never followed a specific economic construction policy consistently for five years. Apart from the economic rehabilitation period immediately following the revolution, China has been through a highly unstable series of economic policy phases, including the first five year plan period marked by the "General Transitional Policy," the second five year plan period characterized by the "Great Leap Forward," the economic readjustment period following the failure of the "Great Leap Forward," and the period of confusion during the Cultural Revolution. Clearly, China

---

1. Erich Fromm, *May Man Prevail? An Inquiry into the Facts and Fictions of Foreign Policy* (New York: Doubleday and Company, Inc., 1961).

cannot afford to undergo all this instability again. Today, China is in a position to participate fully in international affairs, while at home the people can no longer be enthused by the Mao Tse-tung type of revolution, envisaging an utopia in poverty. Under these circumstances, China can only hope to ensure the success of the revolution by bolstering it with material wealth rather than ideological or moral strength through the implementation of a full-scale economic construction program. Thus, China today has no alternative but to walk the long way toward an open society by carrying out the Four Modernizations program, whatever difficulties that may involve and whatever vicissitudes may lie ahead.

What will become of China tomorrow? After a quarter century of turbulence and faced with various difficulties today, the country may look forward to eventually developing a unique socialist society, but such a rosy prospect is still far off. At present, Chinese society is undergoing changes involving symptoms of something similar to Soviet revisionism. This tendency may be inevitable in socialism, although the society of China differs in some basic respects from that of the Soviet Union. Some of the choices made by the Peking leaders, whether they are aware of it or not, make one feel that they are going beyond Soviet revisionism and trying to find a solution in the Yugoslav type of mixed economy. In China's case, this path runs very close to reviving the old China, since Chinese society is a traditional, agrarian one with many elements inherently inimical to socialism. When the national policy of the Chinese Communist party is swallowed up in this traditional society, China will be a vast, commonplace developing country with an immense population in Asia.

What will become of China is of vital concern not only to the Chinese themselves but indeed represents the greatest question in the history of civilization in the twentieth century. Perhaps China may also turn out to be the biggest "North-South problem" in the present world.

CHINA'S FUTURE AND RELATIONS WITH THE SOVIET UNION

Sino-Soviet relations, which will have much to do with internal political trends in China, must be of vital interest to the United States, Japan, and other Western countries. Today, relations between

China and the Soviet Union are so strained that we may well say they are in a state of cold war with each other. Peking's conflicts with Moscow have always been related to policy arguments within the Chinese Communist party (CCP), and whether true or false, charges of intimacy with the Soviet Union have always been hurled at such losers in intraparty policy fights as Wang Ming, Gao Gang, Peng Dehuai, Liu Shaoqi, and Lin Biao when they were condemned. There is no denying that Peking's view of and policy toward the Soviet Union have been closely related to policy struggles within the CCP. We cannot ignore the historical fact that relations with Moscow have been a more or less constant factor built into the internal behavior of the party.

If a significant change in Sino-Soviet relations is conceivable, to what extent might they improve? Will they change so importantly that the United States will be compelled to radically amend its world policy? Will there be a monolithic Sino-Soviet unity again that will be firm enough to threaten Japan's security?

To make valid predictions on these questions, it is essential to analyze the structure of Sino-Soviet discord. Sino-Soviet antagonism today consists of conflicts at four different levels, one resting upon another and forming a complex whole: (1) conflict between the two peoples or their nationalisms, (2) conflict between the two states or their egoisms, (3) conflict between the ideologies of the two countries or between their respective "heresies," and (4) conflict between their governments or between their foreign policies. These may be called respectively nation-to-nation conflict, state-to-state conflict, party-to-party conflict, and government-to-government conflict.

Referring to the first—nation-to-nation conflict—which is the deepest-rooted, the history of contacts between the Chinese and the Russians in the last 300 years is full of conflicts. The two great peoples have lived opposite each other on the Eurasian continent with the vast Mongolian territory lying between them as a sort of intermediate zone, and their competition for the control of this area has led to the hot rivalry between the two nations.

The second conflict, state-to-state, is based on the first and has been carried on historically over border and territorial issues. Indeed, it quickly damped the Leninist spirit of internationalism intoned in the Karakhan Manifesto (1919) following the success of the Russian Revolution. The subsequent emergence of Stalinism in the Soviet

Union and Maoism in China provided ideological justifications to their respective nationalisms or state egoisms, making them more exclusive of each other in their conflict at the interstate level. Generally, journalists and foreign policy experts tend to call diplomatic or intergovernmental conflicts discords "interstate." But what I mean by the "state-to-state conflict" here is one between two states aware of their different stands based on their respective nationalisms and ideological justifications, rather than a conflict in intergovernmental or diplomatic relations (which belongs to my fourth category).

The third conflict, party-to-party, refers to what began as the Sino–Soviet dispute in 1956 and is still continuing as an ideological conflict between the Communist parties of the two countries. In the general context of Sino–Soviet antagonism, the conflict at this level theoretically seems to be subject to change. Partly because Sino–Soviet relations have often depended on internal fights within the Communist parties of the two countries (especially that of China), it is always possible that this third conflict could be significantly affected by developments in such intraparty struggles and leadership changes.

The fourth conflict, government-to-government, can change not only in accordance with leadership changes and new developments in the party of each country but also with changes in international relations.

From the above considerations, it may be reasonable to assume that the Sino–Soviet conflict at the nation-to-nation level will probably remain irreconcilable. The conflict at the state-to-state level also will be hard to resolve unless, in some distant future, the existing social, political, and economic gaps between the two countries are filled. On the other hand, the conflict at the third level, party-to-party, may change as the result of a leadership change; and the government-to-government conflict is subject to change at any time. It should be remembered in this connection that the current Sino–Soviet antagonism began with Mao Tse-tung's intense antipathy against the Soviet Union and the latter's reaction to it and represents the culmination of a process in which the Sino–Soviet conflicts at the above-mentioned four levels have been growing in a complex, integrated form. Hence, Sino–Soviet conciliation was quite impossible while China was under Mao's leadership and will remain very difficult so long as the CCP leadership persists in its present Maoist view of the Soviet Union. Within the limits of the fourth conflict, however, it is theoretically possible to think of some improvement in Sino-Soviet relations under the impact of some international developments, such as an unfavorable turn in Sino-U.S. relations.

As we have seen, China today is undergoing extensive de-Maoization at home, and it is no longer possible to reverse this trend. Leading the nation in this direction is Teng Hsiao-p'ing. With respect to his leadership and its future, it should be noted that although he is indispensable to China today, his intense personality often jars with his colleagues. After attending the twenty-first Congress of the CPSU in 1956, where de-Stalinization was launched for the first time; Teng spoke severely of the evils of personality cult in a report on amendments to the party rules delivered before the Eighth Congress of the CCP that year. In the early 1960s, while playing a leading role in China's dispute with the Soviet Union (at Sino-Soviet talks held in the summer of 1963, for example, he had a hot wrangle with CPSU Politburo Member Suslov in Moscow), he supported Luo Rui, then PLA chief of general staff, in his argument for a united front with the Soviet Union in the Vietnam War. Luo lost his position on account of this proposal and was not reinstated until 1975. This shows that Teng's view of the Soviet Union was basically different from that of Mao Tse-tung, who refused to regard the Soviet Union as a socialist society and flatly rejected the idea of an anti-imperialist united front with that country.

Thus, so far as the influence of China's internal affairs on relations with the Soviet Union is concerned, it should be noted that circumstances are maturing in favor of possible improvements in Sino-Soviet relations at the party-to-party as well as the government-to-government level. Under these maturing circumstances, China will—in the 1980s, at least—try to form its relations with other countries while paying constant attention to the "Soviet card." Despite the historic rapprochement with Peking, the U.S. Congress approved the Taiwan Relations Act by an overwhelming majority. Faced with this unexpected development, China was extremely careful in the spring of 1979 to serve notice of its intention of letting the Friendship, Alliance and Mutual Assistance Treaty with the Soviet Union expire, thus avoiding excessive provocation to Moscow and paving the way for Sino-Soviet negotiations at the vice-ministerial level. This suggests that Peking already has the "Soviet card" in its hands, and we should always remember that it is China itself, after all, that ultimately holds that card.

Of course, it may be argued that Sino-Soviet relations are generally unlikely to improve, since China today must depend on Japan, the United States, and other Western countries for assistance in the implementation of its Four Modernizations program, or that China will continue to need an outside archenemy to keep the people united in surmounting internal difficulties arising in the course of national modernization. As we have seen, however, analysis of the structural makeup and historical background of the Sino-Soviet antagonism indicates that important circumstances are now maturing in favor of possible changes in the conflict. Personally, I feel that a significant change might occur in Sino-Soviet relations in the late 1980s—sometime after 1985—when China will probably be faced with still greater difficulties in carrying out the Four Modernizations and may no longer feel freshness in relations with the West and also when Teng Hsiao-p'ing's present leadership will have to be replaced with a new group of leaders in Peking. Around that time, the Soviets also will probably be switching their current military expansion policy involving aggressive strategy in Asia due to a slowdown in the growth of the Soviet economy. When both countries thus find themselves in serious economic difficulties, will they continue to antagonize each other as they do now?

Since a wishful expectation of continued antagonism between the two countries lies at the basis of U.S. world policy today and since a significant improvement in Peking-Moscow relations can be a diplomatic threat to Japan, we tend to accept too readily the desirable prospect of a world with Sino-Soviet antagonism.

International communism and relations between socialist countries are no better than common international relations in changeability and amplitude of change. Today we look with amazement at the fact that Albania, which used to be China's only reliable ally and served as its mouthpiece for a very long time in its dispute with the Soviet Union, is now seriously at odds with Peking and is hurling strong accusations at the Chinese Communist party. President Tito of Yugoslavia, who had been Peking's long-time enemy, accused of "modern revisionism" and also annoyed by attacks from Albania "in his backyard," visited China at a late stage in his career, where he received a big welcome and had opportunity to look north from the top of the Long Wall with a great emotion in his heart—a very ironic historical event.

Finally, I would like to point out that there is a basic difference between the stands on Sino-Soviet relations held by the United States and Japan, although they are bound together in the U.S.-Japanese-Chinese coalition, which might be viewed as an antihegemonist alliance. Located in East Asia, Japan has to deal far more extensively with China and the Soviet Union than does the United States, which as a global superpower is in a position to carry on a détente policy in the Europe-Atlantic area and an antihegemonist policy in the Asia-Pacific area, dealing with the Soviet Union and China across the Atlantic and the Pacific, respectively. Geographically destined to form a triangle with the Soviet Union and China in East Asia, Japan is in a more exposed position than the United States in dealing with these two Communist powers. It is important to note that the Washington-Tokyo-Peking coalition, though very convenient to the United States as the basis of its Asian policy aimed at counterbalancing the influence of the Soviet Union as a global superpower, is not equally convenient to Japan. This represents a potential new conflict within the U.S.-Japanese security system, since there are some areas of diplomatic relations with the Soviet Union and China in which Japan will find it impossible to share the U.S. stand completely. In other words, Japan has much less freedom than the United States in taking advantage of the tense relationship between Moscow and Peking and even manipulating it to some extent. Therefore, Japan needs a diplomatic strategy flexible enough to withstand possible changes in Sino-Soviet relations. At a time when friendly ties are being formed with China, Japan should give sufficient consideration to this foreign policy task of vital importance.

11 COMPREHENSIVE MUTUAL SECURITY INTERESTS OF THE MAJOR INDUSTRIALIZED DEMOCRACIES

James W. Morley

> *Dr. James W. Morley, professor of government at Columbia University, in this concluding essay examines the common interests of the United States, the other NATO nations, and Japan and explains why these industrialized democracies have committed so little to the common defense of their obvious mutual interests. Professor Morley points out that the comfortable habits of three decades, in which the United States shoulders the major military and economic burdens for its allies, must give way to a new sharing of responsibilities. Using a new and broader definition of "comprehensive mutual security," in the light of the new threats—particularly the threat of interruption of the flow of oil from the Middle East—Morley proposes a new strategy by which allied strength can be maintained simultaneously in Asia, Europe, and the Middle East and suggests a new way for the major powers to consult with each other on major security questions.*

Many of the advocates of trilateralism in the early 1970s believed that once the industrialized democracies of North America, Western Europe, and the North Pacific realized how much they had in common, and how extensively their economies and cultures were interacting with each other—in a word, how "interdependent" they were—they would see the wisdom not only of harmonizing their economic policies, but eventually of broadening their mutual concerns to include security as well. Zbigniew Brzezinski asserted in 1973, for example, that the "linkage" of these concerns already existed.[1] But so far, this expectation has been disappointed. Even with trilateralists in the State Department and the White House, U.S. summit conferences with Japan and Europe have confined themselves largely to economic matters, and even private groups like the Trilateral Commission have touched on security only gingerly. Why should this be so?

Richard H. Ullman argued from the beginning that the expectation was unrealistic.[2] The interests and capabilities of the three potential partners are simply too different. The United States, he pointed out, being a superpower with global interests and military forces capable of supporting them, naturally does have a deep concern for the security of both Western Europe and Japan. The countries of Western Europe, however, are not in the same situation as the United States. A number of these have global economic interests, but each is dependent on U.S. support, none is more than a regional military power, and none has the energy or the inclination to engage itself in security problems on the other side of the world. And Japan, while economically a great power, militarily does not have even regional pretensions. This "substantial asymmetry," he concluded, makes the security triangle more rhetorical than real. It lacks a West European–Japanese leg.

THE CONSTRAINTS THAT HAVE DIVIDED

It is perfectly clear that, similar though the major industrialized democracies (which for convenience we may refer to as the MIDs) have become in many respects, their different histories and geopolitical positions have indeed impeded the development of a common security consciousness. In the recent past, for example, each has given a somewhat different priority to its military defense. In the dark days following the end of World War II, there was little inclination on either side of the globe to do more than try to find one's way back to some kind of normalcy—to clear away the rubble of war and get on with the peacetime job. In Germany and Japan, occupa-

---

1. Zbigniew Brzezinski, "U.S. Foreign Policy: The Search for Focus," *Foreign Affairs* 51, no. 4 (July 1973): 725.

2. Richard H. Ullman, "Trilateralism: 'Partnership' for What?" *Foreign Affairs* 55, no. 1 (October 1976): 1–19.

tion directives enforced demilitarization. In the rest of Europe and in Canada and the United States, popular sentiment moved in the same direction. Swords were beaten into plowshares, and the fields of peace were readied for cultivation.

The Cold War ended all that, but in different ways for each of us. The United States reacted most strongly, raising its defense budget dramatically. It vastly strengthened its armed forces and offered its support for a global mobilization. The reaction in Europe was more moderate. Most European states accepted the U.S. offer of military assistance and alliance in the form of NATO, and the gradual rearmament of Germany was approved; but given the memory of war's devastation, the proximity of the Soviet power, the division of Germany, and the consequently deep appeal of détente, the share of resources allocated to defense was not so great in Europe as in America. Efforts to build a European defense community in the early 1950s grounded on the shoals of nationalism, and in the mid-1960s, France even pulled its forces out of NATO.

The Japanese response to the Cold War was even more restrained. The National Police Reserve instituted in 1950 was converted into the Self-Defense Force, with ground, naval, and air branches; and in 1952 Japan did enter into alliance with the United States. Nevertheless, budgeting for defense has been stabilized for years at the lowest level proportionate to the economy of any major state in the world, and constitutional provisions and public attitudes have placed unusual restraints on both the quality and deployment of even the small forces that have been raised.

For the Americans, whose confidence was high and whose economy was strong, an adequate defense seemed worth whatever it would cost. To the Europeans and the Japanese, it was not. They had suffered such catastrophic destruction during the war and their populations had been so demoralized by wartime death, destruction, and, for Germany and Japan, defeat that top priority had to remain what it had been before, the reconstruction of the economy and the rebuilding of the domestic political order. In Japan, in fact, even the desirability of defense was rejected by a majority of the people well into the 1960s. Thus, a pattern was set many years ago in which the incapacity and unreadiness of Europeans and Japanese to defend themselves was made up for by the United States. This enabled the Europeans and the Japanese to take defense matters less seriously than they would otherwise have been forced to do and to pursue an overall policy of economizing, concentrating their priorities on economic development.

The differential impact of these priorities on the security consciousness of each of the MIDs was compounded by the rise in that period in Japan and Europe of isolationist attitudes, which had characterized the United States a generation earlier, but had lost their force in the wartime and postwar years. Trade and travel have grown so much since World War II that one is inclined to forget that the expansion of the postwar economic relations of the European states and Japan was accompanied by a contraction in other concerns. In political and military terms, one should recall, Japan was a greater power in the first half of the twentieth century than it is today. It defeated China in war as early as 1894–1895. It fought Russia to a draw in 1904–1905. It sent a squadron to the Mediterranean to help its British ally in World War I. It was a charter member of the Council of the League of Nations. And in the late 1930s and early 1940s, it fought its way to domination over nearly all of Asia, bidding to be one of the three or four superpowers of a new world order. The contrast with its course in the post–World War II period is dramatic. Traumatized by defeat, most of its empire shorn away, and confronted by victors whose power had immeasurably increased, Japan gave up its dream of political power. Instead, it attempted to build a vast network of economic and cultural interchange as isolated from international politics as its alliance with the United States would permit. In spite of—or, as the Japanese would say, because of—the vulnerability that its global economic interdependence creates, throughout most of this period, it has been extremely reticent to protect its political interests by any action that might offend others. It has preferred instead to suffer losses where it must aggreeably and to place its trust in a diplomacy of "friends with everyone."[3]

Just as Japan has not been the world actor it once was, so too the European states are no longer the Asian actors they were in the days of empire before World War II. Most of the colonies that tied them to Asia have attained independence. The British are no longer the informal arbiters of the region as they were in the nineteenth century. The French and Dutch administrators have long since departed. European traders and investors still frequent the great entrepots of

---

3. This phrase is Okita Saburo's in "Natural Resource Dependency and Japanese Foreign Policy," *Foreign Affairs* 52: no. 4 (July 1974): 724.

the East, but their fleets do not follow. Since the French withdrawal from Vietnam in 1964, European states have shown little interest in the security of the Asian region except as it might distract the United States. It is hardly surprising that in their allegiance to economic goals and their renunciation of world leadership, the European states and Japan, on opposite sides of the globe, have failed to take the mutuality of their security very seriously.

These attitudes on the part of the Europeans and the Japanese were balanced by the almost opposite attitude in the United States. A relatively isolationist, economic power in the nineteenth and early twentieth centuries—assuming then that the world should welcome its economic thrust and refusing to interest itself seriously in political and military affairs beyond this hemisphere—the United States emerged from World War II as the single most powerful country in the world, confident of its abilities and determined thereafter to play a world leadership role. If economies were weak, it would aid them. If countries were threatened by military aggression, it would come to their defense. As a result, a pattern came to be set by which the then less confident policies and weaker economies of Japan and the European states (and others as well) were supported in their economist, isolationist positions by the willingness of the United States to bear a historically unprecedented share of the collective security burdens, in terms of both budget and geographical commitment.

One must recognize also that a better understanding among the three major democratic centers has been impeded by a serious institutional inadequacy, an inadequacy resting on a conceptual ambiguity. For the relationship we have been speaking of is no simple geometrical triangle. One angle gives no problem. It is clearly Japan, a single country with a single government to deal with. But the angle we referred to first as North America, and then for convenience as the United States, must unquestionably represent two countries, the United States and Canada, which while they have a great many common interests, do also have other interests less in common and certainly have governments with independent views and authorities. Troublesome enough, but Europe is the more difficult problem. Who speaks for Europe?

For military security purposes, most West European states (excluding, however, Ireland, Spain, Sweden, and Switzerland) coordinate their activities under the North Atlantic Treaty Organization (NATO). Forces assigned to it are led by the supreme commander of the Allied Forces in Europe. Policy is entrusted to the North Atlantic Council, made up of the permanent representatives from member states and a Secretariat and meeting on occasion with foreign ministers and heads of government. But NATO is not a supranational entity. Each member state continues to raise its own forces and to deploy them as it sees fit. It assigns some to NATO (except in the case of France, which assigns none), but reserves others for its own purposes, which may or may not be consonant with those of its NATO colleagues. If one were concerned with military security alone, the West European partner would seem to be for some purposes, especially for threats within the confines of Europe, the thirteen European government members of NATO as they relate to each other in the North Atlantic Council and in other circumstances, especially for threats beyond the confines of Europe, the fifteen or seventeen governments of the Western European states, acting in their individual capacities.

The confusion is compounded by a second ambiguity: Who speaks for economic issues related to security—for example, military production or supply? The European Community (EC) embraces only nine of the fifteen Western European states—or seventeen if Greece and Turkey are included. The EC has succeeded, for example, in establishing a common market, negotiating associations with certain LDCs and inaugurating a dialogue with the Arab states and ASEAN. The meetings of its foreign ministers have increasingly taken up economic issues with a defense relevance, such as the possible imposition of restraints on food sales, trade credits, and high technology exports to the Soviet Union in the face of the Afghan crisis. Nevertheless, the EC does not usually include military security within its purview and in any event does not replace the governments of its member states as political power centers.[4] In the seven nation summit conferences since 1975 it has not been the EC that is represented, but only its bigger members, acting independently—the United Kingdom, France, the Federal Republic of Germany, and Italy.

Observers differ as to the significance of these institutional complexities. Most have believed that they are a substantial barrier to the evolution of the Western European states into a more cohesive com-

---

4. Michael B. Dolan and James A. Caporaso, "The External Relations of the European Community," *Annals of the American Academy of Political and Social Sciences* 440 (November 1978): 135-155.

munity. A few have argued that the existence of such diverse institutions has provided essential flexibility, enabling the states to shift from one forum where a decision may be blocked to another where it may be facilitated.[5] But probably few would deny that these complexities complicate international relations. The Japanese government, at any rate, has had some difficulty in sorting all this out, as is clear from its experience in the EC-Japan trade negotiations throughout the 1970s. In spite of the growth in economic interdependence between Japan and the European states in this period and in spite of the mutual desire to put this trade on a more mutually satisfactory footing, the effort to negotiate a communitywide agreement with Japan has so far failed, leaving trade to be conducted according to agreements that had been negotiated with individual state members.[6]

A GROWING CONSCIOUSNESS OF MUTUALITY

And yet, as one lists the factors that over the past generation have constrained the industrialized democracies from perceiving or acting in their mutual security interests, one is immediately reminded of how much several of them have been eroded. The OPEC crisis of 1973 awakened the world, as the Japanese might say, like water poured in a sleeper's ear. The post–World War II shift from coal to oil as the industrialized democracies' basic energy source had been accomplished so smoothly and the oil suppliers had been so accommodating at that time that the vulnerability into which the MIDs had been slipping went largely unrecognized—until OPEC threatened to turn off the spigot. Even then, the allies were perplexed about what to do, seeing the threat as largely economic and therefore perhaps best handled by economic measures of conservation, stockpiling, assistance to the suppliers, and the like. But the Iranian Revolution in 1979 has shown how inadequate these measures were; and now the Soviet invasion of Afghanistan puts the oil supply from the Per-

    5. The positive case is argued in Glenda G. Rosenthal and Donald J. Puchala, "Decisional Systems, Adaptiveness, and European Decisionmaking," *Annals of the American Academy of Political and Social Science* 440 (November 1978): 54-65.
    6. Hosoya Chihiro, "Relations Between the European Communities and Japan" (paper presented to the XIth World Congress of the International Political Science Association, Moscow, August 12-18, 1979).

sian Gulf in a wholly new jeopardy. Neither the United States, Western Europe, nor Japan can now escape from the questions: What must be done to protect oil supplies in the Persian Gulf? And who is to do it?

These questions have a special urgency because they come at a time when there is widespread recognition that the continuing increase of Soviet military power and the greater willingness of the Soviet Union to use its own or proxy forces to attempt a shift in the regional power balance in the Third World pose a significantly greater threat to MID security than was formerly felt. Japan is directly affected, for example, by the strengthening of Soviet deployments in the Southern Kuriles, and augmentation of the Far Eastern fleet based at Vladivostok and Petropavlovsk, and the powerful support given to Vietnam in its war to establish predominance over the Indochinese peninsula. European states are especially deeply concerned by the Soviet activities in Angola, Ethiopia, and elsewhere in Africa. The United States feels challenged by the Soviet's Cuban proxy in the Western Hemisphere. And all of the MIDs recognize the danger posed by Soviet activities in the Middle East.

Thirty years ago, the response to what was then perceived to be a global Soviet threat was the sharp increase in the U.S. military budget, the formation of a network of mutual security arrangements pivoted on the United States, and the deployment of American forces to forward bases the world over. The heightened threat perception of the 1980s, however, can hardly be met in the same way. For one thing, the economic gap among the MIDs has been closed. The per capita GNP of each of them is now roughly the same. The German and Japanese economies, while smaller than the American, are widely seen as fundamentally stronger. The argument that a disproportionate share of the new burden should be borne by the United States, therefore, has lost persuasiveness.

For another reason, the prevailing attitudes are not what they were. In the United States, the weakening of détente has not led simply to a revival of the old Cold War attitudes. There is a heightened sense of danger and a revived readiness to increase military strength and take on new duties in the Middle East, but there is at the same time, partly as a result of the military failure in Vietnam and the economic weakness revealed in the current recession, a consciousness of limitation quite unknown in the first Cold War period. The United States is ready to do more, but the scale and direction of its efforts will be heavily affected by the willingness of the allies to act more equitably where shared interests are concerned.

Fortunately, there seems to be a growing understanding of the changed circumstances in both Japan and Western Europe. In Japan, the widespread pacifism and passivity of the early postwar years has been giving way to a new realism.[7] The self-defense forces and the U.S.-Japan Security Treaty are now being supported by the overwhelming majority of the Japanese people.[8] The Japanese Maritime Self-Defense Forces this past winter for the first time engaged in the multinational Rimpac training exercises with the United States, Canada, Australia, and New Zealand. And the opposition parties agreed in January for the first time to the creation of a special committee on security affairs in the Diet. Few leaders are calling for a dramatic change in the military budget or a significant expansion in the area for which Japan should accept some defense responsibility, but there are an increasing number of persons in the highest places who recognize Japan's dependence on the world security environment and who call for a more politically activist foreign policy. Two years ago, the then director general of the Japan Defense Agency, Kanemaru Shin, proclaimed on his return from Europe, "The security of the world is tied with one string."[9] In a speech this past March, former Foreign Minister Miyazawa Ki'ichi referred to what he boldly called the "alliance relationship" among the three democratic power centers and called for "closer consultation and coordination . . . particularly in regard to such political and security-related issues as the Afghanistan problem."[10] And during the course of the past winter and spring, the late Prime Minister Ohira's denunciation of the Iranian seizure of the American Embassy, his condemnation of the Soviet invasion of Afghanistan, and his announcement that his government would take "appropriate measures" to help persuade the USSR to withdraw all show a new toughness in Tokyo.

The change is evident in Western Europe, too. While there is a deep reluctance in Europe to antagonize the Soviet Union and

---

7. For the background of this change, see James W. Morley, "A Time for Realism in the Military Defense of Japan," in Franklin B. Weinstein, ed., *U.S.-Japan Relations and the Security of East Asia: the Next Decade* (New York: Westview, 1978).

8. Research Institute for Peace and Security, *Asian Security, 1979* (Tokyo, 1979), p. 170.

9. *Yomiuri*, July 1, 1978, p. 7.

10. Miyazawa, "To Meet the Challenge" (speech to the Trilateral Commission London Plenary Meeting, March 23-25, 1980) (mimeo).

acknowledge the tenuousness of détente, the sending of fleet units by several of the allies into the Persian Gulf area, the willingness of most of the EC countries to impose at least some penalties on the Soviets for their Afghan move, and the interest of European leaders in discussing such topics at the EC meeting in Venice in June 1980 confirm the view that the major European democracies have come to recognize that their mutual security concerns do indeed extend beyond Europe. The fact that these same subjects could be added to the agenda of the seven nation summit conference that followed shows that a new sense of the mutuality of their security interests is affecting all three of the democratic power centers.

COMPREHENSIVE SECURITY

Given these changed circumstances, the time has clearly come when we should be examining as carefully as we can the real extent of the common security interests of our three centers and raising the question of whether some new institutional arrangements are needed to advance them. To begin with, we must come to a common understanding that we are not just talking about military matters. Access to energy and other natural resources, markets, technology, and capital are as vital to the national survival of our democratic industrialized states as the physical defense of national territory. The problem is that we are so used to thinking of oil as an energy problem or trade and capital flows as economic problems, and we are so accustomed to turning to scientists, engineers, and economists for the explication of their technical complexities, that we frequently fail to appreciate that each may—and usually does—have a national security aspect.

In Japan, the phrase "comprehensive national security" has come into widespread usage to refer to some of these aspects.[11] It began chiefly as an informal budgetary conception, relating expenses for defense to those for such "grey area" items as were perceived to have a bearing on the nation's overall security such as cultural exchange, development aid, research and development, and reserves of oil, food, and other raw materials.

---

11. See, for example, Saeki Ki'ichi, ed., *The Search for Japan's Comprehensive Policy Guideline in the Changing World: National Priorities for the 21st Century* (Tokyo: Nomura Research Institute, September 1978), p. 27.

This has proved to be a useful device for focusing the nation's attention on the security problem in a meaningful and acceptable way; and on July 2 this year, a prestigious private advisory group recommended that comprehensive national security be made an important new governmental policy focus. The establishment of a national security council was proposed, its province to include all matters of vital concern to the nation's livelihood, such as relations with the United States, policies toward the Soviet Union and the PRC, the strengthening of Japan's own self-defense efforts, the stabilization of energy and food sources, and the handling of large-scale earthquakes.[12]

Each nation at any one time would have its own list of areas that it feels are vital to its security, but if one views national security from this comprehensive point of view, one must acknowledge immediately that the interests of the three democratic power centers are not only overlapping, but are inextricably interlinked.

For more than thirty years, for example, Japan, the Western European countries, the United States, and Canada have acknowledged that the sale of strategic goods by any one of them to the USSR or the PRC may affect vitally the security of the others, and they have worked to harmonize their relevant export policies within the Coordinating Committee (COCOM) and the China Committee (CHINCOM). The organization of an international nuclear regime that would guarantee to each (and to others) the fullest possible development of the peaceful uses of nuclear power while providing safeguards against the proliferation of nuclear weapons has also been a strong mutual security interest, one that has already manifested itself in the signature by most of these countries of the Non-Proliferation Treaty, the institution of the International Atomic Energy Agency, and most recently their participation in the International Nuclear Fuel Cycle Evaluation program. Their participation in the Law of the Sea Conferences also has been motivated not only by their more purely economic interests in the extraction of marine and sea bed resources for productive purposes, but also by their directly security-related concerns—for example, in the extension of national sovereignty over larger and larger areas of the hitherto open seas and

---

12. Report of the Comprehensive Security Research Group, appointed by former Prime Minister Ohira and Inoki Masamichi, *Mainichi shimbun*, July 3, 1980 (morning edition), p. 1.

the possibility of new regimes by which passage through strategically important straits may affect their defense capabilities.

Similarly, each has participated heavily in the efforts to restructure the international economic order, whether it be through the GATT, the IMF, or the various agencies at work on the North–South problem — in major part, of course, for economic purposes, but who could deny that the healthy resolution of the issues involved is vital to the ability of each country to provide the goods and services to its people that will both motivate and enable them to defend themselves? And surely it is obvious that the mutual concern for their oil supply, which brought about the establishment of the International Energy Agency and the agreement on conservation, stockpiling, and the like, stems in real part from their mutual recognition that the supply of each depends on the action of all and that without a guaranteed supply, the security of none is possible.

The provision of military and development assistance by any one of these countries is clearly of common security interest. It can serve to stimulate the international environment in ways that enhance the security of all, or it can — in some cases by granting and in other cases by not granting — exacerbate the tensions that others fear. The regular participation of these countries in the Development Assistance Committee of the OECD therefore clearly has security as well as economic implications. And after all, how effective can the political policy of any one of the industrialized democracies be if decisions as to recognition and cooperation — or withdrawal of these as in response to the Iranian seizure of American Embassy personnel, the Vietnamese invasion of Cambodia, or the Soviet invasion of Afghanistan — are not taken in close consultation with the others?

But, it may be said, institutions already do exist for such consultation. Why should anything more be done? The answer is that most of these institutions were set up almost exclusively to meet needs identified in the economic and political fields. Consequently, economic and political technicians are sent to talk to their counterparts about the economic or political consequences of action. Security specialists are rarely included in such delegations, and the security relevance of the issues confronted is often not taken up — at least not directly. Moreover, these various issues are not generally considered as integral parts of a comprehensive mutual security interest, which must embrace military defense issues as well.

THE NUCLEAR QUESTION

As a matter of fact, the more specifically mutual military defense issues of the MIDs are not taken up anywhere. Does this indicate that in fact these countries do not have important military concerns that are mutual? I do not believe so.

Symbolically, the Strategic Arms Limitation Talks (SALT) have come to be taken as the centerpiece of American-Soviet détente, the evidence that the two superpowers, for all their rival ambitions and enormously destructive capabilities, are sincere in their professed desire to avoid plunging the world into a nuclear holocaust—and indeed may eventually even find a way together to reduce the nuclear stockpiles they have accumulated. The difficulties in negotiating SALT II, therefore, created deep uneasiness in Europe and in Japan—as elsewhere. The preliminary public criticism and the subsequent shelving of consideration of the SALT II Treaty by the U.S. Congress in the wake of the Soviet invasion of Afghanistan in late 1979 deepened the sense of insecurity in both Europe and in Japan. Our allies know full well that when the elephants fight, the grass gets trampled.

They are anxious, therefore, to see SALT reinvigorated but of course not if it is symbolic only. They share, after all, a direct, practical interest in the United States' maintaining at least parity in the central strategic nuclear balance with the Soviet Union. It is in large part America's maintenance of this position and its readiness to use it in Europe's and Japan's defense that justifies the trust each of the allies has placed in its mutual security arrangements with the United States. Given this vital dependency, it is surprising that the Europeans and the Japanese have not been more interested in the details of SALT, where, since 1969, the limits on the central nuclear build-up have been negotiated.

It is difficult to imagine that this can continue. While Europeans and Japanese clearly wish to leave the negotiation and maintenance of the central nuclear deterrent balance to the United States, they have become increasingly uneasy, especially since the deployment of the SS20s began, that the United States may not be able to keep up the strategic forces required, that it may decouple these forces from the defense of the European theater, or that in its readiness to strike a central balance, it may enter into negotiations concerning or ignoring the variable range weapons without sufficient sensitivity to the impact on the theater balances.[13] The United States has tried to counter these fears by insisting in SALT that the independent nuclear fears of Britain and France as well as its own forward-based systems (FBS) should be excluded from the negotiations and by offering to strengthen these systems by stationing in Europe a new force of Pershing II and cruise missiles. But the new missiles are not yet deployed. The Soviets are maneuvering to have the decision reversed. The British are looking seriously at Tridents. The French are pushing ahead with their own neutron bomb. The French and Germans are exchanging views separately with the Soviet Union. Thus, the question of Europe's defense is placing an increasing strain on NATO, with some elements continuing to call for reliance on the overseas U.S. strategic arsenal, others for building a theater balance of Europé-based forces, and others for minimizing weaponry and emphasizing détente. Under these circumstances one can not imagine future U.S.-Soviet SALT negotiations without a strengthening of the interallied consultative machinery and, some would say, more or less direct participation by the major European powers. Nor can one imagine that the Japanese can remain indifferent to these developments, for the central balance affects their security as much as that of the Europeans, and the concepts and policies being fought out about the Eurostrategic balance have obvious relevance to the western Pacific theater as well.

Of course, Japan has no nuclear weapons of its own. Indeed, it has pursued a firm policy of the three nots: It will not possess nuclear weapons, it will not make nuclear weapons, and it will not allow them to be deployed on its soil. And since the return of Okinawa to Japanese administration in 1972, the United States has kept no nuclear systems there either. But that is not to say that the Japanese would not be vitally affected by any limitations SALT may impose on American intermediate range nuclear weapons systems, for it is confronted by massive Soviet deployments based only a few miles away in Siberia. As a result, if Japan were to suffer a Soviet attack beyond the capacity of its own and conventional American forces to resist, its safety would have to be found most immediately in the

13. Christopher J. Makins, "Bringing in the Allies," *Foreign Policy* 35 (Summer 1979): 91-108; and Robert J. Pfaltzgraf, Jr., "Western Europe and the SALT II Treaty: an American View," *The Fletcher Forum* (Winter 1980): 99-108.

nuclear-armed carrier forces of the U.S. Seventh Fleet and under certain circumstances in U.S.-based bombers, ICBMs, and nuclear-armed submarines that are part of the central strategic umbrella.

Japanese security is also affected indirectly by the back-up these Soviet forces could give to the Democratic People's Republic of Korea, should the DPRK again become engaged militarily with the ROK. Japan has always had a special security interest in the Republic of Korea. Since 1952, South Korea has consistently been included within the perimeter of the "Far East," the region for whose security Japan has offered the United States the use of its bases. As recently as 1977–1978, Japan showed the liveliness of its interest in Korea by expressing deep concern over President Carter's announced intention to reduce American ground forces there, forces that for many years have been augmented by the U.S. deployment of theater nuclear weapons.

In addition, there is the question of the People's Republic of China. China, of course, has proclaimed that it will never be a first user of nuclear weapons, but it has shown no interest in participating in SALT or even in signing the NPT. It has already built a nuclear force capable of striking as far away as Eastern Europe, most of Asia, and Alaska and Hawaii; and in May 1980 it successfully tested an ICBM. In view of the hostility that has characterized Sino–Soviet relations since the late 1950s, the USSR has consistently argued that in striking a strategic nuclear balance, the PRC must be calculated on the anti-Soviet side. But for the United States and its allies, the question is not so simply resolved. While Chinese nuclear weapons are at the moment benign and the strategic interests of the PRC and the MIDs are in many ways "parallel," there are areas of divergence and ambiguity, such as Korea, Taiwan, and Indochina, and there remain serious uncertainties about China's future course. In these circumstances, and given the stake that Europeans and Japanese have in the size and effectiveness of the U.S. nuclear umbrella, it would seem that the evaluation of China's nuclear capacity and decisions about possible countermeasures are as much concerns of Japan and of Europe as of the United States.

There can be no doubt that SALT agreements between the United States and the USSR and deployment of Soviet, Chinese, or American forces affecting the balance of central strategic or theater nuclear forces within the western Pacific will vitally affect Japanese security. While the Japanese have so far shied away from serious involvement with these issues, the community of interest they have in these matters with U.S. allies in Western Europe seems undeniable.

THEATER DEFENSE

Just as the Japanese and Europeans have a deeper mutual interest than either has yet articulated in the maintenance of the central strategic balance and in theater nuclear deterrence, so too have they a greater mutual interest than so far perceived in the overall defensive capability, conventional as well as nuclear, that each is able to mount in its own theater. The principal responsibility for theater defense is, of course, borne by the theater states and their allies. So far, the Western European states have not evinced much interest in Japan's defense problems, nor has Japan shown much interest in those of Western Europe. To a certain extent, in fact, they have acted as rivals, each side recognizing that the United States has major commitments to the other, but each at one time or another feeling undercherished in its suit for U.S. military attention and fearful that in time of crisis the United States might be too busy elsewhere to respond to its needs effectively.

During the Indochina War, it was the Europeans chiefly who were worried, fearing that the United States was allocating so much of its attention, budget, manpower, and material to the Asian–Pacific theater that it was allowing its central strategic forces to decline and failing to modernize sufficiently its military forces in Europe. The Japanese have never seen it that way. To them, Europe has always seemed to be the primary theater for Americans. For years they read with apprehension the annual Defense Department posture statements, in which it was emphasized that the United States was prepared to fight only one and a half wars at a time, that the "one" war was assumed to be a "NATO war," and that therefore not only was the United States most heavily deployed in Western Europe, but in time of emergency was committed to "swing" over even its Pacific-based forces to the NATO theater. For a while during the 1970s, U.S. withdrawal from Indochina and from Taiwan and the reduction of ground forces in Korea led many Asians to conclude that a permanent U.S. withdrawal from Asia was actually in progress.

Since 1979, the United States has moved strongly to assuage these fears. It has increased the U.S. defense budget. It has agreed to beef up its forces in Europe. It has halted the U.S. force reduction in Korea, successfully renegotiated the U.S.-Philippines Defense Treaty, made other improvements in the U.S. posture in the region, and at last, in the spring of 1980, reportedly dropped the obligatory "swing" strategy, deciding to exclude its Pacific-based forces from those it is obligated to use for Europe's defense.[14]

The dropping of the obligatory "swing" strategy does help to strengthen the equality of America's commitment to the two oceans, but it hardly solves the fundamental problem of too few forces for too many needs. Rather, that problem has been highlighted: Now the Europeans can count on less American support than before. And our principal allies and friends in the western Pacific, while pleased with the change, are well aware that the old strategy has been dropped not so much out of a heightened recognition of their local needs as in response to newly competitive ones in the Middle East. A new third front has opened up, threatening the security of all three of the industrialized, democratic power centers. Under the balance of forces that had formerly obtained in that region, the United States was able to meet its own and its allies' military requirements in the Middle East by only occasional visits by units under the Pacific command. But with the Iranian Revolution and the movement of Soviet and Soviet-backed military forces, two powerful aircraft carrier groups have been deployed from the Seventh Fleet, a rapid deployment force is in the making, and more or less permanent facilities are being sought in the region.

The reason for such a powerful response is obvious. Since the OPEC crisis of 1973, all industrialized states have become acutely aware of their dependence on energy suppliers. Among all suppliers, none are so vital to each of the democratic centers as the Muslim states in the Middle East. Were there to be a prolonged interruption in the flow of oil from this area, as might be occasioned, for example, by a spread of the Iranian style disorder or by external attack, the effect on the security of the MIDs—and others—would be profound.

As U.S. Defense Secretary Harold Brown put it, "If the industrial democracies are deprived of access to those resources, there would almost certainly be a worldwide economic collapse of the kind that

---

14. Richard Burt, "U.S. Strategy Focus Shifting from Europe to Pacific," *The New York Times*, May 25, 1980.

hasn't been seen for almost 50 years, probably worse.... There's nothing our allies can do in the coming decades that would save them from irreversible catastrophe if it were cut off."[15]

In fact, so disastrous would a cutoff be that none of our states has been able adequately to come to grips with it. Each has taken modest steps to cultivate the Middle East countries with trade and aid, and each has tried to arouse its own people at home to the need to conserve oil and to develop alternative energy sources, but neither the NATO countries nor Japan has found a way to free itself from vital dependence on the Middle East within the foreseeable future. And with the advent of revolution in Iran and a military crisis in Afghanistan, the United States has felt forced to move into the Middle East forces originally recognized as essential to the defense of the Far East and Western Europe. This can be no more than a stopgap solution.

What is needed is a mutual understanding among the industrialized democracies that the maintenance of an adequate defense force in each of the three theaters—Western Europe, the western Pacific, and the Middle East—is vital to the security of each of us. This can perhaps best be seen if one considers the possibly adverse outcomes if defensive balances are not kept. If the defensive balance is not kept in Europe, for example, there are two possible adverse outcomes: The opponent may feel encouraged to undertake hostile action there to the damage of Europe or to shift his western forces southward to the Middle Eastern front or eastward to the western Pacific front, thus upsetting the balance in these regions. A failure to maintain the balance in the western Pacific area sets up a similar possibility of damaging the defense of Western Europe or the Middle East as much as Japan. And in a similar way, an imbalance in the Middle East threatens to upset the defense capability on all three fronts.

Consider, second, the situation that may develop if the theater defense is weakened and an attack came either in that theater or in another and the response is to swing forces away from the unthreatened theaters to the threatened one.[16] The war is immediately escalated in the theater of first action, and a new danger is incurred that it may well spread to these other theaters to deter the "swing."[17]

15. As reported by Richard Halloran in *The New York Times*, February 15, 1980.

16. It should be noted that in dropping the former "swing" strategy, the United States is giving up the *obligation* to swing its Pacific-based forces to NATO's defense not the option to do so if it chooses.

17. The Atlantic Council Policy Study, *Securing the Seas*, by Paul H. Nitze, Leonard Sullivan, Jr., and others (Boulder: Westview, 1979), p. 221, adds another reason for not

Finally, consider the situation in which a defensive balance is kept in each theater. The likelihood of war is seriously reduced, and even if it should come, the Soviet Union would be hindered from concentrating its forces lest it be counterattacked in other theaters. The essential point is that it is very much to the advantage of Western Europe and Japan as well as the United States to keep the Soviet theater forces divided, facing three fronts—the European, the Middle Eastern, and the western Pacific—and pinned down on each by forces sufficiently strong to deter any moves to concentrate forces or cross borders. But how is adequate defensive strength to be maintained in each of the three theaters?

There would seem to be at least three options. One is for the United States unilaterally to so expand its effort that it can hold the Middle Eastern front without drawing down the forces committed to the Far East and to Europe. This is wishful thinking; there will immediately be demands in America that our allies do their share as well. A second option might be for the Europeans and the Japanese to join with the Americans to build a joint force for the Persian Gulf; but given the divergence of views in Europe, the complexity of combined operations, and particularly the unwillingness of the Japanese to consider sending troops abroad, this too seems unrealistic. The realistic option would seem to be more complex—for the United States and certain countries, such as Britain and France, which may be so disposed, to send forces into the region and for the other European states and Japan to compensate for these redeployments by increasing their own capabilities for defense in their own regions. But for this to be accomplished successfully, extensive consultation among all of the powers concerned is required. Thus, in spite of the attitudinal differences and institutional weaknesses that in the past have caused the Europeans and the Japanese to seek their security separately from each other, the mutuality of their security interest has become as demonstrable as that of their political and economic interests, and the recognition of that fact is beginning to take hold among leaders on both sides of the globe. What then is to be done?

---

diverting U.S. naval forces from the Pacific to the Atlantic in time of a "NATO" war—the need to reassure the PRC, so that it will remain outside the Soviet orbit.

A SECURITY SUMMIT

This is not the time for building elaborate formal structures—a new multilateral or NATO-Japan collective security treaty. The Europeans and the Japanese know far too little about each other. The threat perception is not high enough. The constraints are far too strong. Advocates of such a proposal should bear in mind that even after more than twenty-five years of close cooperation between the United States and Japan, there is still no joint command or agreed force commitments to their mutual defense. Moreover, given the division of comprehensive security responsibilities in Europe between the EC, NATO, and other bodies and the continuing parochialism of the security concerns of the smaller European states, neither NATO nor the EC would seem to make a really satisfactory partner.

What is needed, rather, is a looser facility, an arrangement for intergovernmental consultations that facilitates the exchange of ideas on all kinds of comprehensive security issues, from the economic to the military, but respects the integrity of each government's concerns and decisional processes. Fortunately, there is already an institution in place that should be readily adaptable for this purpose—the annual seven nation summit conference. Organized in 1975 to take up economic questions of mutual interest, by 1980 it had proved flexible enough to add a session on political issues. There would seem to be no reason why in the future the agenda could not include comprehensive security as well.

Summits, of course, have no supragovernmental authority. They commit no budgets, stockpile no oil, and move no ships. On the other hand, they already include the core group of major industrialized democracies—the United States, Canada, the United Kingdom, France, Germany, Italy, and Japan. They help to legitimize the topics they take up. They help to form as well as symbolize certain attitudes. They help to focus the attention of the world. They serve to mobilize the energies of their own governments. They can, therefore, especially if given regular staff support at the working level, help each government to identify concrete policies that would not only improve its own security, but at the same time would be mutually supportive of the community as a whole.

Such consultations, of course, should supplement, not replace, other relationships. The era when the world might have been divided into exclusive blocs has passed. Today, the external needs of every state, and particularly those that are highly industrialized and open, such as the major democracies, are so diverse that no single association can satisfy them. France, for example, sells weapons to Saudi Arabia in exchange for oil, sends its troops to French-speaking Africa, and maintains a nuclear deterrent—all outside NATO. The United States has security understandings throughout the world, each separate from the others—as exemplified by its adherence to the NATO and U.S.-Japan Mutual Security treaties. Outside the field of military security, the situation is more complex, so that a modern state is like the hub of a wheel, linked to the world around by many different spokes. For any of the industrialized democracies, their relationship with each other is only one such spoke, but it is a spoke that is indispensable.

APPENDIX: Data Tables

COMPARISONS OF DEFENSE EXPENDITURES, 1979

Country	$ Million	Percent of GNP (1978)
United Kingdom	17,572	4.7
France	18,776	3.3
Germany	24,391	3.4
United States	114,503	5.0
Japan	10,083	0.9

Note: National currency figures have been converted into U.S. dollars using the rates prevailing at the end of the first quarter of the relevant year.

Source: The Military Balance 1979–1980 (London: International Institute for Strategic Studies, 1980).

1979 PROVISIONAL DATA FOR ODA NET DISPERSEMENTS

Country	Percent of GNP	$ Millions
France	0.59	3358 (1978: 2705)
Germany	0.44	3350 (1978: 2347)
Japan	0.26	2638 (1978: 2215)
United Kingdom	0.52	2067 (1978: 1456)
United States	0.19	4567 (1978: 5664)

Notes: "Aid" or "assistance" refers only to flows that qualify as "ODA"—that is, grants or loans (1) undertaken by the official sector, (2) with promotion of economic development and welfare as main objectives, or (3) at concessional financial terms (if a loan, at least 35 percent grant element). In addition to financial flows, technical cooperation is included in aid.

Sources: Information and data are from *Development Cooperation: 1979* published by the OECD. Provisional 1979 data are from OECD official news bulletin.

These figures are in current—that is, 1979—dollars. Exhange rates are annual averages from the IMF International Financial Statistics.

The United States does not include its Ex-Im Bank figures in its ODA figures.

APPENDIX: DATA TABLES 221

ENERGY R&D EXPENDITURES, 1979 (expressed in $ millions and percent of R&D budget)[a]

Energy Source	U.K.[b] $M	U.K.[b] %	Germany[b] $M	Germany[b] %	Japan $M	Japan %	U.S. $M	U.S. %	France[b,c] $M	France[b,c] %
Total Government Energy R&D Budget	389.1	100.0	1048.1	100.0	919.3	100.0	3783.4	100.0	573.6	100.0
Group I (conservation)	34.7	8.9	45.1	4.3	51.3	5.6	211.7	5.6	71.3	12.0
Group II (atomic/fossil)	132.4	34.0	598.2	57.1	571.6	62.2	1061.5	28.0	416.5	72.0
Group III (new: solar, etc)	19.1	4.9	46.4	4.4	38.5	4.2	624.2	16.5	57.0	10.0
Group IV (advanced nuclear breeder reactor)	178.4	45.9	255.7	24.4	243.3	26.5	1229.3	32.5	27.5	5.0
Group V (other)	0.02	—	10.4	1.0	3.5	0.4	23.4	0.6	1.1	—
Group VI (supporting technologies)	24.5	6.3	92.3	8.8	11.1	1.2	633.3	16.7	71.3	12.0

a. Figures are in current dollars (1979). Exchange rates are annual averages from the *IMF International Financial Statistics*.
b. The contributions of European Community members do not include expenditures on European Community programs.
c. Since France is not an IEA member, statistics for France were taken from *Energie: La Voie Française*, published by the Ministry of Industry in Paris. It should therefore be noted that inconsistencies between French statistics and those of the IEA members (e.g., Groups I, III, and VI) may result from marginally different criteria for grouping expenditures. Conservation, for example, is considered part of Supporting I technologies in the French statistics.

Source: *IEA 1979 Review of National Programmes* Paris: OECD.

GLOSSARY

ANZUS	Tripartite treaty between Australia, New Zealand, and the U.S.
ASDF	Air Self-Defense Force (Japan)
ASEAN	Association of Southeast Asian Nations
ASW	Anti-Submarine Warfare
CCP	Chinese Communist Party
CHINCOM	China Committee (to coordinate Western trade with the PRC)
COCOM	Coordinating Committee (for Western trade with the USSR)
COMECON	Council for Mutual Economic Assistance (Soviet bloc)
CPSU	Communist Party of the Soviet Union
DPRK	Democratic People's Republic of Korea (North Korea)
EC	European Community (formerly European Economic Community)
ECCM	Electronic Counter-Counter Measures
ECM	Electronic Counter Measures
GATT	General Agreement on Trade and Tariffs
GNP	Gross National Product
GSDF	Ground Self-Defense Force (Japan)
ICBM	Intercontinental Ballistic Missile
IEA	International Energy Agency
IMF	International Monetary Fund
IRBM	Intermediate Range Ballistic Missile
LDC	Less Developed Country
LDP	Liberal Democratic Party (Japan)

MITI	Ministry of International Trade and Industry
MSDF	Maritime Self-Defense Force (Japan)
MST	Military Ship Transport
NATO	North Atlantic Treaty Organization
NHK	Japan Broadcasting System (Nihon Hoso Kaisha)
NPT	Non-Proliferation Treaty (Nuclear)
NTT	Nippon Telegraph & Telephone Public Corporation
OECD	Organization for Economic Cooperation & Development
P3C	Reconnaissance & Patrol Aircraft (U.S.)
PRC	People's Republic of China
Rimpac	1980 joint Allied naval exercises in the Pacific
SALT	Strategic Arms Limitations Treaty
SAM	Surface-to-air-missile (USSR)
SDF	Self-Defense Forces (Japan)
SSBN	Nuclear powered ballistic missile submarine
UNCTAD	United Nations Conference on Trade & Development

INDEX

Afghanistan, Soviet occupation of, 2, 3, 11, 40, 57, 59, 87, 134, 140, 158, 166, 203-204, 206, 209, 214
Aircraft industry, Japanese, 151
Air Self-Defense Force, 149-50, 163
Albania, 195
Alliances. *See* relevant nations
Allies, 4-5, 16, 19-20, 24, 62
  balance in economic power of, 17, 214
  common economic interests of, 1, 24, 42
  and China, 72, 183
  and "comprehensive national security," 207-208
  economic and political power of, 18
  effect of inflation on, 19
  inequality among, 4-5, 110-111, 117-121
  future military goals, 17-19, 21
  military regionalism among, 198-201, 212-13
  proposed summit conference of, 216
  See also Oil, Security interests
Antisubmarine warfare, 70-71
Arms control, 25n5
ASEAN, 24-25, 31, 84, 178-79
  and USSR, 31, 178-79

Asia
  balance of military power in, 7, 29-32, 45-50, 71-74, 82, 84, 90-91
  economic balance in, 37-38, 76
  foreign investment in, 67, 69
  political stability of, 89-91
  See also Southeast Asia
Asian policy, U.S., 63-67, 68, 69, 81, 82, 88-91. *See also* Nixon Doctrine
  and U.S. global policy, 68, 84-85
  and Thailand, 73, 75, 79
Asian Security 1979, 172, 180

Baikal-Amur Main Railway, 172, 174f
Balance of payments for Japan, 124, 133, 135, 141
Balance of military power (U.S. and U.S.S.R.), 2-3, 7, 27-28, 29-32, 45-50, 180-82, 183
  of strategic forces, 3, 7, 22, 27, 45, 166, 209
  between U.S.S.R. and West, 3, 19, 166
  effect on global relations, 28, 128-29, 210

225

and Japanese foreign policy, 46-50, 53-55, 211-12
in Pacific, 71, 79-81, 83, 180-82
Barnett, Robert W., 25n5
Bipolarity. See Cold War
Brezhnev Doctrine, 166
Brezhnev, Leonid, 30n2, 179
Britain. See United Kingdom
Brown, Harold, 44, 141, 213-14
Brzezinski, Zbigniew, 198
  The Fragile Blossom, 58, 135
Burma, 69, 75

Cambodia and Vietnam, 31, 72-73, 177, 179
Cam Ranh Bay, Soviet military bases at, 7, 29-30, 178
Canada, 21, 201, 216
"Carter Doctrine," 11, 11n2, 13
Carter, James Earl, 11n2, 16, 30n2, 82, 134, 211
Chen Yun, 187, 190
China. See also Allies
  allied aid to, 24, 33, 35, 72, 195
  modernization of armed forces, 72, 84, 211
  social, political, and economic changes in, 10, 32, 34-35, 38, 185-195
  and Taiwan, 72-74, 170, 190
  territorial claims, 75-76, 171
  and Vietnam, 34-35, 38, 175, 176-78, 189
  and West, 60, 72, 183, 190
China and Japan, 12, 34, 95, 177, 187, 192, 195-96
China and U.S.S.R., relations between, 32, 40-41, 191
  and Asian relations, 70, 72, 84, 171, 175
  beneficial effects of, for West, 10, 195
  and possibilities for reconciliation, 10, 33, 175, 192-96
  as reason for Soviet military build-up, 8, 29, 72
  and Vietnam-Cambodia conflict, 31, 33, 36, 72, 176-78
  and international Communist leadership, 171, 193

China and U.S., 31, 33, 35-36, 84, 133-34, 141, 195
  effect on U.S.S.R., 35-36, 171-72, 194-96
  effect on Taiwan, 37, 84, 194
China Sea, 76
Chou En-lai, 186, 187, 189
Cold War,
  U.S. reaction to, 16-17, 199
  and Asian relations, 90-91
Collective defense. See Security interests, allies
COMECON, 177
Communist nations, relations among, 69-70, 195-96
Communist insurgency.
  See Insurgency
Communist Party, of Japan, 54, 59, 62, 157-58
"Comprehensive national security"
  in Japan, 48-50, 206-207
  as model for allies, 206-207
Conflict cause-issue approach, 48-50
Constitution, Japanese, 5, 144, 144n1, 146-47, 160-61, 160n2, 161n3
Credibility, U.S., 133-34, 182
Crown Colony of Hong Kong.
  See Hong Kong

Danang, Soviet military bases at, 7, 29-30, 178
Defense. See Military policy
Defense expenditures, allies, 219 (table)
Defense White Paper (1977), 148
Democratic Socialist party (Japan), 61, 137, 158
Detente, 3, 48, 53-55, 162, 196, 206, 209
Development Assistance Committee of OECD, 208
Ding Ling, 186-87
Dulles, John Foster, 110

Economic and political interests, U.S., 64-65, 67-68, 93
Economic development
  in Asian nations, 69, 74-75, 77-79, 126-27
  and political stability, 126-27, 189-91

INDEX

and social-political problems, 74–75, 126–27, 188, 189–91
Economic diplomacy, 119–20
Economic frictions. *See also* Protectionism, 76
as result of oil prices, 39, 121–24
between U.S. and Japan, 78, 84, 113–14, 121–25, 133, 135, 136, 138–39
as result of U.S. economic decline, 125, 138
Economic relations. *See also* Trade
and Asian security, 48, 55
effect of oil market on, 122–24, 208
between Japan and Europe, 203
between Japan and U.S., 33, 57, 78, 84, 94, 96–99
Economy, Japanese, 42, 55–57, 93–94, 119–20, 121–24. *See also* Balance of payments, Trade
post WWII growth of, 58, 90, 96–99, 98 (fig. 6-1), 100–101 (fig. 6-2), 102–103 (fig. 6-3), 200
Economy, Japanese
and oil, 38–39, 58–60, 105–106, 121–24
and U.S., 96–103, 110–111
Encirclement, Soviet fears of, 8, 183
Energy research and development, 221 (table)
"Equal partnership," crisis in, 131–32
Ethnic and religious tensions in Indonesia, Malaysia, and Taiwan, 75
Europe, as military theater, 27, 209–210
European nations' attitude towards U.S. policy, 16, 41
European Community (EC), a6, 202
Exchange rates, 96, 113

Federal Republic of Germany. *See* West Germany
First Defense Build-up Program (Japan), 156
Fishing rights, and U.S.S.R. and Japan, 169
Fourth Defense Program (Japan), 148
Foreign Exchange Control and Trade Law, 97

Foreign policy, Japan
change in, 12–13, 52–53, 55–57, 94–95
and detente, 53–55, 162
and domestic public opinion, 53–57, 60–62
and economic diplomacy, 23, 119–20
Foreign policy, U.S., 68, 84–85, 132–34, 182. *See also* Isolationism, Vietnam syndrome, Economic and political interests, and Asian policy
Foreign relations, U.S.S.R., 31. *See also* Balance of military power, China and U.S.S.R.; Detente; and Japan and U.S.S.R.
with Japan, 34, 166–70
new alliances in Asia, 72, 179–80
with North Korea, 32, 38, 175–76
policy of, 3, 166, 183
with Vietnam, 30–31, 32, 38, 176–79, 183, 204
Fragile Blossom, The (Brzezinski), 58, 135
France, 16, 21, 216
Fraser, Douglas, 138
"Free ride" hypothesis, 109–111, 135, 143, 159
Fromm, Erich, 190
"Fukuda Doctrine," 12, 95

Gang of Four, 186, 189
Gaulle, Charles de, 60
Greater East Asia Coprosperity Sphere, 62
Gromyko, Andrei, 170
Ground Self-Defense Force, 148–49, 163
Group '77 and Japanese foreign policy, 53
Guidelines for U.S.-Japan Defense Cooperation, (1978) 13, 19, 23, 159, 161

Hangzheu Incident of 1975, 189
Hart, Gary, 160
Hong Kong, 37, 69, 126
Hua Guofeng, 187

Indian Ocean, 7, 29, 39–40, 71. *See also* Military policy, U.S.

Indonesia, 69, 75
Inflation, and allied economic strength, 19
Insurgency, political
in Burma, Indonesia, Malaysia, and the Philippines, 75
in Thailand, 36, 75
Interdependency of allies, 197-98
International Atomic Energy Agency, 207
International institutions, 201-203, 206-208
International monetary system, 96
International Nuclear Fuel Cycle Evaluation, 207
Investment in Asia. See Asia
Iran and Iranian crisis, 2, 11, 39, 87-88, 121-22, 139-40, 203, 213-14
Isolationism
in Europe and Japan, 200
in U.S., 7, 89
Italy, 216

Japan, 5, 6, 19, 23, 42, 44, 59-62, 85, 198-217 passim. See also Economy, Military policy, Military power, and Foreign Policy
and allied military policy, 21, 120-21
constitution of. See Constitution
internal politics of, 42, 61-62, 74, 109, 117, 127-28, 142, 144, 156-58, 205
and Korea, 76
political leadership, 127-28, 142
security issues, 48-50, 58-60
self-image, 53-55, 58
U.S. attitude towards, 137, 139
and U.S. military policy, 23, 32-33, 41, 45-46, 47-50, 57, 83-84, 93-94, 109-110
Japan-U.S. relationship, 4-5, 8, 32-33, 87-129, 131-32. See also "Free ride hypothesis," "Nixon shocks," Trade
basis of, 92-107
cultural differences, 91-93, 107-109
economic relations. See Economic relations, Economic frictions
and global relations, 115-16, 121
problems in, 107-115, 117-129, 133-135, 136-40, 196
Japan and U.S.S.R., 34-35, 40, 45-46, 47, 57-58
Japan as No. One (Vogel), 58
Japanese, The (Reischauer), 58
Japanese Socialist party, 54, 62, 109, 128
Japan: the Government – Business Relationship (U.S. Department of Commerce), 135
Joint Defense Guidelines. See Guidelines for U.S.-Japan Defense Cooperation
Jones Report, 138

Kanemaru, Shin, 205
Karakhan Manifesto (1919), 192
Kennan, George, 90
Memoirs, 90n1
Kim Il-sung, 175-76
Komei party, 61-62, 137, 158
Korean War, 4, 30, 66, 144
Kuriles Islands, 7, 71, 168-69
Kurisu, Hiro'omi, 155

"Latent capabilities gap," 90
Law of the Sea Conference, 207
Lee, Prime Minister, 74
Liberal Democratic party (Japan), 12, 15, 54, 61, 117, 142
"Linkage politics" between U.S. and Japan, 124-25, 134
Long Term Defense Program (NATO), 22
Luo Rui, 194

Magnet theory, 128
Malacca Straits. See Straits of Malacca
Malaysia, 69, 75-76
Manila Pact, 81
Maoism, 186-96 passim
Mao Tse-tung, 170-71, 185-93 passim
Marcos, 74
Maritime Self-Defense Force, 149-50, 163
Marxism, 170
Masataka, Kosaka, 99n10
Matsu, 170

Memoirs (Kennan), 90n1
Midterm Defense Estimate (1980-84), 162
Middle East. *See also* Oil, Persian Gulf
  allied military policy in, 21, 203-204
  as military theater, 13, 14-15, 204, 213-14
Military policy, Japan, 83, 88-89, 118, 151, 156
  analysis of, 145-163
  change in, 12-13, 32-33, 117-21, 205
  and domestic legal issues, 145, 147, 155, 160-61, 163, 199
  domestic public opinion of, 12-13, 31, 41, 47-49, 52-53, 58-60, 117, 136-37, 143-44, 145, 147, 155, 157-58, 199, 205
  expenditures for military, 5, 49-50, 155-57, 159, 162-63, 220 (table)
  internal debates about, 46-50, 109, 144-45, 157-58, 205
  U.S. attitude towards, 109-110, 117-18, 120-21, 125-26, 140-41, 143-44
  and U.S. military policy, 45-50, 96, 99, 104-105, 117-18, 137-38, 148-56 passim, 159-62, 210-11
Military policy, U.S. *See also* Japan; Military policy, Japan
  defense commitments, 134, 182
  European reaction to, 16, 41
  multitheater strategy, 14, 18-19, 214-15
  in Pacific, 22, 31, 83, 135
  and political climate in U.S., 14-15, 17, 28
  "swing" doctrine, 8, 212-14
  apparent withdrawal from Asia, 7, 134, 212
Military power, Japan. *See also* "Latent capabilities gap"
  analysis of, 105, 147-50
Military power, U.S.S.R. *See also* Navy, U.S.S.R.
  build-up in, 2-3, 7, 8, 28, 29, 57, 70-71, 180-82, 183, 204
  on China front, 172-75
  in East Asia, 6-7, 29-32, 70-71, 176-79, 172, 173f, 178

  in Pacific, 6-7, 30, 70-71, 80-81, 180-82
  and Soviet global strategy, 3, 9, 40, 166, 183, 204
Military power, U.S., 80, 94, 103-104
  in Asia, 30-32, 57, 79-81
  in Indian Ocean, 39-40, 80-81, 83
  in Pacific, 30, 45-46, 79-81, 83, 180, 182
Minorities, Chinese, 75, 179
Modernization of forces
  Chinese, 72, 84
  Soviet, 71
  Japanese, 148-49, 152, 153
Monetary system, international, 96
Multipolarization theory, 60
Multitheater strategy, 14, 18-19, 212-215
Muslims in Indonesia and Malaysia, 75
Mutual security interests. *See* Security interests
Mutual Security Treat. *See* U.S.-Japan Security Treaty

Navy, U.S.S.R., 69-71, 80-81, 149, 178, 180-82, 204, 181f
NATO, 13, 15, 16, 19, 201-202, 216
New World Note 173 (N. Pedrova), 44n1
Nippon Telephone and Telegraph Public Corporation issue, 138
Nixon Doctrine, 7, 45, 64, 66, 133, 135
"Nixon shocks, the," 57, 113, 133, 134
Nonnuclear principles of Japan, 145, 210
Non-Proliferation Treaty, 207
North Atlantic Treaty, 4
North Korea, 36-37, 38, 171, 175-76, 183.
  See also South Korea
North-South problem, 68, 208
  effect on oil market, 123
  and Japanese foreign policy, 53-54, 56-57
Nuclear weapons, 77-78, 80, 108-109, 207, 211.
  See also SALT, Balance of military power
  and Japan, 5, 77-78, 145, 210

Nuclear power, 108–109
  in Asian nations, 39, 77, 83
Nunn report, 136, 160

OECD (Organization for Economic Cooperation and Development), 76
Ohira, Masayoshi, 62, 94–95, 95n5, 127–28, 140, 205
Oil, 2, 38–39, 57, 75–77. *See also* Middle East, Persian Gulf
  allies' dependence on, 11n1, 19, 22, 39–40, 105–106, 122–23, 203, 213
  effect of, on Asian economy, 77, 83
  effect of, on international economy, 28, 208
  and Japan, 58–60, 105–106, 121–24
  strategic significance of, 11, 13, 21, 213
Okita, (Foreign Minister), 13, 139
Olympic boycott, allied reaction to, 16
OPEC (Organization of Petroleum Exporting Countries), 2, 28, 57, 59–60, 106, 115, 203
Ostpolitik, 16

Pacific Study Group, 160
Paracel Islands, 75
Park, 74, 15–26
Pedrova, N.: *New World Note 173*, 44n1, 44
Peng Zhen, 186, 190
People's Republic of China. *See* China
Persian Gulf. *See also* Middle East, Oil
  allied dependence on, 11, 39–40, 105–106
  U.S. role in, 105–106, 205–206
Philippines, 69, 74, 75, 76, 83
Political interests. *See* Economic and political interests
Political leadership, lack of, 127–28, 142
Political stability, 69, 74, 126–27, 189–91
Politics, internal. *See also individual nations*
  in China, 184–95
  in Japan, 42, 61–62, 74, 109, 127–28, 142, 144, 156–58, 205

  in U.S., 127–42
Pol Pot regime, 72
Protectionism. *See also* economic frictions
  Japanese, 97, 98 (Table 6-1), 122–23
  problems of, 24, 29, 83
  Western, 33, 76–77, 83

Quemoy, 170

Rapid Deployment Force (U.S.), 40, 213
Rearmament
  of Japan. *See* Military policy, Japan
  of West Germany, 4, 199
Regional cooperation in Asia, 76, 84
Regionalism, military, 3, 85, 198–201, 212–13
Reischauer, Edwin O.: *The Japanese*, 58
Rimpac maneuvers, Japanese participation in, 13, 146, 151, 205

SALT, 209–211
  and U.S.–Japan alliance, 78, 128
Scenario-contingency approach, 47–48, 49
Schlesinger, James, 43
Sea Lanes, security of Japanese, 39–40, 48, 83
Security interests, allies, 2, 20, 59–62, 126, 198–217
  and collective security, 17–18, 59–60, 111–112, 126
  in light of differing postwar priorities, 198–201
Security interests, regional
  European, 6, 41–42, 212
  Japanese, 6, 46–50, 58–62, 212
Self-Defense Forces, 5, 22, 199, 143–63 passim. *See also* Military policy, Japan
Senkaku Islands, 75
Shigeru, Yoshida, 110
Siberia, development by U.S.S.R., 35, 38, 169
Singapore, 37, 69, 72, 74, 77, 126
Sino–Japanese Treaty of Peace and Friendship, 177
Sino–Soviet Treaty of 1950, 167

Socialist-Komei axis, 61, 137, 158
Southeast Asia
  role of ASEAN, 24-25
  and U.S.S.R.-China rivalry, 33, 36, 72, 171, 176-79
  U.S.S.R. military role in, 29-30, 176-79
South Korea
  economic development of, 37, 39, 69, 73, 75, 76-77
  and Japan, 70, 76, 211
  military strength relative to North Korea, 31, 36-37, 73
  political stability of, 74, 126-27
  U.S. military presence in, 8, 18-19, 24, 32, 36-37, 43-44, 73, 81, 83, 134, 141, 176, 211
Soviet Collective Security Plan, 179
Spratley Islands, 75
Stalinism, 192
Status of Forces Agreement, 161
Straits of Malacca
  Soviet military presence in, 7
  strategic importance of, 39
Strategic forces. *See* SALT, Nuclear weapons, Balance of military power
Subcommittee on Defense Cooperation, 159
Summit conference. *See* Allies
"Swing" doctrine, 8, 212-14. *See also* "Carter Doctrine"

Taiwan, 37, 39, 69, 72-74, 75, 76-77, 83, 84, 126, 170, 194
Taiwan Relations Act (U.S.), 194
Taiwan Straits crisis, 66
Tanaka-Nixon conference (1973), 134
Tariffs. *See* Protectionism
Teng Hsiao-p'ing, 44, 171, 178, 187, 190, 194
  economic policies of, 34, 38, 185-191
Thailand, 69, 70, 72-73, 74, 75, 83
  and U.S., 81, 83, 179
Theater Defense. *See* Multitheater strategy
Theaters. *See* Europe, Middle East
Third World, 9, 68, 204
Three Arrow Study, 154
Tian An Men Square Incident, 189

Tito, 195-96
Trade, international, 67, 76, 83, 122-24, 190
  between Japan and U.S., 97-99, 100-101 (fig. 6-1), 102-103 (fig. 6-3), 135
Trade conflicts. *See* Economic frictions, Protectionism
Trans-Siberian Railway, 172
Treaty of San Francisco, 167
Trilateralism, 197-98
Tsurmi-Ingersoll agreement, 134

Ullman, Richard H., 198
"unarmed neutrality," 54, 56, 62
UNCTAD, 53, 68
United Kingdom, 16, 21, 216
United States. *See also* Economic and political interests, Asian policy, Foreign policy, Military policy
  economic health of, 22, 125, 138-39
  expectations of allies, 126, 135
  international economic role, 29, 53-55, 96-97, 125, 201
  international political role, 19, 22, 57, 58, 99-104, 110-11, 132-33, 198-201
U.S. Annual Report on Defense (1981), 160
U.S.-Japan Security Relationship: The Key to East Asian Security and Stability. *See* Nunn Report
U.S.-Japan Security Treaty, 2, 4, 5, 23, 30, 90-91, 143-63 passim, 217
  Japanese public opinion of, 12, 31, 52, 55-56, 60-62, 109, 112, 137, 205
  and U.S.S.R., 167, 170, 179

Vance, Cyrus, 139
Vietnam
  and Cambodia, 31, 72-73, 177, 179
  and China, 176-78, 189
  and Southeast Asia, 36, 72-73
  as Soviet ally, 30-31, 38, 171, 176-79, 183, 204
  and Thailand, 75, 83, 179
  U.S. involvement with, 18-19, 30, 134

"Vietnam" syndrome, 8, 79, 204
Vietnam War, 4, 30, 42, 66, 158
Vogel, Ezra: *Japan as No. One*, 58

Warsaw Pact nations, 41
Weinstein, Franklin B., 20-21n3, 24n4

West Germany, 16, 19, 21, 216
World Economy, 28, 42, 96-97, 113-15, 124, 208.
  See also Exchange rates

Yamashita, (Japanese Defense minister), 46

RAYMOND H. FOGLER LIBRARY